BEING
QUA
BEING

BEING QUA BEING

A Theory of Identity, Existence, and Predication

Panayot Butchvarov

INDIANA UNIVERSITY PRESS
Bloomington & London

This book was brought to publication with the assistance of a grant from the Mellon Foundation.

Copyright © 1979 by Panayot Butchvarov

Manufactured in the United States of America

Library of Congress Cataloging in Publication Data
Butchvarov, Panayot Krustev.
Being qua being.
Includes bibliographical references and index.
1. Identity. 2. Reality. 3. Metaphysics.
4. Predicate (Logic) I. Title.
BD 236.B87   111   78-13812
ISBN 0-253-13700-4 1 2 3 4 5 83 82 81 80 79

To Vanya and Christopher

CONTENTS

ACKNOWLEDGMENTS

Early versions of portions of this book have been read at a number of universities. I am grateful to the philosophers at those universities for their helpful comments and questions.

A version of some of the themes in chapters one and two appeared as an invited article, "Identity," in *Midwest Studies in Philosophy*, Vol. II, "Studies in the Philosophy of Language," 1977, and was reprinted in *Contemporary Perspectives in the Philosophy of Language* (Minneapolis: University of Minnesota Press, 1978). I acknowledge with thanks the permission of the editors of *Midwest Studies* and of the University of Minnesota Press to use parts of that article.

To the graduate students in several seminars devoted to the topics in this book, I express my affection and deep appreciation. I have also benefited much from discussions with Dennis Bradford and Deane Curtin, who wrote their doctoral dissertations on related topics.

Albert Casullo read an early version of the manuscript. My colleague Evan Fales read the penultimate version. I owe both of them a special debt of gratitude for their incisive criticism.

BEING
QUA
BEING

Introduction

I shall introduce the subject of this book by recalling four puzzles that infect the very foundations of metaphysics.

Sometimes we seem to think about, or imagine, or perceive, or, less fundamentally, talk about what does not exist, e.g., Santa Claus or the pink rat a delirious man supposedly hallucinates some morning. How is this possible? Even if there are mental images and sense-data, it is not a mental image a child thinks about when he thinks about Santa Claus and it is not a sense-datum the delirious man fears when he fears the rat he hallucinates.

Sometimes we think about, or imagine, or perceive, or, less fundamentally, talk about *a* and *b* (e.g., the Morning Star and the Evening Star) as if *a* and *b* were two things, although in fact, a fact perhaps even known to us, they are one thing. How is this possible? How is it possible that what the statement "*a* is *b*" says should seem quite different from what the statement "*a* is *a*" says? An aspect of this puzzle is that sometimes we seem to think, or imagine, or perceive, or say that *a* is F (e.g., that the Evening Star is visible tonight), but not think, imagine, perceive, or say that *b* is F (e.g., that the Morning Star is visible tonight), even though *a* and *b* are one and the same thing; and that there also seem to be cases in which *a* is necessarily F while *b* is not necessarily F, although *a* is the same thing as *b*.

We also perceive, or think, or say that things have various properties, e.g., that Socrates has a certain color, and we ordinarily express this with statements of the form "*x* is F," e.g.,

"Socrates is white." But how are we to understand this relationship of *having* that seems to hold between, e.g., Socrates and a certain color? Is it not itself *another* property, albeit a relational one, which its terms now have to each other, and if so are we not swept along on an infinite regress?

Even if this third puzzle is resolved, it already contains the seed of a fourth. For Socrates to be white, he must indeed have a certain color, but it is also necessary that this color *be* white. How are we to understand now this "relationship" between Socrates' color, i.e., that very color one sees when one sees Socrates, and *its* being white? (A no less traditional, but more complicated, example of supposedly the same relationship is that between Socrates and his being a man.) When one *recognizes* Socrates' color as white, what does one come to so *cognize?* Surely not that two distinguishable even if not separable things, as *Socrates* and his color have often been supposed to be, enter in a certain relation, for Socrates' *color* is not distinguishable from, and therefore, unlike Socrates, cannot intelligibly be said to *have,* white color. (Similarly, it has been supposed, Socrates is not distinguishable from his being a man and therefore cannot intelligibly be said to *have* any such property as being a man.)

These four puzzles concern, respectively, the concepts of existence, identity, accidental predication, and essential predication. The first puzzle has long historical roots, reaching as far back as Parmenides, but was forced upon the attention of twentieth-century philosophy by Meinong. The second puzzle is of recent origin, having first been formulated clearly by Frege. The distinction between accidental and essential predication is due of course to Aristotle.

Several preliminary explanations of my terminology are needed. Some philosophers, including Meinong, restrict the concept of existence to concrete, spatiotemporal individual things, and use the term "subsistence" for the "being" of things that are not concrete, or spatiotemporal, or individual; but I believe it is better to distinguish between kinds of existent things,

rather than between kinds of being. I do not use the terms "accidental" and "essential" as synonyms, respectively, for "contingent" and "necessary," as many contemporary philosophers do;
my use of them, though not unrelated, is to be understood in
terms of the Aristotelian examples I have given. By "predication" I do not mean the relation between the subject term and
the predicate of a sentence, or a certain action of a language-user,
but the relation, if any, between what the subject term and the
predicate stand for. And by "identity" I mean what is usually
called "numerical identity." A statement such as "This book is
the same color as that book," often described as asserting qualitative identity, is paraphrasable much more perspicuously as
"The color of this book is the same as the color of that book." The
unwillingness to acknowledge this fact, due mainly to insufficient attention to the metaphysical topic of universals, is one
of the reasons for the recent flurry of interest in what has been
called relative identity.[1] To understand what we mean, I suggest,
we must look at what we talk about and not just at how we talk
about it.

We may say that the four puzzles I have described concern four
senses of the verb "to be," since all four of the corresponding
concepts would often be expressed in English with forms of that
verb. If so, then we may also say that an inquiry into those four
concepts, insofar as it is inseparable from the inquiry into the
features of the world that make their application possible, is an
inquiry into being qua being. But my mention here of the verb
"to be" and its senses is intended to be merely suggestive and
will not serve as a foundation for anything that will follow.*

The inquiry into being qua being has been identified with

---

*It is often supposed that the verb "to be" has a fifth sense, that of class-
membership. But, I suggest, to say that *a* is (an) F in the "sense" that *a* is a
member of the class of F's is to say either that *a* is (an) F in the sense of essential
predication or in the sense of accidental predication, or, if the class of F's is
defined by enumerating *m, n, o. . . .* as its members, that *a* is identical either with
m, or with *n*, or with *o. . . .*

metaphysics. But it would be better to use the term "metaphysics" more broadly, namely, for the branch of philosophy that has as its subject matter the nature of the world, or of reality, rather than the nature of our knowledge, or of our language, or of our sciences about the world. We may then distinguish several levels of metaphysical inquiry. On the least fundamental level metaphysics is concerned with the most general description of the actual world, with the most general kinds of things there are and with the way they fit together. It asks such questions as whether God exists, whether there are both minds and bodies or only minds or only bodies, and if there are both minds and bodies, how they are related. On this level it is closely connected with epistemology, since the main philosophical difficulties such questions pose for us are epistemological in character.

On a more fundamental level, presupposed by the first, metaphysics inquires into the nature of all possible, or at least all conceivable, comprehensible worlds, and thus only indirectly into the nature of the actual world. Can there be a world that consists only of individuals and not also of properties and relations? Or a world that consists only of properties and relations? Can there be nonidentical but indiscernible things? Questions related to those on the previous level can now be asked in complete independence from the usual epistemological considerations. Can there be a world unless there is God? Can there be a world without bodies? Without minds? On this level metaphysics is closely connected with logic. (Immediately following his introduction of the notion of a science of being qua being Aristotle offers a defense of the laws of noncontradiction and excluded middle.) But this connection is no more limited to formal logic than the notion of necessary truth is limited to the truths of formal logic. The criterion of possibility on which it would rely can hardly be mere formal consistency; it must be conceivability or comprehensibility (not of propositions, but of what propositions purport to describe), for, whether we like it or not, we have no other general and ultimate criterion of possibility.

This is why, on this level, metaphysics is also connected with phenomenology, i.e., with the philosophical description of the most general character of the objects of consciousness qua objects of consciousness.

On the third and most fundamental level metaphysics is concerned with the concepts and principles on the basis of which the questions belonging to the other two levels, i.e., the questions about what things there are or at least there can be, must be answered. Instead of these questions, it asks, what is it for something to be in a world, or for something to be a world? It is on this level, I suggest, that metaphysics is best described as the inquiry into being qua being, or, we might also say, as protometaphysics. Any conception of a world presupposes the conception of what it is for something to exist in that world. Any conception of a thing presupposes the conception of what it is for it to be the subject of predication, both accidental and essential. Any conception of a thing presupposes the conception of what it is for it to be identifiable, not in the sense of being merely singled out but also in the sense of being singled out again or in a different way, of being recognized, of being the subject of a true informative identity judgment.

It follows that the concepts of existence, identity, essential predication, and accidental predication cannot be understood as standing for constituents of the world, presumably for certain properties or relations. They are the concepts in terms of which we must understand what it is for something to be in the world, what it is for something to have a property or be related to another thing, and what it is for something to be a property or a relation. Yet they apply to any possible world; indeed nothing would be a world were it not for their applicability to it. We may call such concepts, which apply without standing for anything, transcendental. The inquiry into being qua being, or protometaphysics, may then be called a transcendental inquiry.

Now the central thesis of this book is that the concepts of existence, identity, accidental predication, and essential predication are intimately related, and moreover that the concept of identity is basic and the other three are to be understood in terms of it. I shall argue that the four puzzles with which we began admit of a common solution, the key to which is to be found in a careful study of the second puzzle, that regarding identity. It is a solution based on a distinction between what I shall call objects and entities. A similar, but not the same, distinction has often been made, most notably by Meinong but also by recent possible-worlds semanticists, in treatments of the first puzzle, that regarding existence. But there it rests on the proposition that there are things of which it is true that there are no such things, a proposition that, I suggest, cannot be made coherent, let alone plausible, except on the basis of considerations external to the topic of existence.[2] A similar, but again not the same, distinction has also been made, e.g., by Carnap[3] and Sellars,[4] in treatments of an aspect of the second puzzle, namely, the seeming failure of the principle of the indiscernibility of identicals in intentional and modal contexts; I have in mind the distinction between individuals and individual concepts. But if an individual concept is indeed a *concept*, or at all like a concept, then it is not the object of the propositional attitude, or the subject of the modal property, with respect to which the principle seems to fail, and therefore its relevance is obscure. If it is not really a concept, then how does it differ from the individual with which it is associated? Again, I believe that these questions can be answered only on the basis of considerations both far more general and much deeper than the seeming discernibility of identicals in intentional and modal contexts.

It is with respect to the second puzzle itself, in the context of an inquiry into the general topic of identity, that the distinction needed for the common solution of all four puzzles can be made both clear and plausible. This will be attempted in chapters one, two, and three, where the application of the distinction to the first puzzle, that regarding existence, will also be outlined. The topic of existence will be accorded further, detailed treatment in chapter four. The distinction will be applied to the topic of essential predication in chapter five. Its application to accidental predication, however, is more complex and will occupy us in chapters six, seven, and eight. It requires that we consider the questions whether the notion of a material substance is intelligible and whether properties are universals; the reason is that the problem of accidental predication concerns a relationship of which no definite conception can be formed unless it is determined what its relata can be. And in the appendixes I shall consider briefly two issues that are closely related to the main theses of this book but cannot be fully discussed within its bounds.

The fact that all four puzzles admit of a common solution constitutes, in itself, a major argument in favor of that solution. But in philosophy such an argument is never sufficient; the methods of philosophy are quite unlike those of science. The distinction between objects and entities on which the solution rests must have independent and deeper support. I shall argue, especially in chapter two, that it is grounded in the very nature of conceptual cognition, and that the four puzzles are symptoms of the extraordinary nature of the application to the world of our conceptual apparatus, and, in particular, of the application of the concept of identity. They cannot be solved by ingenious reformulation or mild theoretical innovation. They concern the very foundations of thought and reflect a certain instability, unsettledness in them. The solution must go to those foundations; it can hardly be found in the structure that rests upon them. It must be a radical solution. I shall therefore be compelled to introduce notions and propose theses of unusual difficulty. That they be explained as adequately as their nature allows is the responsibility of the author. That they are unusually difficult, however, is an unavoidable consequence of the nature of the problems they are designed to solve.

It is for this reason that in the earlier chapters I shall often appeal to familiar examples, especially of individual identity (e.g., the Evening Star and the Morning Star) and of nonexistent things (e.g., Santa Claus), which eventually I shall argue are inappropriate. I shall also require notions (e.g., that of singling out) that I believe can be made clear only by the uses to which they are put throughout the book, not by explicit initial explanation. And even though an entire chapter is devoted to it, the foundation of almost all the views I shall defend, namely, the distinction between objects and entities, cannot be fully understood in abstraction from its applications to the topics discussed in the later chapters. On the other hand, these discussions might appear sketchy, perhaps even high-handed, unless regarded as intended to derive whatever substance they possess mainly from that distinction.

CHAPTER ONE

The Apparent Distinctness of Identicals

I

I shall begin with several historical references in order to bare some of the roots of what will follow.

In *Tractatus* 5.5303 Wittgenstein wrote: "Roughly speaking, to say of *two* things that they are identical is nonsense, and to say of *one* thing that it is identical with itself is to say nothing at all."[1] Nevertheless, it remains true that we do have the concept of identity, that it is absolutely fundamental to our conceptual framework, and that our understanding of the world depends largely on its informative applications. In the *Philosophical Investigations* Wittgenstein did come to appreciate this fact. He continued to hold the second half of his Tractarian view but also seemed to acknowledge that the concept of identity has another sort of application in which we say of what in some sense are two things that they are identical. He wrote:

> 215. But isn't *the same* at least the same? We seem to have an infallible paradigm of identity in the identity of a thing with itself. I feel like saying: "Here at any rate there can't be a variety of interpretations. If you are seeing a thing you are seeing identity too."
>
> Then are two things the same when they are what *one* thing is? And how am I to apply what the *one* thing shows me to the case of two things?[2]

Wittgenstein was by no means the first to feel the tension between the two applications of the concept of identity. In his *Treatise of Human Nature* Hume had written:

> ... the view of any one object is not sufficient to convey the idea of identity. For in that proposition, *an object is the same with itself*, if the idea express'd by the word, *object*, were no ways distinguish'd from that meant by *itself*; we really shou'd mean nothing, nor wou'd the proposition contain a predicate and a subject, which however are imply'd in this affirmation. One single object conveys the idea of unity, not that of identity.
>
> On the other hand, a multiplicity of objects can never convey this idea, however resembling they may be suppos'd. . . .
>
> Since then both number and unity are incompatible with the relation of identity, it must lie in something that is neither of them.[3]

In the *Encyclopaedia of the Philosophical Sciences,* Hegel had argued:

> SELF-IDENTITY . . . becomes an Identity in form only, or of the understanding, if it be held hard and fast, quite aloof from difference . . . no mind thinks or forms conceptions or speaks, in accordance with [the law of identity, A is A], and . . . no existence of any kind whatever conforms to it. Utterances after the fashion of this pretended law (A planet is—a planet; Magnetism is—magnetism; Mind is—mind) are, as they deserve to be, reputed silly.[4]

And in the *Science of Logic* he had asserted:

> . . . the fact is that *experience* contains identity in unity with difference and is the *immediate refutation* of the assertion that abstract identity as such is something true, for the exact opposite, namely, identity only in union with difference, occurs in every experience.[5]

II

The cases to which we may apply the concept of identity fall into two kinds, which I shall call formal identity and material identity. And I shall call the respective sorts of statements formal identity statements and material identity statements. Formal identity statements usually have the form "x is (is identical with, is the same as) x", and material identity statements usually have the form "x is (is identical with, is the same as) y." Occasionally, however, the form of the statement is misleading. "War is war" need not be a formal identity statement,[6] and "Scott is Sir Walter" (or "To be a bachelor is to be an unmarried man") need not be a material identity statement.* It is rhetorically convenient, even though philosophically superficial, to begin our account of the concept of identity with a consideration of certain features of identity statements.

Material identity statements do not assert of one thing that it is the same as itself, for they are not formal identity statements. Nor do they assert of two things that they are the same, for sometimes material identity statements are true. And, of course, they are not about three or more things, or, usually, about nothing at all. What then do they assert? How are such statements possible? How can there be statements which, if true, are about one thing and, if false, are about two things? How is it possible that what such a statement is about depends in part on the truth-value of the statement—a drastic sort of dependence, one in respect to number?† I believe that we must follow Hume, Hegel, and Wittgenstein in taking these questions very seriously, and not be

---

*According to Russell, ". . .so long as names are used *as* names, 'Scott is Sir Walter' is the same trivial proposition as 'Scott is Scott.'" (*Introduction to Mathematical Philosophy* [New York: Simon and Schuster, 1971], p. 175.) And in "On Sense and Reference" Frege had observed that "If the sign '*a*' is distinguished from the sign '*b*' only as object (here, by means of its shape), not as sign (i.e. not by the manner in which it designates something), the cognitive value of $a = a$ becomes essentially equal to that of $a = b$, provided $a = b$ is true." (Peter Geach and Max Black, eds., *Translations from the Philosophical Writings of Gottlob Frege* [Oxford: Basil Blackwell, 1970], p. 57.)

†"A principle that I have repeatedly used to eliminate false theories of reference is the principle that the reference of an expression E must be specifiable in some way that does not involve first determining whether the proposition in which E occurs is true." P. T. Geach, *Reference and Generality* (Ithaca: Cornell University Press, 1968), p. XI.

swayed by facile answers or preconceived notions. And our first task must be to identify as generally as possible, yet with reasonable clarity and especially in fresh, philosophically neutral terms, the feature of material identity statements that demands philosophical account.

Frege held that although, if true, such a statement may only be about one thing, that thing may be given to us in many ways, it may be presented to us in many modes, and the subject terms of the statement express two such different ways of being given or modes of presentation, even though they refer to only one thing.[7] But while this view does, I believe, identify the feature of material identity statements we find puzzling, it also proposes an account of that feature insofar as it includes the claim that ways of being given or modes of presentation are themselves things in the world. (Frege called them senses, but made clear that senses are objective, not psychological or even language dependent.)[8] But these two parts of his view can be separated. The part we require at this stage could be reformulated as follows: in a true material identity statement the referent of the subject terms is given or presented to us as two distinct things would ordinarily be given or presented to us. But because of epistemological caution regarding the terms "given" and "presented," I shall instead employ the following, I believe equivalent, formulation: the feature of material identity statements that demands philosophical account consists in the fact that although, if true, such a statement may only be about one thing, what it is about *appears* to be two distinct things.* (Of course, as with any other appearance, one need not be misled by this appearance; one may know perfectly well that it is a mere appearance.) Unlike a false material identity

---

*"Identity is a rather puzzling thing at first sight. When you say 'Scott is the author of *Waverley*,' you are half-tempted to think there are two people, one of whom is Scott and the other the author of *Waverley*, and they happen to be the same. That is obviously absurd, but that is the sort of way one is always tempted to deal with identity." Bertrand Russell, in *Logic and Knowledge*, ed. R. C. Marsh (London: George Allen and Unwin, 1956), p. 247.

statement, what it is about only appears to be two things. Unlike a formal identity statement, what it is about *does* appear to be two things. The subject terms of a material identity statement refer to what appear to be (and if the statement is false, really are) distinct things. In a formal identity statement they refer to what appears to be and also is only one thing. This is why language forces us to employ plural expressions ("they," "identicals") in describing the subject matter of material identity statements (e.g., the Evening Star and the Morning Star) but not in describing the subject matter of formal identity statements, a fact familiar to writers on identity and a cause of irritation to those who regard formal identity as the paradigm of identity.

It is instructive to note the striking analogy in this respect between material identity statements and singular existential statements. If the statement "*a* exists" is true, then it is natural to suppose that its subject matter is *a*, that the statement is about *a*. But if the statement is false, then we are inclined to say that it cannot be about *a*, since there is no such thing as *a*. Yet there is nothing else it can be about, since nothing else is mentioned in the statement. What we may say initially is only that what the statement is about appears to be *a* although of course it cannot be *a*, indeed cannot be anything. We face here the spectacle of a statement such that we must know whether it is true in order to know what if anything it is about. We face the phenomenon of the apparent existence of nonexistent things.

If the statement "*a* is *b*" is true, then it is about the same thing the statement "*a* is *a*" (or "*b* is *b*") is about and also says about this thing what the latter statement says, namely that it is identical with what may only be itself. Yet certainly "*a* is *b*" says something very different from what "*a* is *a*" says. *a* and *b* appear to be, are thought, perceived, and talked about as if they were, distinct things, even if we know that they are not. We face here once again the spectacle of a statement whose subject matter depends on its truth-value. We face the phenomenon of the apparent distinctness of material identicals. If the statement "*a* is *b"* is true then it is about one thing, and if false then it is about two things.

The term "appears" in the above formulations is not intended to bear special philosophical weight (as it often does in the philosophy of perception). It may be understood in what R. M. Chisholm has called its comparative sense,[9] as long as we do not confuse it with its application to perceptual illusions. Material identicals appear distinct in the sense that they appear to us in thought, (nonillusory) perception, or discourse, as distinct things appear. A related notion is Saul Kripke's notion of the "epistemic situation" in which we make a material identity statement. For example, he speaks of a possible world in which we would have "evidence qualitatively indistinguishable" from the evidence we actually have for the identity of Hesperus and Phosphorus, even though in that world different planets are seen at the appropriate places and times.[10] For reasons to be given later, I believe that Kripke is wrong in supposing that what a statement asserts and the modal status of what it asserts can be divorced from the epistemic situation in which it is made.

Such a use of the term "appears" seems to me a natural and conveniently brief way of describing that which occasions, renders needed, indeed alone makes intelligible the characteristic function of material identity statements: that if considered in themselves or as they occur in other statements the subject terms of a material identity statement are understood exactly as pairs of names or descriptive phrases that refer to distinct things are understood; that until and unless we discover that they are identical, material identicals are normally perceived, thought about, and referred to in discourse as if they were distinct, as distinct things are perceived, thought about, and referred to in discourse; that their identity is at least initially an open question, something to be determined; that *prima facie* they are distinct things. If material identicals did not appear to be distinct, there would be only formal identity statements and the concept of identity would have application mainly in logicians' discourse. The function of material identity statements is precisely to assert of what *appear* to be, and thus could be taken to be, two things that *in reality* they are one thing.

What I have attempted to convey by speaking of the apparent distinctness of material identicals might have been expressed more elegantly by speaking of the *distinguishability* of material identicals. Even if the statement "*a* is the same as *b*" is true, we might have said, *a* and *b* are distinguishable, and this fact is the mark of a material identity statement. But then we should have sacrificed logical coherence for superficial elegance. For we must not allow that material identicals are distinguishable either in the sense that they are nonidentical or in the sense that though identical they violate the principle of the indiscernibility of identicals. And what else could we mean, at this point in our inquiry, by their distinguishability?

We could also have achieved elegance of style by saying that a material identity statement appears to be about distinct things, rather than that what such a statement is about appears to be distinct things. But even though the two formulations are probably equivalent, the latter is preferable. It alone goes to the heart of the matter. And it also avoids a possible trivialization to which the former formulation is subject, since there might be a sense in which any statement of the form "x is y" appears to be about distinct things simply in virtue of its grammatical form. (Korzybski argued, for example, that this is true even of formal identity statements such as "$1 = 1$"; hence his conclusion that these statements are false.)[11]

It should be obvious that, as it is ordinarily understood, a statement such as "The Evening Star is the same (planet) as the Morning Star" appears to be about distinct things. Even our normal visual experiences of what the statement is about are quite like our seeing different planets at different times, and we certainly would take them to be experiences of two planets if we lacked the requisite knowledge of astronomy. But the case of an a priori and necessary statement such as "$18 + 13 = 31$" is not significantly different.* Ordinarily, we think of the numbers 18 + 13 and 31 exactly as we think of pairs of different numbers such as 19 + 14 and 31, 17 +13 and 31, 18 + 15 and 31, etc., and might take for granted that they were different if we lacked the requisite knowledge of arithmetic.

The sense in which what a material identity statement is about appears to be distinct things may become clearer if we note that it is quite inapplicable to the subject matter of paradigmatic, explicitly formal identity statements. A necessary feature of this sense is the fact that to suppose that a material identity statement is false (even if one knows that it is not) is precisely to suppose that it is about distinct things, about something other than what it would have been about had it been true. To suppose that "The Evening Star is the same (planet) as the Morning Star" is false is to suppose that it is about two planets. But this is not a trivial consequence of the fact that the statement is an *identity* statement. For to suppose that a *formal* identity statement is false is *not* to suppose that it is about two distinct things. If one were to suppose that "The Evening Star is the same (planet) as the Evening Star" is false, it would not follow at all that the statement is about something other than what it would have been about had it been true. Specifically, it would not follow that the statement is about two planets, any more than that it is about three, or four, or five planets. The statement would still be only about the Evening Star, for there is nothing else it could be about. It would still be about only one entity, and its supposed falsehood would have to consist (if in anything at all) in some peculiar metaphysical feature of that entity,† not, as in the case of a false material identity statement, in the fact that it asserts of two things that they are one.

---

*Compare Frege's examples in *Translations*, pp. 11, 57, and in *The Basic Laws of Arithmetic*, trans. Montgomery Furth (Berkeley and Los Angeles: University of California Press, 1967) pp. 6, 35.

†E.g., in something analogous to the perpetual disintegration consciousness suffers, according to Sartre.

Why is there such a striking difference between material identity statements and formal identity statements? It might be thought that the reason is that, unlike the former, the latter are self-evident or trivial. But to speak of the self-evidence or triviality (and not merely necessary truth, like that of "18 + 13 =31") of an identity statement is at best an obscure and epistemologically tendentious way of speaking of the fact that what the statement is about does not even appear to be two distinct things. For what would it be for an identity statement to be self-evident or trivially true if not to be such that what it is about does not even appear to be two distinct things? If there is room for the notions of self-evidence and trivial truth, surely it is to be found where there is no appearance that might mislead us in regard to what is really the case. (This is why a statement such as "2 + 2 = 4," to say nothing of "1 + 1 = 2," is probably a formal identity statement, at least as it would be understood by a reasonably schooled adult.)

We may say therefore that "Scott is Sir Walter," or "To be a bachelor is to be an unmarried man," would be a formal identity statement only if so understood that what it is about does not appear to be two distinct things, that even if one were to suppose it to be false one would not be supposing it to be about two distinct things. Presumably, that is how Russell understood the former statement when he claimed that "as long as names are used as names" it is "the same trivial proposition as 'Scott is Scott.'" And we may say that "War is war" would be a material identity statement (if an identity statement at all) only if it is understood in such a way that what it is about does appear to be two distinct things, that if supposed to be false the statement would be supposed to be about two distinct things. Thus it is not the syntactical form of an identity statement that determines whether the statement is formal or material, but what its subject matter *appears* to be—and this depends on how the statement is understood. (Even "The Evening Star is the same as the Morning Star" could be so understood that it would be a formal identity statement.) I shall return to this point shortly. But here perhaps it helps to clarify my assertion that a material identity statement is one such that what it is about appears to be two distinct things. This assertion may now be taken as a definition of a material identity statement. Of course, we would not have arrived at such a definition, nor would it have had a clear application, if it did not apply to most statements of the form "x is y." But it allows for someone's finding that what a certain statement of the form "x is y" is about does not appear to him to be two things. Such a person would not understand the statement so that it is a material identity statement. We could also say that he would not use the sentence for making a material identity statement, or that he would not express a material identity proposition or judgment with that sentence.

III

The problem of material identity is how to account for the apparent distinctness of material identicals. Clearly, it admits of two general solutions. First, one may attempt to show that the appearance of distinctness is a mere appearance, perhaps one generated by the manner in which the identity statement is expressed in language. This was Frege's and Russell's approach. The difficulty such a solution faces is how to explain the appearance away without misrepresenting what the identity statement asserts. Second, one may claim that material identicals appear distinct because they are distinct, and attempt to show how nevertheless they can be identical. This seems to have been the approach of Hegel and, perhaps, the later Wittgenstein, both of whom regarded formal identity statements as senseless or at least degenerate, and attached the greatest importance to material identity statements, thinking of them as constituting the very backbone of thought and discourse.

There are other, more specific statements of the problem of material identity. Frege observed that what I have called material identity statements may be informative and a posteriori, while formal identity statements are neither. That the Morning Star is the same as the Evening Star is a discovery of astronomy. That the Morning Star is the same as the Morning Star is not a matter of discovery at all. But, we should note, many material identity statements (e.g., "18 + 13 = 31") are not a posteriori and, in one sense of this vague word, also not informative. And if logical truths have an ontological ground, then, in another sense, even formal identity statements could be said to be informative.

It has also been supposed that, unlike formal identity statements, material identity statements are often contingent. While the Morning Star could not have failed to be the same as the Morning Star, it could have failed to be the same as the Evening Star. For, it would seem, either the statement "The Morning Star is the same as the Evening Star" is so understood as to entail that the planet at a certain place in the morning sky also occupies a certain particular place in the evening sky, or it is not so understood. If it is so understood, then of course it is contingent, since it entails a contingent statement. If not so understood, then it is not really the statement that those who claim it is contingent have taken it to be. For a statement cannot be divorced from the way in which it is understood and thus from the situation in which it would ordinarily be made. The notion of a statement is not purely "metaphysical," but also "epistemic." I shall return to this topic. But here it would suffice to repeat that in any case many material identity statements (e.g., "18 + 13 = 31") are not contingent.*

And, it has been claimed that material identity statements do not legitimize unrestricted substitutivity of their terms in modal and intentional contexts. Even if a is the same as b, there are

*This fact should also discourage frothier suggestions such as that what "a is b" is about appears to be distinct things just in case "a" and "b" designate different things in some "possible world," even though the same thing in the actual world; or just in case a and b are only partially coincident "transworld heir lines" of "manifestations" or "embodiments" of individuals in various possible worlds; or just in case a and b have different "counterparts" in some possible world.

statements in which "*a*" occurs where it cannot be replaced by "*b*" without change of truth-value. It may be true that it is neces-sary that *a* is F, but false that it is necessary that *b* is F; it may be true that S believes that *a* is F, but false that S believes that *b* is F. How is this possible? Does it not contradict the principle of the indiscernibility of identicals, which, unlike that of the identity of indiscernibles, seems indubitable? But while these problems must receive solutions, they would be, as a matter of philosophical strategy, a grossly inappropriate starting point for an investigation of material identity. They are inextricably tied to topics extraneous to that of identity, such as the nature of mental acts and their objects, necessary truth, and the notion of property (it has been argued that nonsubstitutivity is incompati-ble with indiscernibility only if every open sentence expresses a property). And it is reasonable to believe, as I shall argue in chapter three, that their solution would rest in part on the solu-tion of the general problem of material identity.

The fact is that while the informative, a posteriori, and seem-ingly contingent character of some material identity statements, and the restrictions on the substitutivity of the terms of all such statements, are puzzling, they are merely symptoms of the fundamental puzzle, namely, how can identicals appear to be dis-tinct? Some such statements are informative and a posteriori be-cause we find nothing in our notions of the things described as identical from which we could infer that they are identical; and this is so because these notions appear to be notions of distinct things. Some material identity statements are taken to be contin-gent because material identicals appear to be distinct things; and, in the case of certain categories of things, namely, those that may be perceived and therefore imagined, we tend to assume that if they appear to be distinct then it is logically possible that they are distinct. ("What is imaginable is logically possible.") And names of material identicals seem to fail to be intersubstitut-ible *salva veritate* in intentional and modal contexts because, since such identicals appear to be distinct things and thus could be taken to be really distinct, what one knows or believes about the one need not be what one knows or believes about the other, and what seems to be necessarily true of the one need not seem to be necessarily true of the other.

IV

Frege claimed that the statement "*a* is *b*" is informative, unlike the statement "*a* is *a*," because "*a*" and "*b*" have different senses although, if the former statement is true, they have the same reference.[12] Unfortunately, he said very little about the nature of senses, and inevitably a criticism of his theory is in danger of being directed at something he did not mean. Nevertheless, we can say with some confidence that it is faced with the following dilemma. Let the senses of "*a*" and "*b*" be modes of presentation of their reference or ways in which their reference is given;[13] or ways of determining their reference;[14] or their meanings or intensions ("individual concepts");[15] or states of affairs or contexts in which their reference is found in the world. If the senses of "*a*" and "*b*" are really different from their reference, then it must be explained why and how the distinctness of the senses should produce an appearance of distinctness of the references. For "*a* is *b*" is a statement about *a* and *b*, e.g., certain planets, not about modes of presentation, or about ways of determining the reference of "*a*" and "*b*", or about meanings or intensions or individual concepts, or about states of affairs or contexts; and it is *a* and *b* themselves that appear distinct, not just some modes of presentation, or ways of determining reference, or meanings or intensions or individual concepts, or states of affairs or contexts.* On the other hand, if the senses are not really different from the

*Cf. David Wiggins: "As Frege himself remarks, 'If words are used in the normal way what one intends to speak of is their reference'; and nothing might seem more self-evident than this. Why then should *the way* in which the subject(s) in the sentence 'The evening star = the morning star' are picked out by definite descriptions affect what is *said* about it (them)?" ("Identity-Statements,"

reference, then it would seem that the distinctness of the senses of "*a*" and "*b*" is simply a distinctness of *a* and *b* themselves. But then how could the statement "*a* is *b*" be true? My claim is not that Frege cannot avoid this dilemma, but that he says nothing to suggest how he could do so.

Nevertheless, the dilemma is instructive. Indeed, something like its second horn is the chief issue before us. It can be understood quite generally. All cases of material identity, we may say, involve certain "things," other than the identicals themselves though "associated" with them, which are really distinct. These "things" may be meanings (descriptive contents) of expressions, or ways of determining the reference of expressions, or modes of presentation of the identical entity, or different spatial or temporal parts of the identicals, or properties or relations of the identicals, or states of affairs in which the identicals enter. And their "association" with the identicals may be a semantical or epistemic relation, or an ordinary relation, or exemplification of a property or of a relation, or constituency in a state of affairs.

Can we now say that the apparent distinctness of material identicals is due to the real distinctness of such associated things? For example, that the apparent distinctness of the color of this page and the color of the next page, both of which let us suppose are the same shade of white, is due to the real distinctness of the two pages? Or that the apparent distinctness of the Morning Star and the Evening Star is due to the real distinctness, say, of morning and evening? But if I know that John both owns the house at the corner and is married to Jane, the real distinctness of the two states of affairs need not have the slightest tendency to produce an appearance, whether in thought or in perception, of their being two persons, one who is the owner of the house at the corner and the other the husband of Jane.

in *Analytical Philosophy*, Second Series, ed. R. J. Butler [Oxford: Basil Blackwell, 1965], pp. 58-59.) That this, to my mind obvious, point seems in need of emphasis can be seen in John Searle's *Speech Acts* (Cambridge: Cambridge University Press, 1969), where he asserts "Everest is Chomolungma' states that the descriptive backing of both names is true of the same object" (p. 181).

Similarly, the mere difference in meaning (descriptive content) between the subject terms of an identity statement is not a sufficient condition of the appearance of distinctness between their references, between the identicals. It has been noted repeatedly that one may successfully refer to an object with a descriptive phrase that is not true (perhaps even is known to be not true) of the object.[16] And one may use a descriptive phrase for the purpose of making a true statement about an object without referring to, singling out, the object. (I shall say more about this shortly.) If so, then it is to be expected that the connection between the meaning of an expression and its reference would be too loose to allow us to suppose that the difference in meaning between the subject terms of an identity statement is a sufficient condition of the statement's subject matter's appearing to be two distinct things. That this indeed is so can be shown by examples, although with some difficulty, since they must be plausible examples of what in reality are formal identity statements and such statements do not ordinarily occur in natural languages. Consider a lecturer observing the persons in the front row. Were he to say (an unlikely event), "The woman sitting to Jones's right is the same as the woman sitting to Smith's left," he would almost certainly be making, I suggest, a formal identity statement.* He would almost certainly understand the statement he is making in such a way that its subject terms, though obviously very different in descriptive content, do not even appear to differ in reference. He would regard what the terms refer to exactly as he would regard what two tokens of the same referring expression (e.g., those in "The Evening Star is the same [planet] as the Evening Star") refer to, and not at all as he would regard material identicals (e.g., the Evening Star and the Morning Star). If he were to suppose that the statement is false, he would not be supposing that there are two persons the statement is about. He would suppose the latter only if he were to suppose that the *sentence* is used for making a quite different *statement*, one the reference of

---

*Consider the figure a . b and the following statement about it: "The point to the right of a is the same as the point to the left of b."

whose subject terms is understood quite differently. (For example, as it would be understood if, for some reason, when he singled out the person as the woman sitting to Jones's right he could not also have singled her out as the woman sitting to Smith's left.) Indeed, it may even be said that given the way in which he understands the reference of its subject terms, he cannot intelligibly suppose the statement to be false.[17] Whether this further point is useful depends on the sense attached to the phrase "intelligible to suppose," a matter in need of detailed, thorough philosophical investigation that cannot be attempted here.

Nevertheless, while an object's being "associated" with two states of affairs or with two expressions of different meanings is not a sufficient condition of its appearing to be two objects, sometimes the latter does seem to be *in part* due to the former. When does this happen? We may say: only when the object is *also* singled out in two different ways, namely, first as the object "associated" with the one state of affairs or (meaning of an) expression and then as the object "associated" with the other. As we shall see later, saying this does constitute some progress. We may even wish to say that to single out an object in different ways is the same as for it to be given or presented in different modes. This is why I have not also attempted to offer examples of cases in which "association" with such further "things" as modes of presentation fails to produce the appearance of distinctness. But whatever the terminology we employ, and despite the fact that some progress has been made, the appeal to different ways of singling out an object does not provide us with an adequate explanation of the apparent distinctness of material identicals. For what is it for an object to be singled out in different ways? Surely, to be singled out in ways that, considered in themselves, are indistinguishable from singlings-out of *different* objects, to be singled out as different objects would be singled out, perhaps even to be so singled out that one could intelligibly suppose that different objects have been singled out. And how does the fact that an object can be singled out in such ways differ from the fact that it can appear, whether in perception or in thought, to be two or more objects?

The supposition that the apparent distinctness of material identicals can be adequately understood in terms of the real distinctness of singlings-out of the object, or the real distinctness of certain things with which it is associated, seems plausible because we find unproblematic statements such as "The object singled out x'ly is the same as the object singled out y'ly" or "The object associated with x is the same as the object associated with y." (A Fregean, though not Frege himself, might be tempted to state his account of material identity by appealing to the truth of statements such as "The object presented in the x'y mode of presentation [sense] is the same as the object presented in the y'y mode of presentation [sense].")* But while such statements may be unproblematic in other philosophical contexts, they are useless to the account of material identity. For they themselves are material identity statements, and one should not hope to understand the peculiarities of material identity statements in general by appealing to a certain special sort of material identity statement. This is particularly clear with respect to claims that some material identity statements really assert that certain time-stages belong to the same spatiotemporal continuant or that certain sense-data belong to the same family of sense-data. Even if it were plausible to suppose that in a statement such as "Hesperus is the same as Phosphorus" there is reference to time-stages or sense-data, the analysis of the statement as meaning, say, "This time-stage and the one observed this morning belong to the same planet (are parts of the same spatiotemporal worm)" or "This sense-datum and that (remembered) sense-datum belong to the same family of sense-data," would constitute no progress in our

---

*"On this basis, then, what is asserted to obtain by a statement of the form 'A = B' is that the sense expressed by 'A' and the sense expressed by 'B' are senses of the same denotation." (Montgomery Furth, in his introduction to *The Basic Laws of Arithmetic*, pp. xix-xx.)

understanding of material identity, since these latter statements are themselves material identity statements.

V

According to Russell, (1) statements in which the identity sign is flanked by logically proper names are really formal identity statements; (2) statements in which it is flanked by ordinary proper names are statements in which it is flanked by disguised definite descriptions; and (3) statements in which it is flanked by definite descriptions are themselves disguised general particular ("existential") statements, and not identity statements at all. I shall argue against (1) and (3), which are the two views directly concerned with identity.

Russell's notion of a logically proper name is difficult. But I shall not question it. Instead, I shall give examples of statements in which the identity sign is flanked by signs that, even if not logically proper names, are certainly not disguised definite descriptions, and then argue that such statements preserve the apparent distinctness of the identicals and thus are not formal identity statements. Suppose that I assign *ostensively* the name "*a*" to the color of (a sense-datum associated with) this page, and the name "*b*" to the color of (a sense-datum associated with) the next page. So introduced, "*a*" and "*b*" are proper names, not predicates, and no more plausibly regarded as disguised descriptions than any proper names, including Russell's "logically proper names" of sense-data, would be so regarded. I submit now that "*a* is the same as *b*" is a material, not a formal, identity statement. (Of course, it is in no sense *about* the signs "*a*" and "*b*.") That *a* and *b* appear to be distinct should be evident from the fact (to be considered in detail in chapter seven) that most philosophers have rejected the existence of universals precisely because of such apparent distinctness.* They have not been de-

---

*Cf. G. F. Stout, *The Nature of Universals and Propositions* (London: Oxford University Press, 1921, British Academy Annual Philosophical Lecture). I dis-

nying the law of identity. Moreover, I could, though not very lucidly, express the fact that the color of this page (sense-datum) is the same as the color of that page (sense-datum) simply by saying "This is the same (color) as that," referring with "this" to the color of the one page (sense-datum) and with "that" to the color of the other page (sense-datum). Indeed, if we ignore Russell's preoccupation with sense-data, we may also observe that a person could express his belief that the planet he sees now in the evening is the same as the planet he saw in the morning by saying "This is the same (planet) as that," referring with "this" to the planet he sees now and with "that" to the planet he saw in the morning. So used, "this" and "that" may not be logically proper names, but neither are they ordinary proper names or disguised descriptions (as "Hesperus" and "Phosphorus" perhaps are). Yet the statement in which they occur is a material identity statement, the identicals appearing to be distinct.

Does Russell's theory of descriptions solve the problem of the apparent distinctness of material identicals in the case of statements in which the identity sign is flanked by definite descriptions? I suggest that it does not. To begin with, its analysis of such a statement employs the notion of material identity and thus should not even purport to elucidate it. For example, "The F is the same as the G" would be analyzed as equivalent to "$(\exists b):.Fx. \equiv_x.x=b:.(\exists c):Gx. \equiv_x.x=c:b=c$." But the form "$b=c$" is an essential part of this analysis.* The analysis cannot be understood unless this form is understood. How is it to be understood? Only by regarding it as the form of statements such as "Cicero is the same as Tully," "The Evening Star is the same as the Morn-

---

cuss the issue in *Resemblance and Identity: An Examination of the Problem of Universals* (Bloomington and London: Indiana University Press, 1966). In *An Inquiry into Meaning and Truth* (London: George Allen and Unwin, 1940) Russell is explicit in allowing for proper names such as "*a*" and "*b*."

*In "On Denoting" Russell notes that "The meaning of such [propositions as 'Scott was the author of *Waverly*' and 'Thou art the man'] cannot be stated without the notion of identity," but does not seem to appreciate the importance of this fact. (*Logic and Knowledge*, p. 55.) Cf. Wiggins, "Identity-Statements," p. 65.

ing Star," "This is the same as that." Indeed, as we have seen, it could also be the grammatical form of formal identity statements such as "To be a bachelor is to be an unmarried man" and "Scott is Sir Walter." But in the present context it must be understood as the form of genuine material identity statements. This is evident when we think of the bound variables "b" and "c" as pronouns and read the whole statement as follows: "One and only one thing is F, and one and only one thing is G, and the former is the same as the latter."

We could, of course, still in accord with Russell's analysis, say instead, "One and only one thing is both F and G, and nothing else is either F or G." We would still need the identity statement form in order to assert the uniqueness, but no longer in order to assert the identity, of the F and the G. And we could dispense with that form altogether by adopting the early Wittgenstein's convention that the proposition *"Only one x satisfies f ( )"* read: $"(\exists x).fx: \sim(\exists x,y).fx.fy."$[18] Even so, the analysis still misrepresents the sort of situation ordinarily described with statements of the form "The F is the same as the G" in precisely the respect that prompted our inquiry. It analyzes it as a *general* fact. Yet what we ordinarily intend to describe when we say of something singled out by its having a certain characteristic that it is the same as something singled out by its having a certain other characteristic is a paradigm of a *singular* fact. The situation described by the Russellian statement is not an identity situation at all. The one ordinarily described by a statement of the form "The F is the same as the G" is. The difference between the two, even if in some sense an appearance, is nevertheless an essential feature of our experience and thought. This feature must be explained, not ignored.

The failure of Russell's theory of descriptions to reflect the difference between the above sorts of situation is the true source of its familiar failure to do justice to the referring uses of descriptive phrases. I have in mind, of course, Strawson's distinction between referring and nonreferring uses of such phrases, especially as revised and developed by Donnellan,[19] but I shall understand it in terms of a narrower and, I believe, philosophically more fundamental notion of reference, a notion that remains relevant to the metaphysical and epistemological concerns that led to philosophers' interest in the nature of reference. A descriptive phrase, I say, is used referringly only if it is used to single something out and establish it as an object of our thought or perception, to point it out, to fix our attention on it, to place it, so to speak, before our minds. When used nonreferringly, it is merely a means of making an affirmation regarding the properties or relations of what it denotes.* Thus the notion of reference should be sharply distinguished from that of denotation, of an expression's standing for, or applying to, something. To use one of Strawson's examples, the descriptive phrase in "Napoleon was the greatest French soldier" would ordinarily be used nonreferringly, while the descriptive phrase in "The greatest French soldier died in exile" would ordinarily be used referringly. While in the latter statement it would probably serve to single out Napoleon, in the former it would probably be intended not to single out anything but to affirm of Napoleon that he was greater than any other French soldier.

Of course, in special circumstances the phrase could be used referringly even in "Napoleon was the greatest French soldier," namely, when the speaker has singled out someone as the greatest French soldier independently of his being Napoleon. And it could be used nonreferringly in "The greatest French soldier died in exile," if, for example, the speaker makes the statement solely on the basis of general propositions about French military and political history. Russell's theory may not be an adequate account of the *use* of the phrase in this latter case, if Strawson is right that if the description is not uniquely satisfied

---

*So understood, the distinction may be very much in need of clarification, but, I suggest, it is sharp. As expounded by Strawson and Donnellan, it admits of intermediate cases. Cf. Joseph Margolis and Evan Fales, "Donnellan on Definite Descriptions," *Philosophia* 6 (1976): 289–302.

then the result is not (as Russell claims) that a false statement is made, but rather that either no statement is made at all or the statement made is neither true nor false. But, although I shall not argue this here, I am inclined to accept Russell's theory as an adequate account of *the state of affairs* (if any) the speaker intends to describe by means of the sentence in this case. For, since *ex hypothesi* he has no particular individual in mind to whom he attributes death in exile, then, if he has anything relevant in mind (which he may not have), what could it be if not the general state of affairs that someone is greater than any other French soldier and died in exile?

In the rest of this book I shall use the term "reference" and its cognates only in the narrower sense I have just tried to explain. A further explanation of it could be to say that a necessary condition of the referring use of a descriptive phrase is that the user be *acquainted* with the thing referred to, in the sense of "acquaintance" in which Russell used this term, or that he *intuit* the thing, be confronted with it, in Husserl's sense of "intuition." But I shall not presuppose any specific view of the kinds of things with which one can be acquainted or which one can intuit (e.g., sense-data but not physical objects?), or about the kinds of acquaintance or intuition there are (e.g., sense-perception but not imagination?). The development and defense of such views belong to epistemology and the philosophy of mind, not to proto-metaphysics.* Of course, Russell's notion of acquaintance and Husserl's notion of intuition, indeed the general notion of some-

---

*The investigation of these questions in recent decades has been left almost exclusively to the continental philosophers. For example, the classical work on the nature of the imagination is Sartre's. According to Sartre, "The image of my friend Peter is not a dim phosphorescence, a furrow left in consciousness by a perception of Peter. It is an organized form of consciousness which refers in its own way to my friend Peter; it is one of the possible ways of aiming at Peter. Thus, in the act of imagination consciousness refers to Peter directly, not by means of a simulacrum *in* consciousness." (*Imagination: A Psychological Critique*, trans. Forrest Williams [Ann Arbor: The University of Michigan Press, 1972], p. 134.)

thing's being an object before the mind, are far from clear and very much in need of philosophical elucidation (though not more so, I suggest, than are the chief notions in, say, the "historical explanation" theory of reference). But, I believe, they are indispensable for our understanding of the philosophically interesting aspects of the uses of language, as well as of many other philosophical topics, and disdain for them would at best be ostrichlike behavior.

Singling something out must not be confused with *identifying* it. The former is a necessary but not a sufficient condition of the latter. To identify something is to make a judgment about it, whether overtly or not,[20] namely, a true material identity judgment, which may, but need not, be the judgment that the object singled out by the hearer is the same as the object the speaker intended him to single out. To single something out, on the other hand, is not to make a judgment at all, although it may provide some judgment, including one of identity, with a subject. (This is why, even if we need criteria for identification, we do not need criteria for singling something out. I shall return to this point.) Thus the notion of singling something out is logically prior to, and philosophically more fundamental than, that of identifying. And the latter is far broader, and has philosophically far more significant species, than the notion of a hearer's identifying what the speaker has singled out. It seems to me unfortunate that discussions of reference and identification have been preoccupied with the vagaries of this last sort of situation.*

Now Russell's theory of descriptions is incapable of reflecting the distinction between referring and nonreferring uses of descriptive phrases. Indeed, it analyzes all statements containing

---

*A notion of reference similar to ours has been proposed by Jaakko Hintikka in his more recent work (see especially "Knowledge by Acquaintance—Individuation by Acquaintance," in *Bertrand Russell*, ed. D. F. Pears [Garden City: Doubleday, 1972]). I have in mind his notion of individuation by acquaintance. But he does not make the sharp distinction I have just drawn between individuation (singling out) and identification.

descriptive phrases as if these phrases were used nonreferringly.
The analysis it offers of "The F is the same as the G" is a general
particular ("existential") statement, in which no names or descriptions of individuals occur. Clearly, with such a statement no
reference to, no *singling-out* of, an individual can be achieved,
even if the predicate constituting the scope of the quantifier happens to be *true* of some individual. This inability to reflect the
referring uses of descriptive phrases need not be a fatal defect of
his theory of descriptions, for it may be that, as Russell says in his
reply to Strawson,[21] the theory was never intended to apply to
"egocentric" uses of language, and that all referring uses of language are, in his sense, egocentric. It is a fatal defect, however, of
any attempt to account for the apparent distinctness of material
identicals by means of that theory. For material identicals appear
distinct precisely when referred to, singled out—when they appear as distinct objects of our thought or perception. Even if the
statement "The firstborn baby next year will be the recipient of a
gift from the Chamber of Commerce" should seem to someone to
be about two persons, this could easily be taken as due solely to
the surface grammar of the statement, and we may be quite
satisfied with restating it as "One and only one baby will both be
born first next year and receive a gift from the Chamber of Commerce, and no other baby will either be born first next year or
receive a gift from the Chamber of Commerce." For, presumably,
the descriptive phrases used in the former single out no one,
direct our attention to no object, and merely serve to make what
in reality is a general statement. But this is not the case with
statements such as "The color of this page is the same as the color
of the next page" and "The Evening Star is the same as the
Morning Star," in the usual circumstances in which they would
be made. The descriptive phrases in them are used referringly,
and this is why the appearance of distinctness of the identicals
can be eliminated only by misrepresentation of what is asserted.
To analyze such statements as general particular statements, as
statements in which no reference is made to anything, would be

grossly inadequate. And it is precisely in such statements that the distinctness of the identicals is strikingly apparent and the concept of identity finds its primary and indispensable application. For in such statements not only do the descriptive phrases appear to be *true of* different objects (as might be the case even when used nonreferringly), but also they appear to *refer to, single out,* different objects, to draw our attention in *different directions.**

The above argument against the Russellian analysis of material identity statements holds also against Wittgenstein's view in the *Tractatus* that "Expressions of the form '*a* = *b*' are ... mere representational devices. They state nothing about the meaning [*Bedeutung*] of the signs '*a*' and '*b*' " (4.242), that "the identity-sign is ... not an essential constituent of conceptual notation" (5.533). Wittgenstein supports this view by arguing for the possibility of a language in which different signs have different meanings: "Identity of the object I express by identity of the sign, and not by using a sign for identity. Difference of objects I express by difference of signs" (5.53). But to be adequate, a symbolic notation must be capable of expressing that feature of many situations because of which we are uncertain whether we require one sign or two signs in order to describe the situation. It is not because of the presence in my language of different names and descriptions for the same thing that I might wonder whether a certain planet seen in the morning is the same as a certain planet seen in the evening. On the contrary, it is mainly because of such wonderment, and thus of the fact about the world, or our experience of the world, which makes such wonderment possible, that our language contains many names and descriptions for one and

---

*Of course, the misrepresentation need not affect the truth-value of the statement. The apparent distinctness of material identicals is hardly ordinary nonidentity, even if it is more than mere appearance. This is why Russell's theory of descriptions may remain adequate as an account of the truth-conditions of material identity statements. The general distinction on which this point rests is discussed by Strawson in "Identifying Reference and Truth-Values," *Theoria* 30 (1964): 96–118.

the same thing. Once such wonderment has been satisfied, we may indeed not require more than one name for each thing. And it is this fact that renders Wittgenstein's view plausible. We may even say that once we have settled the crucial questions of what entities there are and which objects of our thought and perception are one and the same entity and which are not, we would not need the sign of identity. But it is the settlement of just these questions that constitutes the most fundamental task of understanding and knowing the world, and we need the concept of identity precisely because the world poses such questions to us, not because we happen to describe it in imperfect symbolic notations.

This suggests the nature of the fundamental defect of Russell's and the early Wittgenstein's, though not Frege's, views on material identity. They take for granted that the apparent distinctness of material identicals arises out of certain features of language and therefore is to be explained by considerations *about* language. But the apparent distinctness of material identicals is a fact about the world, or at least about our experience of the world, quite independent of language. This fact can be noticed and examined without reference to language. We need not name or describe the color of one page and the color of another page, or a planet we see at one time and a planet we see at another time, in order to wonder whether they are one and the same and perhaps determine that they are. The apparent distinctness of the colors or of the planets is a matter of experience, absolutely essential to the sort of situation we are confronted with, and not at all due to any names or descriptive phrases we apply to them. If it is to be understood, it must be understood as a fact about the world, not about language. Here, as elsewhere, the linguistic turn, I suggest, was the wrong turn for philosophers to take.

But there is perhaps a deeper reason for Russell's and the early Wittgenstein's views: the puzzling, seemingly incomprehensible nature of material identity. One need not be a linguistic philosopher to feel compelled to deny it a place in the world. We shall see shortly, however, that such a denial is incompatible with the very possibility of conceptual cognition and thus of language itself. In a world without material identity nothing is recognizable, nothing can be classified, nothing can be perceived or referred to twice, no linguistic expressions could be used twice with the same sense or the same reference, no piece of language, or of knowledge, or of thought could last beyond the specious present. We would be in the Heraclitean flux, with its consequences for knowledge and language that Plato so eloquently described in the *Theaetetus*.

VI

I conclude that the first approach to the problem of the apparent distinctness of material identicals, namely, the attempt to show that the appearance in question is a mere appearance, presumably one due to language, is unsuccessful. Can we then go to the other extreme and claim that it is a real distinctness? For example, can we simply acknowledge that the Morning Star is distinct from the Evening Star, and the color of this page from the color of that page? One (perhaps Hegel or the later Wittgenstein) may argue that our supposition that this is unintelligible, as with so many philosophical convictions, is the result of an obsession with an inappropriate paradigm. Philosophers take formal identity as their paradigm of identity and insist that any other kind of identity must be understood as a disguised sort of formal identity. Logicians, it would be said, are particularly subject to this obsession and it is not surprising that we find some of them denying that an identity may be contingent. For is not identity the sort of case that is paradigmatically described with statements such as "*a* is *a*"? And how could such a statement be contingent?

But, one would continue, in reality formal identity statements are at best degenerate statements, and the concept of identity finds genuine application only in material identity statements. The distinctness of identicals is not only an appearance but a natural and essential feature of genuine cases of identity. If *a* and *b* were not distinct, why would anyone wish to say anything about them? Would there be anything that could be said about them, other than the ritualistic "*a* is *a*" or "*b* is *b*"?

Of course, to admit that material identicals are distinct is not to allow that just any two things may be said to be identical. To argue that it is would be another example of the logician's abstract, lifeless thought and discourse. We apply the concept of identity to distinct things, but not to just any distinct things. There are paradigms for its application, and the correctness of a particular application can be judged by reference to its conformity, or at least closeness, to these paradigms. Spatiotemporal coincidence of things of the same sort is one such paradigm. One road's end being the same as another road's end is an unquestionable, primitive case of the application of the concept of identity.* Another paradigm is identity through time. An ashtray being the same as an ashtray seen a moment earlier is an equally unquestionable and primitive case of identity. Neither in the case of spatiotemporal coincidence nor in that of identity through time do we have a natural substitute for identity statements. Not so, however, in the case of the identity of qualities. Indeed, it is correct to say that the color of this page is the same as the color of the next page. But it is equally correct to say that it is exactly like it. And when we come to cases such as mind-body identity, the divergence from the paradigms of identity seems to us excessive. It is not surprising, therefore, that philosophers have almost never questioned identity as spatiotemporal coincidence, have seldom questioned identity through time, have divided over the problem of universals, and usually have rejected mind-body identity.

But, however refreshing we may find such a bold acceptance of real distinctness between material identicals, we must also find it more suggestive than illuminating. Like other philosophical appeals to how our concepts are *in fact* employed, as contrasted with appeals to how our concepts *ought* to be employed, this one would be more a case of youthful exhilaration than careful, de-

---

*We should not suppose that the appearance of distinctness must be absent from cases of spatiotemporal coincidence just because, presumably, there it can be present only in thought, not perception. Consider Frege's example from geometry in *Translations*, p. 11.

tailed thought. We must understand our concepts not just in terms of the commotion of their everyday applications but also in terms of the light they throw upon the world. And as soon as we attempt to do so, we see that the claim that material identicals are really distinct entities is obscurantist. For in what sense are they distinct? In the sense that they are nonidentical, not the same? If so, then obviously the suggestion is absurd. We cannot allow that the notion of identity is self-contradictory. In what other sense may they be distinct? In that they violate the principle of the indiscernibility of identicals? This cannot be the case, not so much because of the self-evidence of that principle as because of the purpose of making material identity statements at all. We assert that *a* and *b* are the same chiefly in order to allow ourselves to say whatever we say about the one also about the other. If their distinctness were supposed to consist in *a*'s being F and *b*'s being G, the point of asserting that they are the same would still be to allow us to say also that *a* is G and *b* is F. The indiscernibility of identicals is not a criterion for the application of the concept of identity. Rather, the applicability of the concept of identity to *a* and *b* is the criterion for regarding *a* and *b* as indiscernible. Were we indiscriminate in our application of the concept of identity, we would find no limits to our application of the concept of indiscernibility. As long as we are willing to assert the identity of *a* and *b*, we are also willing to enforce their indifference in predication. I shall return to this point in chapter three.

We should resist the temptation now to pick up our marbles and quit by simply denying that material identity is genuine, true, or strict identity, reserving the title of "identity" only for formal identity, and calling material identity something else, whether "congruence,"[22] or "a weaker equivalence relation,"[23] or "consubstantiation."[24] Unless such a move were purely verbal, it would constitute an abuse of the natural concept of identity, not a step toward its elucidation.[25] And we must respect the natural concepts in terms of which the philosophical problems that concern us have arisen. The home of the concept of identity is precisely in statements such as "The Evening Star is the same as the Morning Star," not in statements such as "The Evening Star is the same as the Evening Star," even if the latter are not senseless. And its role consists, as we shall see, in a sort of ontological simplification that alone can transform the objects of our thought and perception into a world. We need the concept of identity precisely in order to be able to assert of what might have been supposed to be two things that in fact they are *literally* one thing. And, as I have noted already and will consider in detail in chapter three, an essential aspect of this simplification is the enforcement of indiscernibility. The name we assign to the concept is, of course, immaterial. But to reject it is to deprive ourselves of our primary tool of conceptual understanding. The restriction of the concept of identity to formal identity constitutes just such a rejection. Unless purely verbal, it requires us to regard material identity as a relation, however special and important, between distinct entities. And no relation that holds between distinct entities can allow the ontological simplification and enforcement of indiscernibility that are the *raison d'être* of material identity.

CHAPTER TWO

Objects and Entities

I

We regard the world as consisting of entities, existents, each of which may be singled out, thought about, or perceived in different ways, but each of which is only the same as itself and different from everything else. These entities may be individuals, or properties, or classes; they may be material things or minds; they may be sense-data or numbers. What sorts of entities are included in our conception of the world depends on our metaphysics, but only on the upper levels of metaphysics, not on the foundational, protometaphysical level. For on that level metaphysical systems agree. The world consists of entities, existents, each of which, in Bishop Butler's words, "is what it is and not another thing."

This picture of the world, of course, is not mistaken. What is mistaken is our supposition that it is logically the first picture, that it is logically prior to, and incorporates, any other picture. Specifically, I want to argue, the application of the concepts of identity and existence has to do not with the domain of entities but with another, logically prior domain, or, put differently, though not less figuratively, it has to do with the *conceptual* (not necessarily also psychological or phenomenological or epistemological) transition to a domain of entities from a logically prior and more primitive domain. And the apparent distinctness of material identicals is the real distinctness not of entities but of the constituents of that more primitive domain, while their identity is the result of their emerging from that domain into the domain of entities.

The logically first picture of the world is that of the domain of the objects of the application of our conceptual apparatus. And the most fundamental application of our conceptual apparatus is the application of the concepts of identity and existence. It can also be described as the application of the concept of entity. For an entity may be understood as something that exists and is identifiable, that is, is identical with other, possible or actual, objects of thought or perception. Ordinarily, the applicability of sortal concepts, such as those of a table or a dog, presupposes the applicability of the concepts of existence and identity, that is, the classification of what the sortal concept applies to as an entity.* Indeed, this is true of any concepts whose applicability is regarded as subject to future or other persons' verification, including the ordinary, largely dispositional concepts of observable properties such as colors and shapes. For verification necessarily involves reidentification and thus identification.[1]

Moreover, I shall argue, the concepts of existence and identity themselves presuppose each other in their application, and this is why their roles are both inseparable from and jointly equivalent to that of the concept of entity. We regard an object of thought or perception as existent, as real, only if we regard it as logically capable of being thought or perceived in a number of distinct ways, and thus as logically capable of a number of distinct identifications, a fact particularly eloquently though obscurely emphasized by Sartre.[2] And we have a clear notion of what it is for an object of thought or perception to be identical with another object only if we regard it as existent, as an entity. We have no criteria for the *identity* of nonexistent objects. The concept of identity is not applicable to such objects in material identity statements, and its application to them in formal identity statements, in which the concept of identity has logically guaran-

---

*I shall consider the view, mainly associated with P. T. Geach, that identity statements are logically incomplete unless they specify the sort of the identicals, in chapter three.

teed universal applicability, requires no criteria. To paraphrase Quine's example,[3] are the imagined (not just "possible," as Quine says!) fat man in the doorway today and the imagined bald man in the doorway yesterday the same man or not? There is no possibility of an answer. Nor do we have criteria for the *existence* of objects that we do not regard as multiply identifiable. For example, if we suppose, for whatever reason, that a certain object of perception can, as a matter of logical necessity, be the object of only one act of perception, we find ourselves incapable of giving sense to the question whether it is real or not. And when, despite reasonable efforts, an object of an act of perception is not perceived again, whether by us or by anyone else, then, in the absence of other information, we regard this as a good (though hardly conclusive) reason for denying its existence.

If whatever exists is identifiable (is the subject of true material identity judgments) and also whatever is identifiable exists, then it becomes plausible to suppose that one of these two concepts can be understood, elucidated, in terms of the other. Clearly, we cannot understand the concept of identity in terms of the concept of existence. The latter simply does not possess the sort of rich content that could throw light on the concept of identity, or indeed on any other concept. But there is no similar difficulty about the elucidation of the concept of existence in terms of the concept of identity. We genuinely enrich our understanding of what it is for *a* to exist if we say that it consists in *a*'s being identifiable, i.e., in its being the subject of true material identity judgments of the form "*a* is identical with *x*." Thus, it is the concept of identity that constitutes the cutting edge of our conceptual apparatus. But the adequate explanation and defense of this view may only be given at the end of chapter four, after independent and detailed accounts of the problems of identity and existence have been developed. Here I shall provide only a partial explanation and defense.*

---

*I should warn against a hasty acceptance now of either of the two familiar definitions of existence in terms of identity: "a exists=df. $(\exists x) (x=a)$" and "a

The reason for accepting the proposition that whatever exists is identifiable is implicit in Plato's argument that there can be no knowledge or even language about things in a flux,[4] in Frege's argument that if something is to be accepted as an object it must be capable of being recognized,[*] in Wittgenstein's argument against the possibility of a private language,[5] and in Price's argument for the primacy of recognition in conceptual cognition.[6] It does not consist, of course, in a stipulative definition of "exists" or in a discovery about the ordinary use of that word. It consists in the recognition of the intimate relation between the notion of existence or reality, on one hand, and the notions of knowledge, understanding, judgment, and concept, on the other. If something exists, is real, then it is knowable. If knowable, then it is understandable. If understandable, then judgments about it are possible. To make a judgment about something is to apply concepts to it. A concept must, in principle, be reapplicable. Its reapplicability presupposes the identifiability, the recognizability, of the objects of its application, that is, the truth of certain material identity judgments.

That the above reasoning is correct with respect to properties probably needs no demonstration. Unless a property (e.g., a color) is identifiable (reidentifiable, recognizable), there can be no concept of it, no predicate standing for it, and thus no judgments about it and no judgments in which it is attributed to something else. But our reasoning is no less correct with respect to individuals. Unless an individual is identifiable, i.e., can con-

exists=df. (a=a)." If we assume that the range of the quantifiers and the reference of names are restricted to existent things, then these two definitions are conceptually trivial. If we do not make these assumptions, then both definitions entail that everything, including, e.g., Pegasus, exists. For then the definiens of the second definition would be true for every substituend of "a," and so, by "existential" generalization, would be the definiens of the first definition. Cf. Karel Lambert, "Free Logic and the Concept of Existence," *Notre Dame Journal of Formal Logic* 8 (1967): 133–44.

*If we are to use the symbol *a* to signify an object, we must have a criterion for deciding in all cases whether *b* is the same as *a*, even if it is not always in our power to apply this criterion." *The Foundations of Arithmetic*, trans. J. L. Austin (New York: Harper, 1960), p. 73.

stitute the subject matter of material identity judgments, it could have no proper name; for unless a name can be used again with the same reference it will not be a genuine part of language, and it cannot be used again with the same reference unless there are criteria for the material identity of its reference. Unless an individual is identifiable, it cannot be recognized, we can have no concept of it, in a wider sense of "concept" to be explained in chapter five. No judgment about it can remain in the store of knowledge and thus deserve to be called a judgment, since at a later time there would be no way of telling that the judgment is still about what it was about when made originally. The individual would not be an element of a stable, coherent, lasting picture of the world. And, of course, it would not be the object of public discourse, of communicable thought and knowledge.

It is not surprising, therefore, that individuals enduring through time are ordinarily regarded as the paradigm of real individuals. But the above considerations are broad enough to allow also for momentary individuals. We must not assume that only present individuals can be singled out and referred to; this may be true in the case of perception, but not in the case of imagination or thought. A momentary individual can, therefore, be singled out again and reidentified through imagination or thought, although of course it cannot be perceived again. Moreover, if an individual is to be real, an entity, what is required is the logical possibility of its identification by someone, at some time, perhaps only by God, and not the empirical or even the logical possibility of its identification now, or by me, or indeed by a human being.* Existence is intimately connected with knowability only if the latter is understood as the logical possibility of knowledge by someone, perhaps only by God, and not as the empirical or even the logical possibility of knowledge now, or by me, or by some human being.

An important consequence of the above reasoning is that if a

---

*Compare A. J. Ayer's discussion of the verifiability of statements about the past and about other minds in *The Problem of Knowledge* (London: Macmillan, 1958), chapters IV and V.

thing is identifiable at all, it is indefinitely identifiable. For what could set a limit to the number of logically possible identifications, given that at least one identification is logically possible? If existence is to be understood as identifiability, it must be understood as indefinite identifiability.

But while the above may persuade us that whatever exists is indefinitely identifiable, the converse of this proposition, that whatever is indefinitely identifiable exists, obviously requires further defense. (Are not fictional characters and mythological beings often the subjects of true material identity judgments? If they are, then they are identifiable. And if identifiable, why not indefinitely identifiable?) We shall not be ready for this defense until the end of chapter four. Until then our account of the connection between the concepts of identity and existence will remain provisional. I have argued here for the proposition that whatever exists is indefinitely identifiable in order to demonstrate the fundamental character of the concept of identity, the special role it plays in the application of our conceptual apparatus. That the concept of existence also has such a fundamental character and such a special role requires no argument. That entities are existents, that nothing would be a world unless it consists of entities, are mere tautologies. But that entities are indefinitely identifiable, that nothing would be a world unless its constituents are indefinitely identifiable, are not mere tautologies.

II

I shall refer to the domain of the logically first applications of our conceptual apparatus, that is, the applications of the concepts of identity and existence, as the domain of *objects*, and to the domain that emerges from it by virtue of these applications as the domain of *entities*. The apparent distinctness of material identicals is simply their real distinctness as objects. They are identical only as entities. And we acknowledge our intuition that the ap-

parent distinctness of material identicals is not the real distinctness of certain other entities, whether meanings of words (e.g.,
"individual concepts"), or properties, or relations, or states of
affairs, but of the identicals themselves, by pointing out that an
object is not another sort of entity but rather that which, by the
application of the concepts of identity and existence, comes to be
regarded as an entity.

The distinction between objects and entities is not a real distinction, a distinction between classes of things, but a distinction
of reason, a distinction due solely to the application of concepts.
An object is anything that may be referred to, singled out for our
attention, whether in perception, thought, or discourse; it is anything that may be classified, subjected to conceptualization. If
the concepts of identity and existence are applicable to it, that is,
if it exists and if it is identical with some other objects, then it is
an entity. And it may be an entity of any sort that our ordinary or
philosophical rules for the application of the concepts of identity
and existence allow us to acknowledge—material or mental, objective or subjective, concrete or abstract, "extensional" or "intensional." This is why we can say, without paradox, that material
identity statements are both about objects and about entities. If
true, such a statement is about the entity that is each of the two
objects the statement is also about. And it is about objects because it asserts of two objects that they are one and the same
entity. Unlike a formal identity statement, a material identity
statement is about two objects. And, if true, it is about one entity.

But how are we to understand the above philosophical statements? Obviously, they involve the concept of identity. To say
that the true material identity statement "*a* is the same as *b*" is
about two objects is to say that, as objects, *a* and *b* are not the
same. To say that it is about one entity is to say that as entities *a*
and *b* are the same. Clearly, neither of these can be a material
identity statement. For the distinction between objects and
entities has been introduced precisely for the purpose of
elucidating material identity statements. It has been explained in

such a way that the concept of identity cannot be applied materially (that is, in material identity statements) to objects as objects or to entities as entities.

However, the concept of identity can also be applied formally, that is, in formal identity statements. We may say, therefore, that as objects a and b are not the same in the sense that they are not formally identical (i.e., they are not identical in the way in which Scott is identical with Scott or in the way Scott is identical with Sir Walter), and that as entities a and b are the same in the sense that the entity a and the entity b are formally identical. Indeed, this is exactly as it should be. It is a direct consequence of our distinction between formal and material identity, and of the way in which we have introduced the notions of object and entity. The concept of identity can be applied to entities as such and to objects as such only formally; and it can be applied formally only to entities as such and to objects as such. (The reason we tend to regard formal identity as paradigmatic is precisely that we tend to regard the subject matter of identity statements as consisting of entities—each of which is the same only as itself and different from every other one.) Material identity, on the other hand, is the identity of things considered both as objects and as entities. The concept of identity can be applied to such things only materially; and it can be applied materially only to such things. For the role of material identity is precisely to serve as the bridge between the domain of objects and the domain of entities; while the role of formal identity is internal to each of these domains.

I have also made philosophical statements asserting that a certain object (or a number of certain objects) is (are) a certain entity. What do these statements mean? The answer to *this* question, of course, consists in the whole of the present inquiry. For the question in effect demands an elucidation of the distinction between objects and entities. To describe these philosophical statements as asserting the material or the formal identity of an object and an entity would be a travesty of that distinction. Indeed, no categorization of them in terms of familiar notions would be acceptable or should even be considered. We could say that a certain object is a certain entity in the sense that by virtue of the application to it of our conceptual apparatus, and most directly of the concepts of identity and existence, it is *conceptualized into* that entity. But, of course, the phrase just italicized has no established sense. If we employ it, we must understand it solely in terms of the philosophical picture the present inquiry attempts to convey. In chapter five I shall offer a specific interpretation of certain *nonphilosophical* statements as asserting of an object that it is a certain entity, but still I shall not interpret them as identity statements.

The appeal to formal identity two paragraphs above would be legitimate only if formal identity is clearly distinguishable from, and independent of, material identity. Indeed, it is. The two applications of the concept of identity differ in the most fundamental manner possible: the one has logically guaranteed universality and is not classificatory in nature; the other has no such universality and is classificatory. This should not lead us to deny that there is a connection between the two. For example, we may think of formal identity as a limiting case of material identity, i.e., as the case in which the logical limit of gradual diminution of apparent distinctness is reached. Or we may think of material identity as an extension of the formal application of the concept of identity, namely, to cases in which we are willing to disregard the apparent distinctness of the referents of the subject terms.

But our appeal to formal identity requires an important qualification. The concept of identity is indeed applicable formally to everything without restriction, and thus is applicable formally to objects as such and to entities as such. By appealing to the possibility of such formal applications of the concept, we preserve our account from the incoherence that would result if we supposed the identity or diversity of objects as such and the identity or diversity of entities as such to be material. But even though we can speak coherently of the formal identity or diversity of objects as such or of entities as such in *general* philosophical statements, there are severe limitations on our ability to do so in irreducibly singular statements. In the case of entities as such we cannot construct such statements at all. The reason is not that the concept of identity has no formal application to entities as such, but that reference to entities as such is impossible. Let me explain.

Ordinarily, statements are both about objects and about entities, although not in the same sense of "about." A statement may be said to be about an object in the sense that reference is made to the object, that the object is singled out before the mind. It may be said to be about an entity in the sense that reference is made to an object that happens to be that entity; the terms "reference," "object," and "entity" have been so introduced that the idea of reference to an entity that is not also reference to an object is incoherent. In a third sense of "about," a statement is about a thing, whether object or entity, if its truth conditions involve that thing; this is the sense in which a Russellian translation of a true statement of the form "The F is G" is about the thing, whichever it is, that alone is F and is also G. Now, as we saw in chapter one, in a genuine identity statement, whether formal or material (indeed, we may now add, in any genuine, irreducibly singular statement), the subject terms must be employed referringly. But, clearly, there cannot be reference to entities as such; an expression, whether a demonstrative pronoun, or a definite description, or a proper name, refers to an entity only by referring to an object that is that entity. Therefore, no genuine singular statement of identity, whether formal or material, can be about entities as such. Indeed, there cannot be any statements about entities as such, except in the third sense of "about."*

---

*Of course, entities as such can be *denoted* by definite descriptions. But the ease with which such descriptions, e.g., "the entity x," or even "the entity x as such," can be constructed should not mislead us. A descriptive phrase need not be capable of being used referringly. And even when used referringly, it may misdescribe its referent, it may not fit it; the above phrases may in fact be used to refer to the *object* x.

In the case of objects as such genuinely singular identity statements are of course possible, but still subject to a limitation. We can refer to an object as such with a demonstrative pronoun or a definite description (whether an explicit one such as "the typewriter before me considered as an object" or an ordinary one such as "the typewriter before me" but used to refer to the typewriter before me as an object only). But we cannot give it a genuine proper name. Such a name would be, *ex hypothesi,* inapplicable to the entity, if any, the object happens to be. It would also be inapplicable, of course, to any other object. But from this it follows that the name could be used correctly only once, since, in virtue of the manner in which we have introduced the notion of an object, it is incoherent to suppose that an object can be singled out twice. I have already given reasons why such a "name" would not be a genuine part of a language, why it would not be a genuine name. A genuine proper name names an entity, although only insofar as it can be used to refer to objects that are that entity.*

Our conclusion that we can speak coherently about the formal identity of entities as such in general statements (such as the philosophical statements constituting our account, which prompted our investigation of this issue), but not in genuinely singular statements, should neither surprise us nor appear paradoxical. The view that there are general statements that cannot be instantiated in genuinely singular statements is not unfamiliar. Russell in effect argued that all statements in physics about particles unobservable in principle, all statements about ordinary material things, and all statements about other persons' thoughts and feelings are such, since he held, rightly or wrongly, that what they are about can be known only "by description."[7] The entities such statements are about may be *denoted* by definite descriptions, but they cannot be referred to, singled out before the mind;

---

*It follows that there cannot be a logic of objects and entities, if (some of) its variables would require as substituends referring expressions for entities as such or proper names of objects as such.

therefore, there cannot be genuine, irreducibly singular statements about them. Such a conclusion may be unacceptable for other reasons, but it faces no obvious logical difficulty. It would be puzzling, of course, if there were not an independent explanation of the impossibility of the singular statements in question. But, according to Russell, there is such an explanation, namely, the unobservability of the entities that the statements would be about, the fact that they cannot be objects of "acquaintance." And, as we have seen, there is a perfectly sufficient explanation of the impossibility of irreducibly singular statements about entities as such, although general statements, such as the philosophical statements I have made about them, are quite possible. The very notion of an entity has been introduced in such a way that reference to an entity as such is impossible.

To be sure, there would be a serious logical difficulty for our conclusion, as well as for the Russellian views just mentioned, if we were to adopt the view that a universal statement is an abbreviation of the (finite or infinite) conjunction of all of its singular instantiations, and that a particular statement is an abbreviation of the (finite or infinite) disjunction of all of its singular instantiations. However, this view is both counterintuitive* and circular.†

The above explanations may help us attach sense to an assertion such as that *a* and *b* are two objects but one entity, in that they may elucidate, guide, and render unobjectionable these

---

*"It is true that at first sight the proposition 'All whales are mammals' seems to be not about concepts but about animals; but if we ask which animal then are we speaking of, we are unable to point to any one in particular." (Frege, *The Foundations of Arithmetic*, p. 60.) "It is surely clear that when anyone uses the sentence 'all men are mortal' he does not want to assert something about some Chief Akpanya, of whom perhaps he has never heard." (Frege, *Translations*, p. 83.)

†"It is perfectly clear, I think, that when you have enumerated all the atomic facts in the world, it is a further fact about the world that those are all the atomic facts there are about the world, and that is just as much an objective fact about the world as any of them are." (Russell, *Logic and Knowledge*, p. 236.)

uses of the terms "two," "one," and "are." But do they suggest criteria for determining (1) that *a* and *b* are two objects and (2) that they are one entity? Criteria for determining (2) would in reality be criteria for determining that the material identity statement "*a* is the same as *b*" is true, a topic we shall consider at length later. On the other hand, the criterion for determining (1) is simply the fact that *a* and *b* appear to be distinct things, that they are singled out differently. And, unlike identifying, singling out an object and thus distinguishing it from another object is not a conceptual activity at all, hence not one requiring criteria. The application of a concept to an object presupposes that the object has been singled out; it would be perverse, and in any case contrary to psychological fact, to argue that the object could not have been singled out except through the application to it of some concept. To say this is not, of course, to say that there can be no *explanation* of our singling out of objects,* nor is it to deny that as a matter of psychological fact one could not single out certain objects unless one were in *possession* of an appropriate sortal concept (not: unless one actually *applied* to them that concept!).

Thus the difference between (1) and (2) with respect to criteria reduces to the difference between singling out and identification. And we are now in a position to see the light the latter casts also on the difference between formal and material identity, especially on the fact that the concept of identity has material applications only to existent objects, to entities, but formal applications to both existent and nonexistent objects. Let us return to the quasi-Quinean example mentioned earlier. We can form no clear idea of the difference between the fat man imagined in the

---

*Such explanations are offered, for example, by Gestalt psychologists. For a useful discussion of the issue, see Eli Hirsch, *The Persistence of Objects* (Philadelphia: Philosophical Monographs, 1976), pp. 41–45; he argues that "someone's sortal ignorance with respect to a given object will typically not prevent the object from presenting itself as an articulated unity, as something that stands out from its surroundings" (p. 42). See also his "Physical Identity," *The Philosophical Review* 85 (1976): 357–89.

doorway now being the same as the bald man imagined in the doorway yesterday, and their not being the same even though quite similar. But we have a very clear idea of the difference between imagining two men in the doorway now and imagining only one man in the doorway now.

III

The explanation I have offered of the apparent distinctness of material identicals rests on a proposition that may seem to the reader no less paradoxical and bewildering than Meinong's principle that there are things of which it is true that there are no such things. (The similarity is, of course, not coincidental.) It may be put bluntly and uncharitably as "There are distinct things that are identical." Indeed, the argument for this proposition is quite simple (so is the very similar main argument for Meinong's principle). It consists in the recognition of the fact that the concept of identity is a genuine concept, a principle of classification. If we take this fact seriously, if we grant it honestly and not force it into the logician's mold it does not fit, then our proposition, however puzzling at first, follows straightforwardly. For there would have to be things that the concept of identity classifies, and these may only be pairs of *distinct* things. Yet their classification in terms of the concept of identity could only consist in their classification as identical, i.e., as *one* thing! But, as the example of Meinong's principle has shown, to prove a proposition is one thing, to render it intelligible is quite another.

Our distinction between objects and entities is intended to render the above proposition intelligible. But it itself cannot be properly understood if divorced from the manner in which it was introduced. For then the crucial point that it is a distinction between the two sides of the frontier of conceptualization, not between two regions on one of these sides, not between two classes of things, would be missed. I want to make clear that it is founded on considerations about the nature of the ultimate application of a conceptual apparatus, whether our own or that of any other rational beings, and not on some ordinary psychological, or phenomenological, or epistemological argument.

What we attempt to understand by means of our concepts must not be confused with *how* we understand it. The former is independent of our concepts and their applications. The latter, of course, is not. This should be evident from the possibility of reclassification and of alternative classifications. For a concept is essentially a principle of classification. And while the application of a concept, that is, a classification, is not an actual reordering or regrouping of a subject matter, neither is it ordinarily a mere ritual of labeling. It consists in our coming to see, to understand, what the concept is applied to, that is, what is classified, in a different light, in terms of some, and not others, of the similarities and differences between it and other things. Such alternative ways of understanding or seeing are always possible, even if only one of them is adequate to the nature of the subject matter. Therefore, it is intelligible to distinguish the domain of the application of a concept—that is, the domain of the things of which the concept may either be affirmed or denied, the things that *may* be understood in terms of the applicability or inapplicability of that concept, even if also in terms of that of any one of a number of other concepts—from the domain that results from such correct affirmations and denials, that is, the domain of the things understood in terms of the affirmations and denials of that, and *not* of any other concept. Our distinction between objects and entities is nothing but that distinction in the case of the concepts of identity and existence.

Indeed, such a distinction is only one of reason. In no sense can we say, for example, that a university student considered in abstraction from the correct application to him of the concept of an undergraduate, and the student considered in terms of that application, are two persons; or that the domain consisting of undergraduate students and graduate students, which results from the application to university students of the concept of an undergraduate, is really distinct from the domain of university students, or, e.g., from the domain consisting of male university students and female university students. For the application of a concept may change our understanding of something, but it cannot change the thing itself. If it did, then it would be a case of alteration, not of classification. In the case of the concepts of identity and existence, however, the distinction between the domain of their application and the domain resulting from that application, though still a distinction of reason (otherwise objects would be a sort of *entities*) and the result of a classification, not of an alteration, has the additional characteristic of being a distinction between domains that differ in respect to the number of their members. It is this characteristic of the distinction between objects and entities that makes the appearance of distinctness between material identicals not only intelligible but an actual fact about our thought, perception, and language.

This numerical difference is a direct consequence of the application of the concept of identity. It is only a rather qualified consequence of the application of the concept of existence. To apply the concept of existence to the domain of objects is to classify some of them as existent, as entities, and others as nonexistent. This by itself does not lead to a numerical difference between the domain of the application of the concept and the domain resulting from that application. But in fact the point of the use of the concept is precisely to lead us to suppose that there is such a numerical difference. For the point of its use is to exclude the objects of which the concept has been denied from further consideration, to exclude them from further classification, indeed literally to exclude them from the world. It is a part of the role of the concept of existence to allow us to say that the objects of thought and perception are in a sense fewer than we would otherwise have taken them to be. Therefore, while we cannot, strictly speaking, claim that the domain consisting of existents and nonexistents differs numerically from the domain of objects, we can say that the objects of which the concept of existence has been denied are no longer considered part of the domain of the application of the conceptual apparatus, no longer part of the world.

The numerical difference between the domain of objects and that of entities, however, is a direct consequence of the application of the concept of identity. The number of the *objects* to which the concept of identity is correctly applied is necessarily greater than that of the *entities* resulting from that application. *
For a material identity statement asserts precisely that two objects are one entity. The Evening Star and the Morning Star, if considered as objects, are two objects; but since they are materially identical, they are one entity. The statement that the color of this page is the same as the color of the next page is about two objects but one entity. When the application of certain concepts to a domain produces a domain that has a different number of constituents, it is no longer merely possible, *intelligible,* to distinguish the two domains. The difference between them becomes an actual fact about our thought and language.

Indeed, the general function of the concepts of identity and existence is precisely to transform our experience into a world by reducing the objects of perception and thought to a smaller number of *entities*. This reduction is the first and absolutely indispensable stage of *understanding* what we perceive and think about. It is the most basic conceptual activity. And, like all such activities, it consists in seeing one thing in terms of another, although not, as in the case of other concepts, through the grasp of similarities and the employment of analogies. It consists in our understanding some things through, in terms of, others in the most fundamental way in which this can be accomplished, namely, by regarding them as one thing. It consists in the enforcement of a sort of ontological parsimony, in a rendering of

---

*For formal purposes, we may say that identity is an equivalence relation, and that entities are the equivalence classes generated by that relation. If understood metaphysically, however, this would be grossly misleading. See above, p. 5, and below, Appendix B.

the world more intelligible to ourselves by means of simplification.* A "world" of mere objects, we may say, would be
our world as it would appear to a mind lacking the concepts of
identity and existence. On the other hand, a world of mere
entities would be such that the notions of singling out and referring to its constituents would be inapplicable.†

Thus, the distinction between objects and entities is required
by the very idea of the application of the concepts of identity and
existence. An object is something of which these concepts may
be affirmed or denied. That there are objects is no more questionable than that these concepts have a domain of application.
The distinction between objects and entities is not a distinction
between kinds of *entities*. This is why it need not be offensive to
anyone's robust sense of reality. Nevertheless it provides solutions to the problems of existence and material identity. In the
case of existence, it does so by allowing us to speak of the objects
of the application (whether correct or incorrect) of the concept of
existence without committing ourselves to the existence of such
objects and thus to the redundancy of true singular assertions of
existence and the self-contradictoriness of false such assertions.
And in the case of identity it does so by allowing us to speak of
the distinctness of the objects of the application of the concept of
identity without committing ourselves to the self-contradictory

*Cf. W. V. O. Quine, "Identity, Ostension, and Hypostasis," in *From a Logical
Point of View*. According to Quine, the simplification is accomplished by trans-
forming reference to entities of small spatiotemporal spread (e.g., the momentary
parts of a river, its "stages") into reference to entities of larger spread (e.g.,
rivers). He does not consider the problem of material identity, e.g., the apparent
distinctness of the river-containing-this-stage and the river-containing-that-stage.
It is these latter, and not the river-stages themselves, that would be objects,
according to my terminology.

†Such a world could be described only in completely generalized propositions.
To use Wittgenstein's apt phrase (*Notebooks, 1914–1916*, New York: Harper and
Row, 1969, p. 20), its representation would then be *impersonal*. (Compare *Trac-
tatus*, 5.526.) For an argument against the possibility of such a representation, see
P. F. Strawson, "Singular Terms, Ontology, and Identity,"*Mind* 65 (1956); also
Max Black, *A Companion to Wittgenstein's 'Tractatus'* (Cambridge: Cambridge
University Press, 1964), pp.287–88.

proposition that two things are one thing. Objects are the objects of the application of the concepts of identity and existence. In the case of (material) identity, *of course* there are two such objects in every identity situation. If there were not, why would it even occur to us to consider whether the concept of identity is applicable to the situation? But to say that there are two such objects is not to say that there are two such entities, and thus it is not to say anything incompatible with the fact that if the statement is true then it is about only one entity. In the case of existence, *of course* there are objects to which the concept of existence is inapplicable. If there were not, there would also be nothing to which it is applicable, and thus there would not be such a concept at all. But to say this is not to say that these constituents of the domain of its application *exist*.

But are the notions of identity and existence genuine concepts, that is, are they really principles of classification? The distinction between objects and entities depends on, indeed is equivalent to, an affirmative answer to this question. Yet such an answer is in conflict with our undeniable tendency to think of the existence and identity of what we find in the world as given to us independently of the application of any concepts. And the motive behind this tendency is clear. The applicability of the concepts of identity and existence, unlike that of any other concepts, determines the very constitution of the world, the subject matter of our knowledge, *what* we attempt to understand. And how can that be merely a *way* of understanding the world? But, I suggest, it can and in fact is. To suppose otherwise, that is, to deny that the notions of identity and existence are concepts, principles of classification, would be to suppose that the first and most fundamental questions that we ask about the objects of our perception and thought, namely, which exist and which do not, and which pairs of such objects are really one entity, have no conceptual content and thus are miraculously answered by the objects themselves. Such a supposition could only be described as an example of philosophical primitivism.

That this is so in the case of the notion of identity perhaps requires no demonstration. Its classificatory function is no less evident than that of any ordinary relational concept, even though identity is not an ordinary relation. We classify pairs of objects as cases of single entities very much as we classify pairs of persons as cases of marriage. Any doubts about this would be due precisely to puzzlement over the apparent distinctness of material identicals. The argument behind such doubts could be put as follows: If identity is a genuine concept, then it may only be a relational concept. But even if we grant that formal identity is a relation, material identity cannot be a relation. For what would it relate? Not an entity to itself, for then it would be formal identity. And not two entities, for this would be self-contradictory. Clearly, such an argument would be plausible only if a distinction such as ours between objects and entities is either not recognized or rejected for some other reason. And since to accept this distinction is to accept the classificatory character of the notion of identity, the argument would be little more than a *petitio*.

The case of the notion of existence, however, is different. Its classificatory nature has often been denied, usually in the form of arguments that "exists" is not a predicate. Such arguments require detailed discussion, which will be provided in chapter four. Suffice it here to draw attention to the fact that in common discourse we find logically unproblematic the usual assertions of the existence or nonexistence of God, or of Santa Claus, or of the pink rat one supposedly hallucinates some morning, or of something one has dreamed about; the assertions of existence that are part of the content of statements about various things (e.g., people, countries, situations) beginning or ceasing to exist; and even less usual assertions such as Moore's "This might not have existed," where "this" could even refer to a sense-datum. It is worth noting also that, as used in philosophical discussions, but also in much of ordinary discourse, the term "exists" functions as a synonym of "real," which surely has a classificatory use; that "real" also has more specific, still classificatory but philosophically uninteresting uses, a fact pointed out by J. L. Austin,[8] is irrelevant to its having, in ordinary discourse, a philosophically significant use.[9] And let us make clear that we have no intention of performing the conceptually idle move of speaking of the *being*, or the *subsistence*, or the *ontological status* of the objects to which the concept of existence is inapplicable.

But behind the denial that the notions of existence and identity are principles of classification there may be an even deeper motive that would account for its enormous plausibility and for the extraordinary difficulty of any distinction such as ours between objects and entities. It is the legitimate fear that we may be led to embrace a variety of transcendental idealism. In Appendix B I shall argue that this fear is groundless.

IV

I have tried to explain what objects are. It may be useful to say also what they are not. The notion of an object should not be confused with that of a sense-datum, or of a momentary experience, or of a temporal slice of an entity. Objects, though not qua objects, are what we assert to be the same when we make material identity statements. But no two sense-data may be said to be the same, even if they belong to the same material thing. No two momentary experiences may be said to be the same, even if they are experiences of the same entity. (This is why the simplification of the world effected by the application of the concept of identity must not be confused with a Kantian or Husserlian synthesis of appearances or of intuitions.) And one temporal slice of an entity is no more the same as another temporal slice of that entity than one spatial part of an entity is the same as another spatial part of that entity; what at t_1 is the same as something at t_2 is not the temporal slice but that-whose-slice-it-is.

Moreover, an object cannot be the "accusative" of different singlings-out, it cannot be referred to in different ways, it cannot be the sole subject matter of a material identity statement (though it can be the sole subject matter of a formal identity statement). But a sense-datum, or a momentary experience, or a temporal slice, as these are ordinarily understood, can be singled out and referred to in two or more different ways. For example, even though a momentary experience can be enjoyed only once and only by one person, it can be thought about, studied, and imagined many times and also by others.

Nor are objects intensional entities, at least not if properties, as contrasted with the classes they define, and propositions are the paradigms of such an entity.* "The color of a is the same as the color of b" and "The proposition Mary accepts is the same as the proposition Jane accepts" are examples of material identity statements about intensional entities. In such statements the noun-phrases flanking the identity sign, if used referringly and correctly, would refer to distinct *objects* but, if the statement is true, to one and the same intensional *entity*. Therefore, the notion of an intensional entity is different from that of an object.

Quine has offered the following argument against the view that an appeal to intensional entities would resolve the puzzle about the failures of the substitutivity of identity in modal and intensional contexts.[10] Let "A" be the name of an intensional entity and let p be any true contingent statement. Even though "$A=(\imath x)$ $[p.(x=A)]$" is true and its subject terms designate the same intensional entity, they are not intersubstitutable *salva veritate* in contexts involving modalities and propositional attitudes. It should be clear now that this argument would be unsound if A were supposed to be an object, in our sense of the word. For either "$(\imath x) [p.(x=A)]$" is not used referringly, and then the statement would not be a genuine identity statement; or it is used to

---

*Despite its extensive use by logicians, most notably Carnap and Church, the *general* notion of an intensional entity has not received anything that deserves to be called philosophical elucidation. The same is true of the specific notion of an individual concept. Only the other two alleged species of intensional entity, namely, properties and propositions, have been accorded serious philosophical attention, the former usually in discussions of the ontological topic of universals and the latter in the philosophy of language and the philosophy of mind.

refer to an object other than A, and then the statement would be false if intended to be about objects as objects (as it must be for the purposes of the argument); or it is used to refer to the same object that "A" refers to, and then the statement would be a formal identity statement, its subject terms being intersubstitutable in all contexts as long as they are used referringly in the same way. This is why Quine's argument would not hold against an appeal to objects in accounting for the failures of the substitutivity of identity, even if it does hold against an appeal to intensional entities. We should reach the same conclusion also if the specification of the intensional entity is accomplished not by designation but by stating uniquely determining conditions,[11] as long as the statement of these conditions is thought of as serving the purpose of establishing an object before the mind.

Nor are our objects Meinong's "pure objects" (even though, like Meinong's, they may be said to be beyond being and nonbeing), if a Meinongian object can be singled out more than once and thus be the sole subject matter of a material identity statement. Nor are they Husserl's moments (in *Logical Investigations*) or Husserl's aspects (facets) or Husserl's noemata (in *Ideas*), if a moment or an aspect or a noema may be singled out more than once and thus be the sole subject matter of a material identity statement. And in any case two Meinongian objects, or two Husserlian moments or two Husserlian aspects or two Husserlian noemata would, presumably, never be identical.* This would also be true of Hector-Neri Castañeda's guises or facets, which in the case of physical objects are, as he says, in a sense "parts and parcels" of these objects.[12] But our objects are precisely such that two of them can be literally identical, that they can be the logical subjects of a true material identity statement. We describe their identity as material only to distinguish it from the very different case of formal identity, not because it is not

---

*Husserl is explicit on this regarding moments. See *Logical Investigations* (New York: Humanities Press, 1970; translated by J. N. Findlay), p. 149.

true, or strict, or literal identity. The paradigmatic identity statements are all material. And material identity statements are precisely about two objects, though, if true, about one entity. Indeed, according to our account, two objects are identical because they are one entity, not because they are one object. But it is the objects that are said to be identical; it is primarily to the objects, and only secondarily to the entity, that the subject terms of the identity statement refer. Therefore, to say that a true material identity statement is about two objects but one entity is precisely to say that it is about two objects that are identical.

It should be clear that the view that corresponding to every individual there is an individual concept of that individual, and to that concept a concept of it, and to the latter a concept of a concept of a concept of the individual, etc.,[13] is completely foreign to our theory of objects. Even if we spoke of an object as being *of* an entity, it would be sheer nonsense to speak of an object as being *of* an object. It should also be clear that our notion of an object is different from the notion of a possible (to say nothing of an impossible!) object.[14] Only what can be singled out before the mind is an object. Many uses of consistent and certainly all uses of inconsistent definite descriptions (unless involving misdescription) fail to single out anything.

And, finally, our notion of an object must not be confused with the notion of a mental, or mind-dependent entity. Indeed, an object must be such that it *could* be singled out, that it could be the accusative of an act of perception, or imagination, or thought. But nothing in our introduction of the notion of an object implies that an object *must* be singled out, that it must be such an accusative. Consequently, there is no contradiction in supposing that there are objects that are not perceived, or imagined, or thought by anyone; objects are not logically mind-dependent.* Nor of course are they causally mind-dependent. Objects as such

---

*Clearly the quantifiers in general statements about objects, e.g., in "There are objects that are not singled out by anyone," must be interpreted "nonexistentially." I shall consider such an interpretation in chapter four.

are not entities, existents. Therefore, the notion of causality, of causal dependence or causal independence, whether with respect to a mind or a body, simply does not apply to them. On the other hand, it is trivially true that no example of an object that is not singled out can be given, and that no genuinely singular statement can be made about such an object. To give such an example, or to make such a statement, one must first single out the object.*

*In *A Theory of Possibility* (Pittsburgh: The University of Pittsburgh Press, 1975), Nicholas Rescher argues for "the ontological mind-dependence of nonexistent possibles" but then takes out of the argument whatever sting it might have by adding: "We have no desire to be pushed to the extreme of saying that the 'being' of nonexistent 'possible beings' lies in their being actually *conceived;* rather we take it to reside in their being conceivable" (p. 202).

CHAPTER THREE

Indiscernibility

I

The questions most prominent in the literature on identity have concerned not the apparent distinctness of identicals, as was described in chapter one, but rather the connection between identity and indiscernibility. I shall attempt to answer them on the basis of the account of the apparent distinctness of identicals I have offered. There is, first, the general question whether the concepts of identity and indiscernibility are necessarily equivalent, perhaps one and the same concept, or at least whether one entails, perhaps is included in, the other. There is, second, the question how to understand the seeming counterexamples to the indiscernibility of identicals in intentional and modal contexts. And there is, third, the question whether identity is relative to the sortal characteristics of the identicals, whether a may be the same F, but not the same G, as b; if it may, then one can argue that a and b are identical but discernible.[1]

What does it mean to say that a and b are indiscernible? The usual and for our present purposes satisfactory answer is that a and b are indiscernible if whatever property the one has the other also has. But this answer is satisfactory only if the term "property" is understood in the very general sense of a respect, of whatever sort, in which two things may differ, or of whatever may be the case about a thing, or of whatever may be true of a thing. If so, then it becomes reasonable to regard the principle of the indiscernibility of identicals as equivalent to the so-called principle of the substitutivity of identity, i.e., the principle that coreferential expressions are intersubstitutible *salva veritate* in all propositional contexts, in all statements in which one or both of the expressions occur. For it is reasonable to assume that whatever an open sentence expresses (we may call it a propositional function), even if, strictly speaking, not a property, is a respect in which two things may differ, exception perhaps being made for the open sentences in terms of which the familiar set-theoretical paradoxes arise.*

The connection between identity and indiscernibility is intimate enough to tempt us to identify them. And this temptation is stimulated further by our puzzlement over the concept of (material) identity and by the relative clarity of the concept of indiscernibility. Yet, while we find acceptable the proposition that identicals are indiscernible (the principle of the indiscernibility of identicals), we are uneasy about its converse, that indiscernibles are identical (the principle of the identity of indiscernibles); it seems to us conceivable that two entities may differ with respect to no property, however widely the notion of property is understood, and still be two. But the fact is that neither the indis-

---

*But do we want to say then that there is a respect in which Giorgione and Barbarelli differ, on the grounds that even though they are the same person the name "Barbarelli" cannot be substituted for "Giorgione" in the sentence "Giorgione was so-called because of his size" without changing the latter's truth-value? (Quine, *From a Logical Point of View*, pp. 139–41.) But, I suggest, this sentence is logically incomplete, in that it contains a pronoun ("so") that lacks an antecedent. If the intended antecedent is added, then the sentence would read "Giorgione was called 'Giorgione', and he was so-called because of his size"; and "Barbarelli" can be substituted for "Giorgione" (not of course also for "'Giorgione'") in this sentence without changing its truth-value. Richard Cartwright has argued (in "Identity and Substitutivity," in *Identity and Individuation*, ed. Milton K. Munitz [New York: New York University Press,1971], p. 122) that even though this sentence (his actual example is "Giorgione was called 'Giorgione' because of his size") does express the same proposition that "Giorgione was so-called because of his size" expresses, the fact remains that the latter constitutes a counterexample to the principle of substitutivity with respect to the name "Barbarelli." But this is not so. "Giorgione was so-called because of his size," strictly speaking, expresses no proposition since it is logically incomplete, even though one can *gather* which proposition it is intended to express from the fact that the name "Giorgione" is used to refer to the logical subject.

cernibility of identicals nor the identity of indiscernibles is a part of the concept of identity, of what we mean by "identity." And the reason for this is not that we find discernible identicals or nonidentical indiscernibles conceivable but that (1) we may apply the concept of indiscernibility only on the basis of the applicability of the concept of identity, that is, identity is the criterion of indiscernibility, and (2) we apply the concept of identity without appealing to the indiscernibility of the objects of its application. The concept of identity is a primitive concept, as of course it must be if our account of it as the most fundamental element of our conceptual apparatus is correct. That of indiscernibility has a trivial definition.*

We *enforce* the indiscernibility of what we have already judged to be identicals; we do not discover it. And we do not determine that they are identical by determining that they are indiscernible. The plausibility of the supposition that *any* F that is a property of *a* is also a property of *b*, and vice versa, may only be due to, and is directly proportionate to, the plausibility of the supposition that *a* and *b* are identical. We have no independent means of establishing the former, e.g., by enumeration of properties (which might be infinite in number), nor do we ever attempt to do so. Moreover, given that *a* is F, we often determine that *b* is F solely on the basis of our judgment that *b* is identical with *a*. Consider the color of this page and the color of the next page, which, let us assume, are exactly similar. Are they identical? Some philosophers have argued that they are not, on the grounds that they have different spatial locations, one where this page is and the other where the next page is. But suppose that we ask for the grounds of the claim that the color of this page has a different location from that of the color of the next page. It is evident that the determination whether this claim is true or false depends not on longer visual examination of the colors or of the places the pages occupy. It depends solely on whether we are

---

*"x is indiscernible from y = Df. (F) (Fx≡Fy),"assuming that properties are understood in the broad sense we have explained, but with some provision for excluding the "properties" that give rise to the set-theoretical paradoxes.

willing to assert the identity of the color of this page and the color of the next page. If we are, then we face no difficulty in saying that the color of this page is, *of course*, also where the next page is. And if we do face a difficulty in saying this, then the reason lies solely in a difficulty in accepting the identity of the color of this page and the color of the next page.

We assert the identity of the tall man before us now and the short boy we knew years ago. Was the boy tall, or is the man short? Of course, the answer is neither. Yet, assuming the identity of the two, we insist on finding that they are indiscernible and accomplish this by asserting that the man *was* short but *is* tall and the boy *is* short but *will* be tall, or we say that one and the same individual is both short at one time and tall at another time, thus avoiding the appearance of discernibility. The fact is that we can always accommodate our willingness to assert the identity of two objects by making them indiscernible, and the only consideration that may keep us from making such an assertion is the inapplicability of the primitive concept of identity to the case. Consider two persons, John and Mary. *Prima facie*, they differ in many respects; one is male the other female; one is here the other there; one is tall the other short. But *if* we were willing to assert that they *are* one and the same individual (not just parts of one and the same scattered individual), say Joma, such alleged discernibility would not stop us at all. We could easily avoid the appearance of discernibility by saying that Joma is male here and female there, that Joma is both here and there, though known here as John and there as Mary, that Joma is tall and male here but short and female there. (The parallel with the case of the tall man and the short boy is exact.) Indeed, there is something quite absurd about such a procedure. But what is absurd is not the series of statements that in effect deny that John and Mary are discernible, but the assertion of the identity of John and Mary. If the latter were plausible, so would be the former.*

---

*Of course, a's being F and b's not being F may be appealed to as evidence for the nonidentity of a and b when the latter cannot be determined directly. It is

But why do we enforce the indiscernibility of identicals? What is the explanation of this peculiar relationship between the primitive concept of identity and the defined concept of indiscernibility? I suggest that it consists in the fact that the role of the concept of identity, namely, the simplification of the world, can be performed only if its application is understood to have *as a consequence* the applicability of the concept of indiscernibility. The simplification achieved by means of identification would be worth nothing, it would be idle, a conceptual farce, if identicals were allowed to be discernible. The identification of a and b would not really reduce the complexity of the world if we allowed that, say, a is F but b is not F. This is why we accept the principle of the indiscernibility of identicals.* And the reason we should also accept the principle of the identity of indiscernibles is closely related, though not as direct. If we deny that a and b are identical we would be denying the only conceivable basis on which we could assert that they are indiscernible. Since identity is our only criterion of indiscernibility, the assertion that a and b are indiscernible may only be justified by our finding that a and b are identical. Therefore, the supposition that they are both indiscernible and nonidentical is, though not self-contradictory, conceptually idle.

II

While the principle of the indiscernibility of identicals has not been seriously questioned, and the principle of the identity of indiscernibles has, it is the former, paradoxically enough, that is faced with apparent counterexamples, and the latter is not. The

evidence of *what* or *which* things a and b are, and thus contributes to our determination whether a and b constitute, or sufficiently resemble, a paradigm of identity.

*It is worth noting that the addition of identity to the standard predicate calculus is achieved ordinarily by the addition of the two axioms $(x)(x=x)$ and $(x)(y)$ $[(x=y) \supset (Fx \supset Fy)]$. Without the latter (or an equivalent axiom), the addition would accomplish nothing.

closest we can come to a case of nonidentical indiscernibles is an imaginary world, such as Black's.[2] And serious doubt may be entertained whether such a world is really imaginable, indeed whether it is really logically possible.[3] Black describes a world consisting of two exactly similar iron spheres and nothing else. No contradiction can be derived from the description, unless one begs the question by identifying identity with indiscernibility. Of course, this does not suffice to show that Black's world is logically possible, in the broad sense of this term, for the principle of the identity of indiscernibles may be both synthetic ("synthetic a priori") and necessarily true. Is it imaginable? We may reasonably argue that it is not, and that it seems imaginable only because in fact we imagine a world containing some third thing, namely, the imaginer or at least a point of view. But we need not rely on such a consideration, convincing though it is. We have already given a general reason for the acceptance of the identity of indiscernibles. The criterion for the indiscernibility of the constituents of a world such as Black's could only be their identity. Therefore, to suppose that though not identical they are indiscernible would be idle.

But apparent counterexamples to the *indiscernibility of identicals* need not be imagined; they pervade some major areas of thought and discourse. Sometimes described as opaque contexts, they primarily involve propositional attitudes and modalities. A person may believe that the Morning Star is a planet but not believe that the Evening Star is a planet, even though the Morning Star is identical with the Evening Star. The President of the United States is necessarily the chief executive officer of the United States, but the person born at a certain specifiable time and place is not necessarily the chief executive of the United States, even though he is identical with the President of the United States. Sometimes, in the hope of salvaging the principle of the indiscernibility of identicals, such cases are described instead as failures of the principle of the intersubstitutivity of coreferential terms. And it is argued that even though the latter entails the former, the converse is not the case, for we need not admit that every open sentence stands for a property.[4] But surely such a solution is ad hoc. Even if we deny (as later we will) that every open sentence stands for a property, we must demand to know how identicals may be discernible in respect of whatever the open sentence does stand for or express.

Our account of identity in chapter two provides a direct and natural explanation of such counterexamples to the principle of the indiscernibility of identicals. I have argued that to single out an entity is necessarily to single out an object, though the converse is not the case. A statement in which reference is made to an entity is necessarily one in which reference is made to an object, though the converse is not the case. This does not mean that a referring expression has a double reference. The entity an object may happen to be is not something additional to the object; it cannot be singled out and referred to separately and contrasted with the object. Nevertheless, ordinarily we do not regard what our statements are about as objects, for ordinarily we are interested only in things that, though singled out in one way, we believe may be singled out also in any number of other ways. There are exceptions, however. In some cases we are inclined to regard what is singled out as an object, even though we may also regard it as an entity. Occasionally, the philosophical distinction between objects and entities emerges even in nonphilosophical thought. Contexts in which we think and discourse about what we believe to be nonexistent are obvious examples. But such also are contexts involving modalities and propositional attitudes. The failures of the substitutivity of names of material identicals in the latter contexts are puzzling only if we ignore the fact that identicals are not only entities but also objects. For such failures occur precisely when the property that appears to belong to one of the identicals but not to the other (e.g., the properties expressed by the open sentences "x is necessarily F" and "S believes that x is F") is attributed to a thing only insofar as the latter is regarded as an object. This is true of modal properties. We attribute them to a thing only because of the specific way in which we understand it, think about it, perceive it, single it out, that is, only insofar as we regard it as an object. For example, if we were to say that a certain person is necessarily the chief executive of the United States we would do so only insofar as we think of him as the President of the United States, not insofar as we think of him as the person born at a certain specifiable time and place.* (I shall return to this topic in chapter five.) And, again, we attribute properties involving propositional attitudes to a thing (e.g., to Cicero in the statement that Philip believed that Cicero denounced Catiline) only insofar as we regard it as an object, and not merely as an entity, because such properties are nothing but specific ways in which something is thought of or perceived. Such specific ways of thinking of or perceiving a thing are precisely ways of singling it out, with a different object corresponding to each different way. And insofar as we regard *a* and *b* as objects, they do indeed have different properties, even if they are one and the same entity. This is why their indiscernibility as *entities* is a matter of enforcement, not discovery.

Nevertheless, while in some statements we are primarily interested in material identicals as objects, we are almost always also interested in them as entities. And when the weight of our interests shifts, as it often does, we find ourselves inclined to allow the substitutions that had seemed to us unallowable, to carry out without restrictions the enforcement of indiscernibility that the material identity of the objects legitimizes. Indeed, we are usually inclined to say that it is false that Philip believed that Tully denounced Catiline if he did not know that Tully was Cicero, even though he believed that Cicero denounced

---

*Whether we are *right* in this is not our concern here. I am merely drawing attention to a fact about the reasons that actually govern our application of modal concepts, about the basis of our *knowledge* of logical necessity. This must not be confused with the *nature* of logical necessity. I discuss this distinction in detail in *The Concept of Knowledge* (Evanston: Northwestern University Press, 1970), pp. 99–105, 178–83.

Catiline. But we may also find ourselves inclined to say that after all Philip did believe that Tully denounced Catiline. For was not Tully the same *person* as Cicero? Similarly, we are usually inclined to deny that the person born at a certain specifiable time and place is necessarily the chief executive of the United States. Yet, we may also feel some inclination to affirm this. For is he not the same *person* as the President of the United States? The conflict between such inclinations requires not adjudication but philosophical understanding.

IV

Partly because of their concern over the failures of the substitutivity of identity in modal contexts, some philosophers have recently held that all genuine identity statements (those employing definite descriptions being excluded and analyzed instead in accordance with Russell's theory) are, if true, necessarily true, and, if false, necessarily false. Saul Kripke's defense of this view has attracted particularly great attention and is instructive.[5] The distinction between objects and entities allows us to understand both its plausibility and limitations.

I begin by observing that, indeed, if a true identity statement is understood as being about entities, and not also about objects, it may only be necessarily true. For, so understood, the statement does not even appear to be about distinct entities and thus is understood in such a way that in reality it is a formal identity statement. But insofar as an identity statement is (is understood as being) about objects, it need not be necessary. For it may be only contingently true that two certain objects are one entity. The *object* we ordinarily refer to as the Evening Star is singled out in terms of its position in the sky at a certain time, and the *object* we ordinarily refer to as the Morning Star is singled out in terms of its very different position at a very different time. That they are only contingently identical is no more questionable than that it is only contingently true that a certain planet visible in the morning is also visible in the evening. But if we were to regard the Evening Star and the Morning Star *only* as entities, i.e., if we were to abstract from the objects just mentioned, then of course they would be necessarily identical because they would be formally identical; we would abstract from precisely that which renders them apparently distinct and the statement of their identity material rather than equivalent to, say, the statement "Venus is Venus." A material identity statement would be necessary only if the objects it is about are of certain specifiable kinds, e.g., if they are mathematical objects. (I shall return to this latter point in chapter five.)

Kripke's chief argument depends on the notion of a rigid designator. He introduces this notion in two distinguishable ways, although he seems to think that they are equivalent. First, to say that *"a"* is a rigid designator is to say that it is false that *a* might not have been *a*. In this sense, a definite description involving a predicate F would not be a rigid designator if it is true (as it is in most, but not all, cases) that the F might not have been the F. It also follows that genuine proper names are rigid designators, because with respect to any such name *"a"* it is of course false that *a* might not have been *a*. But the reason for this is nothing more startling than the necessary truth of the law of identity, "(x)(x is x)." It does not follow that if true "*a* is *b*" is necessarily true, even if *"a"* and *"b"* are rigid designators in this sense, for "*a* is *b*" is not an instance of the law of identity. To say that it is, on the grounds that if "*a* is *b*" is true then it is the same proposition as "*a* is *a*" or "*b* is *b*," would be either to beg the question or to appeal to the second way of introducing the notion of a rigid designator. We must not *assume* that to deny that *a* might not have been *b* is to deny that *a* might not have been *a*.

According to the second way the notion of a rigid designator is introduced, to say that *"a"* is a rigid designator is to say that *"a"*designates the same entity in all possible worlds in which this entity exists. It follows trivially that if *"a"* and *"b"* are rigid designators in this sense then "*a* is *b*" is necessarily true if true at all. But the price to be paid for this quick demonstration is that now we can no longer assume that genuine proper names are rigid designators. For to know that an expression is a rigid designator we would need to know that all true identity statements in which it occurs are necessarily true. Therefore, we can no longer argue that a given identity statement is necessarily true if true at all by appealing to the status of its subject terms as rigid designators; such an argument would be circular. Let me explain.

The locution "'a' designates x" is ambiguous. It may mean (1) that there is a semantical rule, a linguistic convention, that 'a' designates x. But it may also mean something importantly different, namely, (2) that x is identical with y and that there is a semantical rule, a linguistic convention, that 'a' designates y. For example, "The Evening Star" (or "Hesperus") designates the Evening Star in sense (1), but it designates the Morning Star in sense (2); it designates the Morning Star in part because of the latter's identity with the Evening Star, not solely because of a linguistic convention as in the case of its designation of the Evening Star. Now if both "a" and "b" are designators of the same thing in sense (1) of "designate," i.e., if by linguistic convention "a" and "b" designate the same thing, then of course "a is b" is necessarily true because it is in effect a formal identity statement, like "Scott is Sir Walter," and we need not appeal to the notion of a rigid designator. But if one or both are designators in sense (2) of "designate," we could know that they are rigid designators only if we knew independently that "a is b" is necessarily true if true at all. For "a" designates x in sense (2) only if x is identical with what "a" designates in sense (1), say, y. And if "x is identical with y" were not itself necessary, then "a" would not designate the same thing in all possible worlds and thus, trivially, would not be a rigid designator, even if in our use of it we intended it to be a rigid designator. For example, to determine whether "The Evening Star is the Morning Star" is necessarily true we would need to *determine* whether "The Evening Star" and "The Morning Star" are rigid designators (and not merely rely on our referential intentions), and to determine that they are rigid designators we would need, in part, to determine that "The Evening Star is the Morning Star" is necessarily true.

Nevertheless Kripke's thesis, if not argument, remains plausible. As he says, if "*a*" and "*b*" name, designate, the same entity, how could "*a* is *b*" be false? Indeed, it could not, if we abstract from the fact that "*a*" and "*b*" also designate objects. As we have seen, once such abstraction is performed, "*a* is *b*" is in effect a formal identity statement and therefore necessarily true. But ordinarily names designate also objects. We understand them, and the statements made with them, only if we know what objects they designate. A true identity statement is both about two objects and about one entity. Our understanding of it, its content, what it asserts, the statement it is, are inseparable from its being about objects, and not merely about an entity, and indeed from its being about these rather than any other objects. If we ignore this fact then we ignore the apparent distinctness of the identicals. And while to do so is, in effect, to regard the statement as being really a formal identity statement, and thus as necessarily true, it is also to regard it as being no longer the same as the original statement. The identity of a statement, *which* statement it is, is a function of how it is understood, and how a statement is understood is a function of what we take it to be about and thus of the context of experiences, beliefs, thoughts, and intentions in which we make it. If it is said that a statement's being about objects is an epistemic matter and that the entities it is about are alone of metaphysical concern, then we should reply that a statement, particularly one of identity, cannot be divorced from such "epistemic matters," that the notion of a statement is partly but essentially epistemic. As the history of modern philosophy has taught us, the distinction between epistemology and metaphysics is not so simple.

V

If the failures of the substitutivity of names of material identicals are due to our sometimes regarding such names as referring
primarily to objects and only secondarily also to entities, another
feature of the concept of identity, pointed out by P. T. Geach, [6]
namely, the logical incompleteness of many identity statements,
is due to our sometimes regarding the subject terms of the statement as referring primarily to entities and only secondarily also
to objects. A material identity statement asserts of two objects
that they are one and the same entity. Some such statements
would be true (false) regardless of the sort of entity the objects
are taken to be, indeed even if we have no idea of their sort. I
shall call such applications of the concept of identity and the
statements expressing them primary. That there are such applications and statements will be argued shortly. But not all applications of the concept of identity are primary. Sometimes the
identity statement would be true if the entity the objects are
asserted to be is taken to be of a certain sort, but false if it is taken
to be of another sort. To use a familiar example, two objects may
be one and the same river but not one and the same water. One
may be bathing in the same river one bathed in yesterday, but
not in the same water. I shall call such applications of the concept of identity and the statements expressing them secondary.
They are neither paradoxical nor even surprising, given our distinction between objects and entities. For an object is essentially
that to which our conceptual apparatus is initially applied, that
which comes to be classified as an entity. And there is no reason
why one and the same object should not be equally legitimately
classifiable in different ways, as different sorts of entity (e.g., why
something I am looking at should not be equally legitimately
classifiable as a river as well as a certain water). Therefore, there
is no reason why it should not be the case that two objects are the
same entity of the F sort but not the same entity of the G sort. In
such cases the bare assertion of the identity of the two objects,

without specification of the sort of entity they are asserted to be, would not have a definite truth-value and thus would not have a definite sense.*

Therefore, with respect to secondary applications of the concept of identity, we may agree with Geach that (1) the form of a logically complete identity statement is "*x* is the same F as *y*," in which "F" is a sortal predicate, not "*x* is the same as *y*"; and that (2) while *x* may be the same F as *y*, it need not be the same G as *y*. John Perry[7] has rejected (1) on the grounds that the incompleteness, indefiniteness, of some statements of the form "*x* is the same as *y*" is due not to indefiniteness of the predicate, as Geach claims, but to indefiniteness of the reference of the terms. (An extreme example would be "This is the same as that," when the context does not make the reference of the pronouns clear.) If so, then the defective character of such statements discloses nothing about the concept of identity; it is merely an example of a failure to which any statement containing referential terms is subject. But it may be perfectly definite which *objects* "*x*" and "*y*" refer to (e.g., which object I am looking at now and which object I remember having looked at yesterday), and yet "*x* is the same as *y*" may still not have definite sense. For are the two objects referred to the same water or the same river? What Perry has shown is that such a statement would be logically incomplete if it is not definite which *entities*, even if it is definite which *objects*, its subject terms refer to. And, of course, for the former to be definite the *sort*(s) of the entities referred to must be definite.

---

*But nothing can be concluded from this regarding what predicates can be regarded as the sortals needed for the completeness of secondary identity statements. In particular, it does not follow that they must stand for natural kinds. Obviously, "red" is not a suitable predicate. "Man" seems to be suitable. But so does "iron sphere," indeed "sphere" itself. These terms are no less obviously individuative, both synchronically and diachronically, than "man" is. This should not be surprising. The individuation of spatial objects is based in part on the individuation of the places they occupy, and those predicates of spatial objects are individuative which include as part of their sense the possession of a more or less well defined spatial location.

David Wiggins has rejected (2) (which he does not regard as a logical consequence of (1), a part of Geach's view he accepts) on the grounds that it violates the principle of the indiscernibility of identicals.[8] But let us interpret (2) to be in effect the claim that the concept of identity may have correct secondary applications to certain objects if the latter are considered as entities of one sort, but not if they are considered as entities of another sort. Then the false identity statement "*x* is the same G as *y*," would not be about the same *entities* as the true identity statement "*x* is the same F as *y*," even though it would be about the same *objects*. And insofar as we are concerned with the entities, rather than the objects, the statements are about, there would be no violation of the principle of the indiscernibility of identicals. The objects the statements are about would be discernible, but also not identical, qua objects; as we have seen, objects as such can only be formally identical, and by definition the objects a material statement is about are not formally identical.

Nevertheless, secondary applications of the concept of identity presuppose primary applications, that is, applications that do not require prior determination of the identicals as entities and thus specification of their sort. In a secondary application we depend on, or take for granted, the *identifications* of the object with other objects in virtue of which it comes to be regarded as an entity of a certain sort. On pain of an infinite regress, some of these identifications must be primary. And that there are such identifications is evident from examples.[9] If I wonder whether what I dimly see lying on a bench in the park is the same as what I saw an hour earlier, the resolution of my wonderment (e.g., by appeal to the testimony of others who kept the thing under continuous observation) may be quite unaffected by the question of whether what I am referring to is a man, or a woman, or a dummy, or a log, or a large package, or a shadow. In examining a strange thing by warily walking around it, I may be quite confident in my judgment that what I am looking at now is the same as what I saw a moment ago from the other side, without being able to apply to it any genuine sortal concept. One may recognize that the color or shape or feel or smell of an object is the same as the color or shape or feel or smell of another object without possessing the appropriate specific (e.g., "red") or even generic (e.g., "color") concept. And small children (perhaps also some animals) are quite capable of judging whether something is the same as something else (e.g., whether a certain trinket is *his*, whether it is the one *he* found), even if possessing no relevant sortal concepts and no relevant linguistic competence. Such identity judgments are the obvious first and absolutely necessary step in the very acquisition of any appropriate sortal concept.

Indeed, without primary applications of the concept of identity, the genesis, the acquisition, of *any* concepts would be impossible. In *Thinking and Experience,* which continues to be the most thorough account of conceptual cognition, H. H. Price describes recognition as the experience of "the same again" and argues that it is necessary both for the possession and the acquisition of concepts. Of course, recognition is not a mere experience, and Price's point is logical, not psychological. Unless one can see that the red color of one thing is the same as the red color of another thing, or that a cat seen from one point is the same thing as the cat seen from another point, one could not acquire the concepts of red and cat.* (This is why, I may add, Wittgenstein's argument against the possibility of a private language, if sound, would also prove the impossibility of any public language.)

---

*In *Relative Identity*, Nicholas Griffin says: "It is hard to see how any sense can be made of the notion of an individual item without individuation, and it is hard to see how sense can be made of individuation without sortals which supply the principles which make individuation possible" (pp. 158-59). But it is even harder to see, I suggest, how we can acquire and apply sortal concepts (consider, e.g., the concept of a mountain) unless we could make identity judgments that do not include a sortal. Regarding the items such judgments would be about, Griffin legitimately goes on to ask, "What are these items? and how much of the world does each take up?" I believe that our theory of objects provides answers to these questions.

It is a familiar philosophical claim that the criteria for the applicability of the concept of identity to a particular case are provided (at least in part) by the sortal concept applicable to the things asserted to be identical. It is a claim of considerable plausibility because it is trivially true for *secondary* applications of the concept of identity. Such an application is, by definition, one in which the truth-value of the statement depends, in part, on the sort of the entity the statement is understood to be about. Thus the features of the entity that would be taken to constitute its sort are part of the truth-conditions of the statement, and can be called criteria of identity. But, again by definition, no such criteria are available for *primary* applications of the concept of identity. Indeed, there are no criteria *at all*, in the usual sense of this term, for such applications. To demand that there be truth-conditions for the applicability of the concept of identity in such cases, other than, trivially, the fact of the applicability itself, would be to ignore its primitive nature. It would also be to ignore the fundamental place it occupies in our conceptual apparatus and to render incomprehensible the application of concepts to the world.

That there are no criteria, in the usual sense of this term, for primary applications of the concept of identity does not imply that such applications cannot be judged as correct or incorrect, that they are not subject to criteria in a broader sense of the term. As with other primitive concepts, e.g., those of red and green, the use of the concept of identity is governed by paradigms, and the correctness of its application in a particular case is a function of the similarity of that case to the paradigms of identity. But this is determined in the case of primary applications not by investigation or argument but by the perception of the similarity and the decision to regard it as sufficient for the classification of the case as one of identity.*

---

*For a discussion of this last point, see my "The Limits of Ontological Analysis," in *The Ontological Turn*, ed. M. S. Gram and E. D. Klemke (Iowa City: University of Iowa Press, 1974). I shall discuss the notion of a criterion of identity in chapter six.

Indeed, someone's assertion that *a* is the same as *b*, if it constitutes a primary application of the concept of identity, may lack definite sense *for the hearer*. Since no indication of the sort of the entity *a* and *b* are asserted to be is provided, the reference of "*a*" and "*b*" is likely to be unclear to the hearer. But from this it does not follow that the assertion would have no definite sense *for the speaker*, or that the reference of "*a*" and "*b*" would be unclear to him, even though he has no relevant sortal concept in mind. Even a statement such as "This is the same as that" can be perfectly clear to the speaker, though totally obscure to the hearer.

CHAPTER FOUR

Existence

I

In chapter two I offered a joint account of the roles of the concepts of identity and existence. Nevertheless, my chief concern there, as well as in chapter three, was with identity. In the present chapter I shall amplify and defend the views on existence already delineated.

There are at least three questions philosophers may ask about existence, and it is important to distinguish them at the very outset. There is first the question, what exists? Of course, most of its applications are to be found in everyday life and in the sciences. Whether the sinister man Mrs. Jones fears exists or not is, fortunately, a question for psychiatrists and detectives, not for philosophers. Whether life exists on other planets is a question for scientists and astronauts. But the question What exists? also has philosophical applications. Whether uninstantiated universals, material objects, and other persons' experiences exist are philosophical questions and can be answered adequately only by philosophical means. But it is not with such questions that I shall be concerned here.

The second question is, what is it for something to exist? In the older philosophical jargon, it would be, what is the content of the idea or concept of existence? In the newer jargon, it would be, what is the meaning or use of the word "exist"? or, what is the criterion or criteria for saying of something correctly that it exists? Clearly, this second question has logical priority over the first. We can hardly determine what exists if we are unclear about what it is for something to exist. Yet it is a question likely to be asked and answered only by philosophers. It has the logical fundamentality that is characteristic only of questions we regard as philosophical.

But a third question is even more fundamental than the second, and an orderly investigation of existence must begin with it. It can be stated in any one of the following forms: What is the *general* status of existence? What *sort* of situation, or fact, or state of affairs, is the existence of something? Is existence a property, an "essence"? What is the logical status of an assertion of the existence of something? What *sort* of concept is the concept of existence? Indeed, is there good sense in calling it a concept at all? Is "exists" a logical (or, in Kant's terminology, real) predicate?

Why is there a philosophical issue regarding the general status of existence? I remarked earlier that the reasons are very similar to the reasons for puzzlement over material identity. Certain statements (as well as beliefs, thoughts, and perceptions) appear to be about something they cannot be about. Certain statements (and beliefs) seem true yet in a way we find incomprehensible. And still other statements (and beliefs) seem to be without truth-value even though with perfectly clear sense. The first, and philosophically most suggestive, class consists of singular true negative existential statements.* We understand what is meant by "Santa Claus does not exist" and also know it to be true. What is the statement about? Santa Claus. Why is it true? Because it says about Santa Claus what is the case, namely, that he does not exist. But if the statement is true, then there is nothing, no one, it is about, and nothing, no one, about which it can be saying what is the case. The second class of statements consists of true singular nonexistential statements that *prima facie* are about nonexis-

---

*I shall mean by "existential statement" one in which a form of the verb "exist" or of one of its synonyms occurs as the main grammatical predicate. What is ordinarily called the existential quantifier I shall call "the particular quantifier"; and I shall call the statements it forms "general particular statements."

tent things. Examples would be "Santa Claus has a beard," "Hamlet is indecisive," and "The rat John hallucinated this morning was pink." How can such statements be true if they are about nonexistent things? For is not being about nonexistent things the same as being about nothing? The third class consists of seemingly truth-valueless singular nonexistential statements that *prima facie* are about nonexistent things. Examples would be "Santa Claus wears an undershirt," "Hamlet usually had eggs for breakfast," and "The rat John hallucinated this morning suffers from heart disease." There seems to be no sense in assigning a truth-value to such a statement because there seem to be no criteria for determining its truth-value. (In the case of statements belonging to the first two classes there are such criteria.) The seeming exception here to the principle of excluded middle is much more extreme than that provided by, e.g., the statement "The sequence 777 occurs in the expansion of *pi*." God may be supposed to see in his mind's infinite eye the infinite expansion of *pi* and thus see whether or not 777 occurs in it. But even God could not see whether or not Hamlet usually had eggs for breakfast.

All three of these classes of statements appear to be about entities but in fact cannot be. I have called this the phenomenon of the apparent existence of nonexistent things, a phenomenon analogous in structure and significance to that of the apparent distinctness of identicals and, as I have suggested, subject to the same ultimate explanation. If the members of the first class were about entities, then they would not be true; yet, obviously they are true. If the members of the second class were about entities, then their truth would constitute no puzzle; yet, it does. If the members of the third class were about entities, they would have a truth-value; yet, they do not. The distinction between objects and entities, which in the context of the topic of existence amounts to the recognition that "exists" is a logical predicate, that the notion of existence is a genuine concept, a principle of classification, that there are nonexistent things, provides a solution to the puzzles regarding all three classes. I shall devote the present chapter to showing that this is so by defending the proposition that there are nonexistent things against a series of actual and possible objections. But before I begin, an explanatory remark is needed.

The reader has no doubt noticed the omission from the above list of the corresponding three classes of universal statements, even though these have received much attention in the literature on the topic of existence: true negative universal existential statements (e.g., "Carnivorous cows do not exist"), true universal nonexistential statements that *prima facie* are about nonexistent things (e.g., "Carnivorous cows are mammals"), and seemingly truth-valueless universal statements that *prima facie* are about nonexistent things (e.g., "Carnivorous cows live longer"). The reason for this omission is that in such purely general statements no reference, in the strict sense of "reference" explained in chapters one and two, is made to anything (unless, irrelevantly, to properties). This is why such statements do not provide plausible reasons for supposing that there are nonexistent things. The apparent reference in them to such things is easily eliminable. For example, the three statements in parentheses can be plausibly replaced, respectively, with the following: "Nothing is both carnivorous and a cow," "If anything is both carnivorous and a cow then it is a mammal," and "If any cow is carnivorous then it lives longer."

Indeed, these classes of universal statements do have the puzzling feature of seeming to resist specification and instantiation.[1] General particular statements of the form "Some carnivorous cows are . . ." and singular statements of the form "This carnivorous cow is . . ." seem to have no clear sense. But, of course, they seem so only because they seem, in the former case, to presuppose the possibility of reference to a nonexistent thing (if some carnivorous cows are . . . then perhaps some other carnivorous cows are not. . . , and we should be able, in principle, to say which are and which, if any, are not) and, in the latter case, actually to make such reference. And ordinarily we do not single out and refer to carnivorous cows. But suppose that we did. Suppose that we found ourselves often dreaming and hallucinating about carnivorous cows, or at least that writers of fiction developed a penchant for carnivorous cows in their choice of characters. I suggest that we would then be able to refer to particular carnivorous cows and thus to make singular statements about them, if we can do so regarding nonexistent things at all. And, by "existential" generalization, these singular statements would lead to general particular statements about carnivorous cows that have perfectly good sense. (Moreover, if we were also to discover that some existent cows are carnivorous then it would be true that some carnivorous cows exist and that others do not.) Thus universal statements about carnivorous cows would no longer have the puzzling feature of resisting instantiation and specification. But they would continue to be puzzling insofar as the required singular statements are puzzling. Would the imagined psychological or literary events indeed make it possible for us, as I have suggested, to refer to, and to make genuine singular statements about, nonexistent carnivorous cows? It is this kind of question that constitutes the core of the problem of the general status of existence, and this is why the latter must be examined with respect to singular, not general, statements that seem to be about nonexistent things.

II

I have suggested that the question whether "exists" is a logical predicate is equivalent to the question whether the notion of existence is a genuine concept, a principle of classification. If this were not so, then it would be unclear why and how the question can constitute a philosophical problem. For "exists" is, of course, a grammatical predicate. And the question whether it is also a logical predicate, if not identified with the question whether it expresses a classificatory notion, could only concern its presence and role in some particular system of logic. In *Principia Mathematica*, it is not a predicate; its ordinary function is assumed by the particular quantifier. But there is no difficulty in constructing a system in which it is a predicate, whether defined or undefined.² Indeed, both as a grammatical and as a logical predicate it is an extraordinary one. As we have seen, at least in universal statements, it has some rather unusual characteristics. And it appears to bear important relationships to logical notions, particularly those of quantification, in a way no ordinary predicate does. But these peculiarities do not suffice for the conclusion that it is not a logical predicate. The important question is whether or not statements of the form "x exists," where "x" takes as substituends proper names or demonstratives or definite descriptions used referringly, should be understood as *describing* x. If they should, then so should be their negations. And since some of these negations are true, the question has the same philosophical cash-value as the question whether there are nonexistent things. But this makes evident that it is really the same as the question whether the notion of existence is a genuine concept, a principle of classification. For to say that a certain notion is a genuine concept, a principle of classification, is to say that its applicability to a thing distinguishes, or at least can distinguish, that thing from other things.

What objections are there to the view that "exists" is a logical predicate, or that the notion of existence is a genuine concept, or that there are nonexistent things?

The most fundamental objection is very general in character. It is not enough that we should be able to formulate the notion of a nonexistent thing without inconsistency and without obviously unacceptable dialectical consequences. We must also understand this notion, we must find it intelligible, intellectually visible. And is it not in fact thoroughly obscure? This objection, which I believe is fatal to any ordinary Meinongian theory, has already been dealt with. For we introduced the notion of a nonexistent thing on the basis of the distinction between objects and entities. A nonexistent thing is an object that is not also an entity. We were led to this distinction primarily by considerations regarding the concept of identity, not the concept of existence; it can be made by reference to the nature of material identity without our even mentioning existence. And these considerations were themselves grounded in a philosophical picture of the nature of conceptual cognition, of the application of a conceptual apparatus, of the conditions that must be satisfied by anything that is to be counted as a world of entities. The fact that the seemingly unconnected problems of existence and identity are solved by the same distinction already throws light on each solution and keeps it from being ad hoc, a mere formulation, a verbal trick. But this would still have been insufficient if the distinction had not been independently grounded in more fundamental considerations. When so grounded, it comes to have, I believe, as much intelligibility, intellectual visibility, as the most abstract metaphysical theses may aspire to.

Moreover, our discussion of identity in chapter one also allows us to see the inadequacy of the main alternative to the view that there are nonexistent things, namely, Russell's theory of descriptions. Our criticism of the latter as a solution of the problem of the apparent distinctness of material identicals is, *mutatis mutandis*, a criticism of it also as a solution of the problem of the apparent existence of nonexistents. The fact is that sometimes we do find ourselves singling out something before our minds, whether in perception, thought, or discourse, asking ourselves whether it exists (is real, is really there), and answering that question in the negative. When we do so in discourse by means of a definite description, the latter is used referringly and therefore, as we have seen, is not subject to the Russellian analysis. And, of course, we often accomplish such reference also by means of indexical expressions such as "this" and "that."

The examples of nonexistent things offered in the literature on the topic of existence are of great variety but unequal value. There are fictional things (e.g., Hamlet), legendary things (e.g.,

Santa Claus), what one recent author has felicitously dubbed "nonesuches" (e.g., the present King of France),[3] impossible things (e.g., the round square), possible things (e.g., the golden mountain), objects of false belief (e.g., that Hitler defeated the Soviet Union), imaginary things (e.g., the home she would like to own), things one has only dreamed about, objects of existentially illusory perception (the pink rat one supposedly hallucinates some morning). I shall not attempt a detailed discussion of the differences and similarities between such examples. Two observations, however, are in order. First, many of these examples are inappropriate because they are not examples of objects, of things that are, or even can be, singled out and referred to. This is clearly the case with impossible things. That we can *use* a descriptive phrase such as "the round square" in grammatical and perhaps even true statements does not entail that we are able to single out something the phrase stands for. And many merely possible things, e.g., the golden mountain, may in fact not be singled out and referred to, even though they could be. They may in fact be nonesuches, like the present King of France. That is, as ordinarily used, the respective descriptive phrases may refer to nothing, whether existent or nonexistent; there may be nothing before the mind they stand for.

The second observation is that many of the common examples of nonexistent things ought to receive prior elucidation by other branches of philosophy if anything of protometaphysical significance is to rest on them. Fictional things are such examples. Unlike hallucination, dreaming, and imagination, fiction is a certain mode of discourse and thus cannot directly acquaint us with objects. Whether, and the extent to which, genuine reference to fictional things is made, the differences between the author's and the reader's reference, what I shall later describe as the analogical applications to fictional things of the concepts of existence and identity, are all issues specific to the philosophy of literature that require independent examination.[4] Other examples are the objects of false belief. If there are such objects at all, presumably they should be understood as nonactual (nonexistent) states of affairs.* But the notion of a state of affairs is faced with serious independent difficulties, made evident already in the controversy between Bradley and Russell regarding the role of relations.[5] And the notion of a nonactual state of affairs is even more questionable. (I shall return to this topic in chapter eight and also in Appendix A.)

The examples of nonexistent things I shall consider are imaginary things, things one has dreamed about, and especially the objects of existentially illusory perception. They are the most obvious cases of nonexistent things actually singled out before the mind. And nonexistent perceptual objects are of special epistemological importance, since perception provides most of the objects of the application of our conceptual apparatus. What I shall say about them will apply easily also to imaginary things and to things one has only dreamed about.

One may experience a hallucination of a pink rat. One may refer to the object of the hallucination (whether during the hallucination or later) with a definite description or an indexical expression. The question of whether the object so referred to exists or not may well command one's thought and, often, one may be able to answer it. This philosophically most fundamental sort of case, discussed in epistemology repeatedly and at very great length, has been largely ignored in the literature on the topic of existence, in favor of anemic examples from fiction and legend. Why is this so? The chief reason, I believe, is the epistemological views about nonveridical perception held by writers on existence. Some of these views are simply irrelevant to the

---

*Meinong calls them objectives that have no being ("The Theory of Objects," in *Realism and the Background of Phenomenology*, ed. R. M. Chisholm [Glencoe: Free Press, 1960]); R. M. Chisholm calls them states of affairs that, though necessarily existent, do not obtain (*Person and Object* [LaSalle, Illinois: Open Court Publishing Company, 1976], chapter IV); Gustav Bergmann calls them complexes that have the mode of potentiality, rather than the mode of actuality (for references to Bergmann, see chapter eight, n. 7).

latter topic. Others are in fact consequences of usually unargued and often only implicit theories about it.

Moore and Russell believed that in existentially illusory cases of perception, what one is directly aware of, and may refer to, is something existent, namely, a sense-datum, and not a nonexistent thing such as a pink rat. This belief, together with their desire to provide a unified account of veridical and nonveridical perception led them to the conclusion that even in veridical cases of perception one is not directly aware of material objects, but only of sense-data, and that apparent references to material objects are to be analyzed away in accordance with Russell's theory of descriptions. Moore wrote:

> Two things only seem to me to be quite certain about the analysis of such propositions [as "This is a human hand"] (and even with regard to these I am afraid some philosophers would differ from me) namely that whenever I know, or judge, such a proposition to be true, (1) there is always some *sense-datum* about which the proposition in question is a proposition—some sense-datum which is *a* subject (and, in a certain sense, the principal or ultimate subject) of the proposition in question, and (2) that, nevertheless, *what* I am knowing or judging to be true about this sense-datum is not (in general) that it is *itself* a hand, or a dog, or the sun, etc. etc., as the case may be. . . . I think it certain . . . that the analysis of the proposition "This is a human hand" is, roughly at least, of the form "There is a thing, and only one thing, of which it is true both that it is a human hand and that *this surface* is a part of its surface."[6]

But even if there are sense-data, surely what one refers to by means of the word "this" in the statement "This is a human hand" is not a sense-datum, which is a mere expanse, whether or not it is a part of the surface of a human hand, but the human hand itself. Surely, also, what one refers to in a hallucination of a pink rat, and perhaps finds terrifying, is not a sense-datum or a part of some surface, but the pink rat itself. And if one were to say "The pink rat in the corner does not exist (is not real, is a mere hallucination)," one would be using the descriptive phrase to refer to the pink rat, not to a sense-datum or a part of some surface. If a sense-datum were to be mentioned, the statement might be, "The pink rat associated with this sense-datum does not exist," in which the descriptive phrase would be used re-ferringly and therefore, as we saw in chapter one, the statement would not be adequately analyzed as "It is false that there is one and only one pink rat with which this sense-datum is associated."

The substance of what I have just claimed is acknowledged, though in different terms and not unqualifiedly, by H. H. Price, to whom we owe the most detailed version of the sense-datum theory. I have in mind Price's notion of perceptual consciousness and especially of the kind of perceptual consciousness he calls perceptual acceptance. Price wrote:

> Let us consider once more the celebrated case of the delirious man who "sees a pink rat". The correct analysis seems to be this: (1) He is acquainted with a pink sense-datum; and about the existence of this ("wild" though it is) there is no doubt whatever. . . . (2) He takes for granted the existence of a rat, and he takes for granted that this rat has a front surface of a certain general sort. . . . This rat is not real. Still, he really does have perceptual consciousness of it, in exactly that sense in which he has a simultaneous consciousness of his table or his boot. (p. 147)
> . . . the curious thing is that perceptual consciousness also *seems* intuitive. In the first place, not only is there no passage of the mind from the sense-datum to the taken-for-granted, both coming before the mind at once as one single complex; but also, within the taking for granted itself there is no passage from the front surface of the material thing to the back and sides and inside. . . . Yet somehow it is the *whole* thing, and not just a jejune extract from it, which is before the mind from the first. From the first, it is the complete material thing, with back, sides and insides as well as front, that we "accept", that "ostends itself" to us, and nothing less . . . (pp. 151–52)
> . . . when I look at a house. . . . What is before my mind is a *house*. . . . And not only so . . . but a particular house. . . . Of course it need not in fact be that particular house, say Mr. Jones's; it may not be a house at all—I may be having an hallucination. (p. 152)[7]

I believe that what Price calls perceptual consciousness in the above passages is what I would call singling out in perception of a material thing, which may but need not exist. I do not agree that it only seems intuitive, nor that it need involve the acceptance or taking-for-granted of the existence of the thing. Price's unwillingness to allow that perceptual consciousness is genuinely intuitive is due solely to his assumption that intuitive consciousness may only have existent things as its objects. His insistence that it involves acceptance of the existence of its object seems to me a mere mistake; the hallucinator would be no less perceptually conscious of the pink rat if he were to doubt or deny that it exists, or even if he knew that he was hallucinating.

Philosophers who find the sense-datum theory distasteful are likely to claim that in a hallucination there is nothing the person singles out, since they mistakenly assume that if there were something it could only be a sense-datum.* Consequently, they are also likely to claim that there is nothing in the hallucination of which the concept of existence may be denied. But, first, it is obvious that the hallucinator takes himself to be singling out something, and to argue that he is not actually doing so would be merely to beg the question by assuming that there are not nonexistent things. And, second, it is equally obvious that, specifically, he takes himself to be *perceiving* (e.g., seeing) something, and to argue that he is not would be either to beg the question again by assuming that there are not nonexistent things or to insist on using the verb "perceive" only with respect to existent things. If the latter (which is largely but not wholly sanctioned by ordinary usage) is the case, then the argument

---

*For example, the so-called adverbial theory of sensing (as expounded, e.g., by R. M. Chisholm, most recently in *Person and Object*, pp. 47–52) does not even pretend to issue from an independent, detailed investigation of the nature of perceptual consciousness. No such investigation is likely to suggest that, for example, saying that one senses redly is more adequate to the nature of sensing than is saying that one senses something red. The theory is explicitly proposed as a *formulation* that avoids, on the level of surface grammar, reference to objects of sensing, which the theory merely assumes may only be sense-data.

could be met by substituting Price's phrase "is (am) perceptually conscious of" for "perceive" or by explaining that "perceive" is used in the sense, certainly present in ordinary usage, in which one may be said to perceive even things that do not exist.*

Indeed, the topic of existence would have received much more illuminating treatments if it had not been for the tendency of epistemologists to insist that in cases of existentially illusory perception either a sense-datum is what is really ("directly") perceived ("sensed") or nothing at all is perceived. I shall not engage here in a detailed discussion of the problem of perception.[8] But perhaps the following remarks are appropriate. (1) The paradigm of an object of perception is what philosophers usually call a material object, a body, something like an animal, or a rock, or a chair, and not a sense-datum, or an appearance, or an idea. (2) It does not follow from (1), nor are there any independent good reasons for holding, that if someone perceives a material object then it exists, unless we assume that there are not nonexistent things; nor does ordinary usage support such a conclusion unequivocally. (3) It does not follow from (2) that there is no need for a category of entities such as sense-data, since the need for this category is epistemological and not metaphysical.[9] It may still be argued that our *knowledge* of the existence and properties of (existent) material objects is derivative, or indirect, and requires for its basis primary, or direct, knowledge of the existence and properties of certain other things that are not material objects but may enter in certain specifiable relations with existent material objects. For sense-data have been introduced as a way of making clear the nature and possibility of our *knowledge* of the existence and properties of material objects, and it is plausible to

*Cf. G. E. M. Anscombe, "The Intentionality of Sensation: A Grammatical Feature," in *Analytical Philosophy: Second Series*, ed. R. Butler (Oxford: Basil Blackwell, 1965). That such a use is nonstandard (as argued, with reference to Anscombe's article, by R. C. Coburn in "Intentionality and Perception," *Mind* LXXXVI (1977): pp. 1–18) is not, it seems to me, of importance to the issues before us; this fact is easily explained by the pragmatic purposes for which we need perceptual verbs.

argue that only the perception ("sensing") of *existent* things can constitute evidence for the *existence* of material objects and for the properties of *existent* material objects.

III

So far I have considered the fundamental and most general objection to the view that there are nonexistent things, namely, that the notion of a nonexistent thing is not intelligible. The chief response to this objection was in effect made in chapter two. In the previous section of the present chapter I have tried to support that response by showing how the notion of a nonexistent thing has a natural application in familiar perceptual situations.

But there have been numerous other, more specific objections. The following three are both the most common and the easiest to meet. First, the view "multiplies entities without necessity." Second, nonexistent things are unobservable, their "being" is unverifiable. Third, the very notion of there being nonexistent things is self-contradictory. I believe that none of these objections applies to the distinction between objects and entities, and thus to our version of the view that there are nonexistent things. Objects that do not exist are not entities at all and have no place in the real world. But at least some are quite observable, namely, whenever we have existentially illusory perceptual experiences. And we do not, of course, apply the concept of existence to nonexistent objects; nor do we apply any equivalent or related notion, such as that of subsistence, being, or ontological status; the statement "There are objects that do not exist" would be interpreted as meaning "Some objects do not exist," and not as "There exist objects that do not exist."

According to a fourth objection, if there were genuine singular existential statements, then if affirmative they would be redundant and if negative, self-contradictory. The argument behind this view is that the subject term of such a statement would have no reference and thus no significance (assuming that it is a proper name or a demonstrative pronoun or a referringly used definite description) unless there really were something it refers to. But if by "there really is something it refers to" is meant that the term does really refer to something, the conclusion does not follow, for the term may really refer to a nonexistent (unreal) thing. On the other hand, if what is meant is that the term refers to an existent, real, thing, then the conclusion does follow, but only by a *petitio*.

P. T. Geach considers the sense of the statement "Cerberus doesn't exist (is not real) like Rover," as it might be made to comfort a child frightened by hearing myths about Cerberus and expecting Cerberus to come to bite him. According to Geach, a proper recasting of the sentence could consist, in part, of saying to the child "When I said 'Cerberus' in that story, I was only pretending to use it as a name."[10] But unless the child were also taught Geach's views about naming, he would find no comfort in this recast verbal performance. A person (perhaps even an animal) may wonder, investigate, and perhaps find out whether a certain object before him is real without engaging in metalinguistic exercises, indeed without talking at all, even to himself.

A fifth objection to regarding existence as a genuine concept arises in connection with quantification. (It is closely related to the third.) If we interpret general particular statements, that is, statements of the form "Something is F" as asserting existence, as equivalent to "There exists a thing which is F," and accordingly also interpret the universal quantifier as ranging only over *existent* things [otherwise we would not preserve the equivalence of $\sim(x)\sim Fx$ and $(\exists x)Fx$], then, clearly, we would contradict ourselves if we were to assert that some things do not exist. Moreover, on this interpretation of general statements, one who accepts nonexistent things must disallow existential generalization [if Fa, then $(\exists x)Fx$] as well as universal instantiation [if $(x)Fx$, then Fa] because of the possibility that "a" refers to a nonexistent thing.

Obviously, the response to this objection would consist in a different interpretation of quantification. We must regard the universal and the particular quantifiers as ranging over objects, not just entities, and thus over both existent and nonexistent things.* Such an interpretation is indeed the more natural one; it fits better the ordinary uses of the words "all," "every," and "some." If we adopt it, then there would be no contradiction in asserting that some things do not exist and no difficulty in allowing the inference from "Fa" to "Something is F," or from "Everything is F" to "Fa," even if a does not exist. But what shall we say about the expression "there is" ("there are")? Indeed, sometimes it is a synonym of "something (someone) is" (or, significantly, of *"es gibt"* in German and *"il y a"* in French), and then we could assert that there are things that do not exist without fear of contradiction. But sometimes it is a synonym of "there exists," and then we could not do so. Nothing of philosophical importance rests on this ambiguity, or on how we may decide to resolve it, or on whether we bother to resolve it.

The semantics of quantification so understood is no less clear, though also no more illuminating, than the semantics of quantification as ordinarily understood. For example, we can say, roughly, that a singular atomic statement of the form "Fx" would be true if and only if the individual designated by its subject term has the property its predicate stands for; that x may be nonexistent is in no way incompatible with its having properties, if it is

---

*The *formal* features of such an interpretation are outlined by Lejewski in "Logic and Existence." See also his "Ontology and Logic" and "Reply" in *Philosophy of Logic*, ed. Stephan Körner (Berkeley and Los Angeles: University of California Press, 1976), pp. 24, 59–61; and Eugene C. Luschei, *The Logical Systems of Lesniewski* (Amsterdam: North-Holland Publishing Company, 1962), pp. 109–18. But, unlike Lejewski, I would regard what he calls empty or nondesignating names as names designating nonexistent things, or mere objects. I shall argue shortly that truth-conditions for singular statements about nonexistent things can be provided and thus that L. Jonathan Cohen's chief objection to Lejewski's account of quantification can be met. (See Cohen, *The Diversity of Meaning*, 2d ed. [London: Methuen, 1966], pp. 275–85). Such an account of quantification must not be confused with the so-called substitutional interpretation. (See, for example, Ruth Barcan Marcus, "Interpreting Quantification," *Inquiry* 5 [1962]: 252–59.) It is an *objectual* but *nonexistential* interpretation.

an object in our sense of the term. (I shall return to this point in my response to the seventh objection.) And we can say that a general particular statement of the form "(∃x) Fx" would be true if and only if at least one individual, whether existent or not, satisfies the propositional function "Fx," while a universal statement of the form "(x)Fx" would be true if and only if all individuals satisfy the propositional function "Fx." On both interpretations of quantification, a general particular statement may be true even if none of the substitution-instances is about an object, whether existent or not, that is singled out or referred to by someone. But is this not paradoxical on our interpretation? The appearance of paradox arises only if we indulge in the incoherent supposition that nonexistent objects are in some sense mind-dependent. (See above, pp. 62–63). On the other hand, the requirement that there be clear conditions for the identity and diversity of the members of the domain of the bound variables is satisfied by objects that do not exist. As I have pointed out (pp. 45–46, 51–52), these conditions for objects as such consist in the truth or falsehood of formal identity statements.

It is perhaps because of their failure to perceive the possibility of such an interpretation of quantification that philosophers who have allowed that there are nonexistent things have also insisted that such things must nevertheless have "being." Such a notion of being is not, of course, a genuine concept, a principle of classification, since it has been explicitly introduced in such a way that nothing could fail to satisfy it.[11]

A sixth objection is that at least some nonexistent things violate the principle of noncontradiction. Russell pointed out that Meinong allowed for objects, such as the round square, which are self-contradictory.[12] Meinong replied that the principle of noncontradiction should not be expected to hold for impossible, or self-contradictory objects.[13] And, in order to forestall Russell's further objection,[14] namely, that the principle applies to propositions, not to objects, he could have added that there is no reason for refusing to allow that contradictory propositions about such an object would both be true. But while this reply does, I believe, blunt Russell's objection, it does not address itself to the deeper question, how can the round square, something self-contradictory, be an object at all? If the round square can be singled out in thought, then we must give up thinkability (conceivability) as the ultimate criterion of logical possibility—and what do we replace it with? If the round square cannot be singled out in thought (as of course it cannot be singled out in perception or in imagination), then what possible sense is there in the supposition that it is an object, that it is *something?* But whatever difficulties Meinong's theory of nonexistent objects may face, ours does not face this one. An object, for us, is only what can be singled out. And nothing self-contradictory can be singled out. The mere fact that we have the definite description "the round square" proves nothing, for, except in cases of misdescription, it may only be used nonreferringly, and the statements in which it would be so used could be understood either, in accordance with Russell's theory of descriptions, as disguised false general particular statements, or, in accordance with Strawson's, as truth-valueless or as not genuine statements at all. (If, as Russell asserts, Meinong's "theory regards any grammatically correct denoting phrase as standing for an *object*,"[15] then we must reject this theory.) Therefore, there can be no genuine, irreducibly singular true statements about the round square. Therefore, there cannot be contradictory singular statements about the round square that are both true. Meinong's loose talk about the round square and the golden mountain, and his apparent assumption that if a sentence is grammatically of the subject-predicate form and moreover seems to be true then there is an object it is about, invite a theory of descriptions such as Russell's.

IV

Yet far more serious objections face us. According to the seventh, no predicates are applicable to nonexistent things. Therefore, nonexistent things cannot be supposed to have properties.[16] And how can something that has no properties be an object of perception, thought, or discourse? A predicate is applicable to something, it can be argued, only if its applicability is, in principle at least, subject to verification, whether by other persons or by oneself in the future. For example, when we say that a certain thing is pink we necessarily allow for the possibility that it may turn out not to be pink, that we or others may discover that it is not pink. One who did not allow for this possibility could not be taken to mean by the predicate "pink" what it ordinarily means. But the possibility of verification of the applicability of a predicate presupposes that the thing to which it is applied is multiply identifiable, reidentifiable, and thus an existent.

Now, indeed, ordinarily the applicability of a predicate does presuppose verifiability. But from this it does not follow that no predicate may be applied to a nonexistent thing. For the dependence of the *ordinary* application of predicates on verifiability may be due not to their meaning, or to the necessary conditions of their applicability in general, but to the nature (actual or assumed) of the objects of such application. Ordinarily, of course, we are interested in and speak of what we take to be *entities*, that is, existent and reidentifiable objects. Therefore, ordinarily the criteria for the applicability of predicates do include future and other persons' observation and thus reidentification. For they presuppose the indiscernibility such reidentification enforces. And to achieve indiscernibility we sometimes must regard certain properties of the object as illusory and the corresponding predicates as not in fact applicable. But nonexistent objects are not entities, they are not reidentifiable. There is no reason why the applicability of predicates to them should be subject to the necessary conditions for the applicability of predicates to entities. Indeed, we find ourselves making such applications with perfectly good sense. We know perfectly well what is meant by saying that a nonexistent object, e.g., a hallucinatory rat, is pink. The fact that saying this is not subject to future or other persons' verification does not affect at all its intelligibility.

For it is due not to failure of sense but to the fact that the hallucinatory rat cannot (logically) be perceived again or by other persons. To insist that for this reason it cannot be said to be pink would be to cut a philosophical pose, not to make a philosophical point.

The eighth objection to nonexistent things (which is related to the seventh) is that they violate the principle of excluded middle. Is the golden mountain large? Usually it would be taken for granted that the question cannot be given a defensible answer. Being merely a possible, some philosophers say, the golden mountain has only the properties (if any) of being golden and a mountain, and their logical consequences. From this it seems to follow that a nonexistent thing violates the principle of excluded middle with respect to at least some properties, and thus that the thesis that existence is a genuine concept is incompatible with one of the laws of thought.

We must make a preliminary observation before we consider the heart of the issue before us. It must not be assumed that the golden mountain may not have some other properties, e.g., being large. For if we use the description "the golden mountain" referringly, then we use it with respect to an object of perception or imagination or thought that may be perceived or imagined or thought of as having such an additional property. It is only when the description is used nonreferringly that this could not be so. And in that case we would not be making a genuine singular statement about a nonexistent thing; we would be, at most, asserting a false general particular proposition. If there are nonexistent things, then the test of what properties they have would be what properties they are perceived or imagined or thought of as having when they are singled out. It is only about objects singled out that we can make genuine singular statements.

But even if nonexistent things do have properties other than those mentioned in the definite descriptions with which we have referred to them, it seems to remain true that with respect to most

properties they possess neither these properties nor their con-
tradictories. As ordinarily thought of or imagined, the golden
mountain, it would seem, is neither large nor not large, and a
hallucinatory rat neither suffers from heart disease nor does not
suffer from heart disease. This seems not only obviously true but
indeed to follow from our own account.

To say that an object that is not perceived or imagined or
thought of as being F, or as having some property that entails the
property of being F, is nevertheless F may only be to say that it is
(materially) identical with some object (perhaps not yet or ever
singled out) that is F. Therefore, to say that the former is F may
only be to say that it is F *insofar as it is an entity*, not insofar as it
is an object. Clearly, then, a nonexistent object that is not perceived or imagined or thought of as being F, or as having some
property that entails the property of being F, cannot be said to be
F. But from this it does not follow that also it cannot be said to be
not F. To say of a perceived or imagined or thought-of object that
it is F is to say either that it is perceived or imagined or thought
of as being F (or as having some property that entails the property of being F), or that it is an *entity* that is F. In the case at
hand, the first disjunct is false by hypothesis and the second is
false by virtue of the nonexistence of the object. Therefore, the
whole disjunction is false. Why should we not conclude that the
object is not F, since the statement equivalent to saying that it is
F is not true? If we do conclude this, then nonexistent things
would not constitute exceptions to the law of excluded middle. It
would be simply false of them that they have any property that
they are not perceived or imagined or thought of as having (or
that is not entailed by a property they are perceived or imagined
or thought of as having).

The above argument rests on two assumptions, both of which
seem to me reasonable but which I shall not attempt here to
defend. First, that a clear distinction can be made between positive and negative properties, and that an object may be perceived
or imagined or thought of only as having positive properties. If

we make this assumption, then we can insist that "F" in the preceding paragraph takes only positive properties as its values. Otherwise the argument would not prevent the violation of the principle of excluded middle. For, if we were to substitute "not-F" for all occurrences of "F" in the preceding paragraph, and if we assume (what may well be the case) that the nonexistent thing is neither perceived or imagined or thought of as being F, nor perceived or imagined or thought of as being not-F, we would be led to the conclusion that it is neither F nor not-F. If we were to suppose that this conclusion does not contradict the principle of excluded middle, on the grounds that property negation should be distinguished from propositional negation (that "a is not-F" is not the same proposition as "it is not the case that a is F"), we could have answered the eighth objection simply by appealing to this distinction. But then we would have faced another objection: that nonexistent things violate the principle that every individual has exactly one member of every pair of contradictory properties. This principle would not be equivalent to the principle of excluded middle: that for every individual and every property the individual either does or does not have the property (or, generally, that every proposition is either true or false), but seems to me equally compelling.

Our argument depends also on a second assumption: that transcategorial predications ("category mistakes"), that is, predications to things belonging to one category, of properties that only things belonging to another category can have, are false, and not neither true nor false. For, in effect, our claim has been that it is false, and not neither true nor false, that a nonexistent thing has any property that it could have only if it were an existent thing. It is analogous in content and in motivation to the claim, for example, that it is false that the number 4 is pink, rather than neither true nor false. The defense of this assumption would be that transcategorial predications are merely obviously, indeed trivially, false, and not radically different in kind from ordinary predications. But we need not develop such a defense here. It is sufficient for our purposes to observe that even though nonexistent things would constitute an exception to the principle of excluded middle if this assumption is rejected, so also would all existent things. For with respect to anything there are innumerable transcategorial predications, all of which would then be neither true nor false. The number 4 would be neither pink nor not pink, and an existent rat would be neither greater than the number 4 nor not greater than the number 4.

I have allowed that we should be willing to attribute to a nonexistent thing not only the properties it is perceived or imagined or thought of as having but also all properties these entail. That something is a rat, even if hallucinatory, entails that it has a backside, and moreover that its backside has a color. Yet, obviously we cannot ascribe any specific color to its backside. Is this not a violation of the law of excluded middle? It is not. It is a violation of what may be called the law of specificity, namely, that every instance of a generic property must also be an instance of a specific property ranging under that generic property. And I find no compelling reason for insisting that this law should be applicable to nonexistent things. Certainly the reason cannot be that counterinstances to the law are unimaginable or inconceivable. A witness to a car accident may report that he saw that the car was dark in color but did not see exactly what color it was. As many persons certainly are, he is likely to be capable of imagining the car as having a dark color without imagining it as having any specific dark color. Of course it must have had a specific color, assuming that it was a real, existent car. But suppose that it was not; suppose that the person merely imagined or hallucinated the accident and the car involved in it. Although there would be no sense in denying that the car he imagined or hallucinated was dark in color, there would also be no sense in affirming that it must have had a specific dark color even though the person did not imagine or hallucinate it as having such a color.*

*"A hare vaguely perceived is nevertheless a specific hare. But a hare which is

Nevertheless, questions such as "Is the golden mountain large?" or "Did the rat he hallucinated suffer from heart disease?," when the objects they are about are not singled out as having these characteristics, as well as the negative answers they should receive according to our account, remain puzzling. But there is a natural explanation of this fact. We are ordinarily interested in entities, not in mere objects, and our ordinary uses of language are regarded as having to do with entities, not mere objects. It should not surprise us that we find sentences intended to be about mere objects puzzling.

V

The ninth objection, directed explicitly to the view that the notion of existence is a classificatory concept, was leveled by Gaunilo[17] against Anselm and by Russell[18] against Meinong. It can be put in our terminology as follows: If the concept of existence is classificatory, then existence is a property. But any property can also be a property of an object *as such*, i.e., independently of whether the object is an entity or not. (In traditional terminology, any property may be regarded as an essence, and thus as part of an essence, including the essence of something whose existence may be in question.) Therefore, any property can be a property of a nonexistent object. But existence cannot be a property of an object that does not exist. Therefore, existence is not a property. The objection appears especially plausible when directed against arguments for the existence of God that rest on the definition of God as the being that has all properties (or some equivalent definition), as well as when stated in the form of a *reductio* such as that a round square exists since it is logically true that the existent round square exists.

We should not attempt to meet the objection by simply denying that every property can be a property of an object as such. We

an object of a vague image is a vague hare." Sartre, *The Psychology of Imagination* (Secaucus, New Jersey: The Citadel Press, 1972), p. 20.

must also have a clear criterion and justification for distinguishing those that cannot from those that can. Nor should we simply deny that, whatever the case with other properties may be, existence at any rate cannot be a property of an object as such. What reason shall we give for this denial, except that it saves us from an unacceptable conclusion? Have we not in fact centered our whole inquiry on the thesis that the concept of existence is a classificatory notion applicable to objects? And what could its applicability to an object consist in if not in the fact that the *object* has the property of existence? Nor should we simply point out that *of course* existence cannot be a property of objects that do not exist, since this would be a contradiction. It is no less true that *of course* every object that has the property of existence does exist. But how could we then refuse to allow that the being that has all properties and the existent round square exist?

To meet the objection we must dig more deeply. We must make clear the sense in which existence is a property and the sense in which it is not. It is a property insofar as the concept of existence is classificatory. It is not a property insofar as it cannot be a property of an object as such, and thus also not of an object of which the concept of existence is to be denied. What properties can be exemplified by objects as such, and thus by objects that do not exist? Our answer must be grounded in the manner in which we introduced the notion of an object. An object is what can be singled out, whether in perception or imagination or in thought, what can be an object of the application of our conceptual apparatus. Clearly, we must allow that objects as such may have any properties in terms of which an object can be singled out, can be perceived or imagined or thought of *as* having, as well as any properties these entail. (We must not confuse singling out an object in thought as having a certain property with thinking *that* it has this property.) Let us call such properties *individuating*. An individuating property is one the possession of which is a necessary (though usually not sufficient) condition of the formal identity of the object, of its being the object it is. That any property the object is perceived or imagined or thought of as having is such a necessary condition follows from the way we have introduced the notion of an object. Individuating properties are to be contrasted with properties that can be attributed to an object only by virtue of its material identity with other objects, that is, only insofar as it is an entity. Clearly, no object as such can have such a property. For example, any irreducibly dispositional property would fall under this category. To attribute to something such a property would presuppose the identifiability of the thing through a stretch of time and space. We may of course use definite descriptions in which such properties are mentioned. But these descriptions would not be used referringly.

Existence is not an individuating property. By definition, an object can exemplify it only insofar as it is an entity. This is why we cannot simply think of, single out, an object as having existence and then infer that the object exists, although of course we can think of any object *that* it exists.* This is why the above simple version of the ontological argument for the existence of God is unsound. Insofar as in the definition of God as the being that has all properties the definiens allows us to single out, pick out God, it is not really understood as including existence. On the other hand, if it is understood as including existence, it is a definite description that may be used only nonreferringly, and on both Russell's and Strawson's theories of definite descriptions the argument would be unsound.† This is also why one cannot prove that a round square exists by appealing to the proposition that the existent round square exists; or that a unicorn exists that

*This, I suggest, is the kernel of truth in Kant's famous assertion that "By whatever and by however many predicates we may think a thing—even if we completely determine it—we do not make the least addition to the thing when we further declare that this thing *is*." (*Critique of Pure Reason*, trans. Norman Kemp Smith, B628.)

†The subtler version of the ontological argument is that we single out (conceive of) God as having some other property (e.g., absolute perfection) which entails, but does not include, existence. My argument commits me, of course, to denying that we can single out an object in terms of such a property.

one shall see in the next thirty seconds by appealing to the proposition that the existent unicorn that one shall see in the next thirty seconds exists.[19] If the subject term is used referringly, then the success of this use depends not on the occurrence in it of the adjective "existent" but solely on the rest of its content. If it is not used referringly, then the sentence is not a tautology but expresses either, according to Russell, a false contingent proposition, or, according to Strawson, a truth-valueless proposition or no proposition at all.

However, more needs to be said in reply to the ninth objection.

VI

Let us recall the three philosophical issues about existence we distinguished at the beginning of this chapter. There is the question of the general status of existence. This is the question with which we have been concerned so far in the present chapter. There is the question of what most general sorts of entities exist. Much of chapters six, seven, and eight will be devoted to it. But there is also the question of the specific content of the concept of existence. Our answer to it was delineated in chapter two. It was natural to suppose at the beginning of the present chapter that the first question is logically prior to the second and third. And, indeed, it is. We can now see, however, that the ninth objection to the view that the notion of existence is classificatory, and thus that the notion of a nonexistent thing is intelligible, can be met fully only if we provide an adequate answer to the third question. For it is not enough to say merely that existence is a nonindividuating property. We must *demonstrate* that this is so by stating exactly *which* nonindividuating property it is. We ought not to be surprised by this turn of our discussion. It should have been clear all along that the conclusive answer to the question whether the notion of existence is classificatory must include, as its final part, an account of exactly which classificatory notion it is. If we do provide such an account, then we show that all nine objections we have considered must be unsound, even if our specific arguments against them are inadequate. If we do not provide such an account, we can derive no real assurance from these arguments even if they are impeccable. There might be a tenth objection that we could not answer. It is time, therefore, that we return to the question What is the specific content of the concept of existence?

Our discussion in chapter two of the connection between the concepts of identity and existence provided an answer to this question that is in accord with the spirit, if not the letter, of one mentioned, though perhaps not espoused, by Plato: being is power.* We may say that existence is power in the general sense that what exists, even if it has finite duration and belongs to the past, is permanently facing us, if not physically or in perception, then in thought, always to be reckoned with, never subject to our whim. And the precise sense in which we should understand this is that the existent, the real, is the indefinitely identifiable. It is that which we may be forced to confront physically or in our perception or thought on indefinitely many occasions. It is thus also that the truths about which are inexhaustible. It is the stable, coherent element in what we perceive or think about.

Clearly, so understood, existence is a property, in the broad sense in which we have been using this term. Equally clearly, it is not an individuating property. It would be senseless to attribute it to an object as such, or to suppose that an object may be singled out, whether in perception or imagination or thought, as having it. Moreover, the concept of existence so understood neither has the narrowness ascribed to it by other accounts nor is subject to the vexing question whether the property of existence

---

*"*Str*. My notion would be, that anything which possesses any sort of power to affect another, or to be affected by another, if only for a single moment, however trifling the cause and however slight the effect, has real existence; and I hold that the definition of being is simply power." (*Sophist* 247, Jowett translation.) The Stranger, however, adds that "we . . . may one day change our minds [regarding this definition]." (Ibid.)

itself exists, whether existence itself is an entity. It can be intelligibly, even if falsely, applied to everything that can be singled
out, by whatever mode of consciousness, though, quite properly,
not to anything else. And the property of existence, namely, indefinite identifiability, like identity, to which it is reducible, is
not itself an object, it cannot be singled out or referred to,
whether in perception or in thought, it cannot be itself a constituent of the world (see above, p. 5, and below, Appendix B).
Thus there can be no question whether it exists, although of
course there is and there ought to be the question whether it is
true that a given object has that property.*

Let us test this answer by considering briefly the ways in
which it fits with the three most common philosophical conceptions of existence.

According to the materialist conception, to exist is to be
spatiotemporal. Clearly, what is meant cannot be the mere possession of spatial and temporal relations to other things. A hallucinatory pink rat does enter into such relations, at least with the
other objects of the hallucination, but does not exist. What is
meant is the *occupancy* of a place and a time, the being *in* space
and time, the possession of a home in the world, and the causal
role this is taken to entail. And how does this differ from the
spatiotemporality of the hallucinatory rat? Surely, in the suggestion of permanency that the notions of occupancy, of being a part

---

*Indeed, so understood, existence loses some of its sublime and mysterious
character, so often ascribed to it by Thomistic philosophers (e.g., by Joseph
Owens, in *An Interpretation of Existence* [Milwaukee: The Bruce Publishing
Company, 1968]), as well as by philosophers in the phenomenological and exis-
tentialist traditions (e.g., by Heidegger, the introduction to whose *Being and
Time* remains one of the most important contributions to the topic of existence,
and by Sartre, in *Being and Nothingness*). The ascription to existence of such a
character is not, of course, an accident or, given the other views of these philosophers, inappropriate. For example, the Thomistic view is inseparable from the
Christian doctrine of Divine creation. And although Heidegger devotes the rest
of *Being and Time* to human existence, to "Dasein," he does so because of his
belief that we can understand being as such only by way of understanding human
being.

of the world, and especially of having a causal role, contain. Of course, this permanency does not consist in infinite duration. It is the permanency of identifiability, especially through indefinitely continuing chains of effects, which, according to this conception, only a part of the spatiotemporal world may be supposed to possess—permanent, indefinite identifiability by oneself or by others, if not always in perception at least in principle always in scientific thought.

According to the empiricist conception, to exist is to be an object of perception. What does this mean? To say that to exist is to be perceived would be grossly inadequate. If "perceive" is used in the sense in which only what exists may properly be said to be perceived, then the formula, though not trivial (it requires us to deny existence to anything unperceived), presupposes the concept of existence and throws no light on it. But if "perceive" is used in the sense in which what is perceived need not exist, then the formula entails the absurdity that the pink rat a delirious man hallucinates exists. Similar objections may be made to a second version of the empiricist conception: that to exist is to be perceivable, to be capable of being perceived. If only what exists may properly be said to be perceivable, then again the formula presupposes the concept of existence and does nothing to display its content. And if nonexistent things may also be properly said to be perceivable, then the formula identifies the concept of existence with the possibility of being an object of perception and thus requires us again to say that the hallucinatory pink rat exists. For, in this sense, hallucinatory rats are very much capable, both logically and causally, of being perceived.

It is only a third version of the empiricist conception that appears at all plausible: that to exist is to be capable of being perceptually singled out and also to be such that an indefinite number of other objects can be perceptually singled out (whether by oneself or by others) each of which is materially identical with the first and with every other member of the set. This formula, I suggest, does express what we ordinarily mean by the existence of *perceivable* objects. Whether it is also an adequate account of existence in general depends on whether empiricism is true, an issue I shall not discuss here.

According to what may be called the Platonic conception of existence, to exist is to be eternal, immutable, nontemporal. Hence the conclusion that only entities such as the Forms or universals exist. The motive behind this view is clear. What could assure indefinite identifiability more obviously than eternity? For example, the number 4 is independent of the vicissitudes of space and time. No change can deprive us of the possibility of contemplating it; it has no position in time and therefore there can be no time at which it could no longer be intellectually visible. It is permanently available to us as a determinate object of thought, to the consideration of which we may endlessly return, which can be singled out in infinite ways, and which confronts us in various thought-situations with a determinate nature independent of our whim. I believe that these considerations justify the application of the concept of existence to eternal entities such as universals, whether or not these are instantiated.[20] But it is a mistake to suppose that they also show that only to such entities is the concept of existence applicable. It seems plausible, but in fact is false, that only what is eternal is indefinitely identifiable. As we saw above (pp. 43–44), even a momentary entity is indefinitely identifiable.

VII

But even if our view of the specific nature of existence as identifiability fits well with the motivations, if not the formulations, of the three major traditional views, it requires further defense. Unlike the proposition that whatever is not identifiable does not exist, which I defended in chapter two, the proposition that whatever does not exist is not identifiable seems implausible. And it is not difficult to see the reason for this. In addition to saying, or imagining, or dreaming, or hallucinating, or thinking that a certain nonexistent object has some ordinary property or relation, we sometimes also say, or imagine, or dream, or halluci-nate, or think that it is the same as some other nonexistent object. A novelist writes that the murderer was in fact the chief detec-tive. Mrs. Jones dreams that the house she had longed for has now been built. A teen-age boy visualizes again today the girl he had visualized with passion yesterday. The drunkard halluci-nates that the pink rat that entered the hole in the baseboard emerges shortly afterwards from the drain in the shower.

But while it is because of such undeniable facts that we may be sceptical regarding the account of existence as identifiability, they do not themselves constitute a reason for rejecting that ac-count. They would do so only if what the novelist writes, or Mrs. Jones dreams, or the teen-age boy imagines, or the drunkard hallucinates could be true. And what is at issue is precisely whether it could be true, whether the concept of identity can be coherently applied to such situations, not whether it is in fact applied to them. This distinction is particularly obvious in its application to a work of *pure* fiction. The question whether the sentences the *novelist* writes are true does not even arise, has no application, literally has no sense, for we take for granted that these sentences are not used for the purpose of making state-ments.[21] And while a *reader* can use such a sentence to make a statement, his use of it would be very different from the novelist's; perhaps it would be best understood as being, even though only implicitly, about what the novelist has written, about the novel.

How then do we determine whether the explicit or implicit identity statements made by the novelist, or those describing Mrs. Jones's dream, the boy's imaginings, and the drunkard's hallucination could be true? Clearly, by describing cases just like these but omitting from the descriptions the question-begging identity statements. The novelist writes about a certain man in one chapter of the novel and about a certain man in another chapter, but writes neither that they are the same or not the same, nor anything else that would entail logically that they are or that they are not the same. Are they the same man or not? We have no answer, not because of insufficient knowledge but because nothing imaginable could count as a reason for an answer. It would be useless to appeal to our knowledge of scientific facts and ordinary probabilities, as we would if concerned with real men, for these facts or probabilities are determined by reference to real, existent things, not by reference to nonexistent, purely fictional things. (But it would not be useless to appeal to logical entailments because nonexistent things, insofar as they are objects in our sense of the term, must be logically possible.)

Mrs. Jones dreams on Friday of a certain particular house, and on Saturday she again dreams of a certain particular house, but she does not dream that they are the same house or anything entailing that they are. Is the house of her second dream the same as the house of her first dream? Nothing would count as a reason for an answer. Certainly no mere similarity between the houses she dreamed about would be a reason for asserting identity. And what additional reason could there be? Exactly the same remarks can be made on the question whether the girl a boy visualizes today is the same as the girl he visualized yesterday, and on the question whether the pink rat the drunkard hallucinates as entering a hole in the baseboard is the same as the pink rat he later hallucinates as emerging from the drain in the shower.

It is convenient to state our conclusion by saying that the concept of identity is not applicable to nonexistent things because there are no criteria for such an application, because there are no criteria of identity for nonexistent things. But I want to make quite clear how I shall use the much abused phrase "criterion of identity." I begin with an explanation of what I shall mean by a sentence of the form "there are criteria for the application of the concept F." I shall mean by a sentence of that form that it is logically possible for someone to distinguish clearly between something's being F and its not being F, if not through perception then at least in imagination or conception; that someone can understand clearly the difference between something's being F and its not being F; that someone can distinguish clearly between perceiving or imagining or conceiving of something as being F and perceiving or imagining or conceiving of it as not being F; that it is clear, determinate what it is for something to be F and what it is for something not to be F. To suppose now that a concept may be applicable to something even if there are no criteria, in this sense, for its application, would be to suppose that although applicable it is logically impossible for anyone to understand the difference between its being applicable and its not being applicable. Such a supposition would render the idea of the applicability of a concept, indeed the idea of a concept itself, totally useless. It can be motivated only by a confusion of the applicability of a concept with the employment of a word. Indeed, we do not ordinarily employ words strictly in accordance with criteria so understood. Language is an activity, performed for a variety of purposes and generally requiring a degree of flexibility incompatible with the constraints imposed by strict rules. But, I would insist, only insofar as our uses of language conform to criteria, in the sense explained, do they constitute, or represent, the application of concepts; only to that extent do they have not only practical but also conceptual worth and are they expressive of understanding.*

If this is what I shall mean by a sentence of the form "There are criteria for the application of the concept F," then what I shall mean by the term "criterion" itself can be explained as follows. If there is a criterion for x's being F then it is clear, determinate, what it is for x to be F. For this to be clear, there must be something about x that, if known, would render the applicability of "F" to x unquestionable. That something is the criterion. It is a

---

*Frege insisted that, with regard to any concept, "the limits of its application should be sharp, that we should be able to decide definitely about every object whether it falls under that concept or not." *Foundations of Arithmetic*, p. 87. He did not mean by a concept a word.

sort of evidence that x is F, but a logically conclusive evidence that x is F. Yet it is not just any deductive evidence, but rather that about x in virtue of which we understand what it is for x to be F. Nor is it any inductive evidence, although its presence may itself be determinable on the basis of such evidence. Ordinary inductive or deductive evidence is such that we must be able to understand independently that which it is evidence for. The criterion is the evidence that if present renders the concept F applicable to x on pain of violating the very concept of F. It may therefore be described as conceptual evidence for x's being F. If nothing would be such evidence then there is no genuine concept of F, and therefore nothing can be intelligibly supposed to be F. This, I suggest, is the legitimate verifiability principle of meaning.*

Since a criterion, so understood, for something's being F is a logically (in the broad sense of this adverb) sufficient condition for the applicability of "F," it must not be confused with what in the literature on Wittgenstein has been called a nondefining criterion.† An *expression* may be quite commonly used with respect to certain things on the basis of some distinctive features they have, but unless these features entail the applicability of the expression they are not constitutive of the applicability of the *concept* expressed and the use of the expression does not represent *understanding* of the things with respect to which it is used.

It may happen that the criterion for the applicability of a con-

*Hence the appropriateness of testing alleged criteria by imagining situations that might serve as counterexamples. This is not mere science fiction, as Quine suggests in his review of Milton Munitz, ed., *Identity and Individuation*, in *The Journal of Philosophy* LXIX (1972): 488–97.

†I discuss this point, as well as the general notion of criterion, in the *The Concept of Knowledge*, pp. 274–87. The tendency of Wittgensteinean philosophers to use a weaker notion of criterion is usually motivated by their desire to short-circuit difficult epistemological issues (e.g., our knowledge of other minds), not, as the extensive literature on the topic makes evident, by any conviction that such a notion is clear. For a useful review of much of this literature, see W. Gregory Lycan, "Noninductive Evidence: Recent Work on Wittgenstein's 'Criteria,'" *American Philosophical Quarterly* 8 (1971): 109–25.

cept F to x cannot be distinguished from x's being F, that it cannot be informatively described. In such a case it is better to speak of x as being a paradigm for the application of the concept F and to appeal for the conceptual justification of any claim to knowledge that x is F to the paradigmatic status of x as (an) F.

The concept of identity is not applicable to nonexistent things because there are no criteria, in the sense I have just explained, for such an application. But why do we nevertheless employ the concept of identity in fiction and in our dreams, imaginings, and hallucinations? The reason, I suggest, is that in many cases a nonexistent thing is singled out not in isolation but rather as a part of what may be called a nonexistent world. A novel is not merely a description of certain nonexistent things; it is a description of a nonexistent world. A dream is seldom about only one thing, or about several unrelated things, although imaginings, and especially hallucinations, often are. We reflect this fact by applying the concepts that are essential to our regarding something as a world, and, of course, the concepts of identity and existence are the fundamental such concepts. But their application to nonexistent things is at best analogical, just as its subject matter is only analogous to a world. We do want to distinguish between what is included in such a "world" and what is not. For example, we want to distinguish between Hamlet's mother and Hamlet's wife. To mark this distinction we speak of the former's "fictional existence," thus showing our clear awareness that the concept of existence can be employed only analogically regarding fiction. We should also speak of fictional identity, to mark that with respect to fiction the word "identity" is also used only analogically. Similar remarks may be made regarding imaginary, hallucinatory, and dream "worlds."

A symptom of the inapplicability, in a literal sense, of the concept of identity to cases involving nonexistent things is that even when we think of such things as identifiable we never think of them as *indefinitely* identifiable. We recognize that nothing would count as returning to the thing again and again, singling it out from any point of view we desire; that it is false that there are circumstances in which we would encounter it again, or that we could track it through space and time and investigate it. And this is exactly what we mean by saying of such a thing that it is unreal, that it does not exist, that we only imagined, or dreamed, or hallucinated, or told a story about it. We regard it as nonexistent precisely because there are severe restrictions on its identifiability, precisely because it is not indefinitely identifiable.

In view of this fact, why should we not be satisfied with the very plausible claim that only indefinite identifiability entails existence, instead of claiming, as we have done, at first sight very implausibly, that even one case of correct identification entails existence, that there is no identity at all without entity? The reason we should not is that where there is no indefinite identifiability, there is no genuine identifiability either. Where there are no criteria for the indefinite applicability of the concept of identity, there are no criteria for even a single application. For what could set a limit to the number of logically possible identifications, given that at least one such identification is logically possible?

Suppose that I see a certain spot on the wall in front of me and wish to assert that it is the same as the spot I saw there yesterday. I may be quite confident in my assertion. But suppose that it is questioned, whether by someone else or by myself. What kind of defense is logically available to me? I could appeal to my continuous observation of the spot during the intervening period of time, i.e., to the identity of the object I see now with an indefinite number of other objects, and to the identity of each of these objects with the one I saw yesterday. I could appeal to other persons' observation of the spot during that period. I could determine that the spot remains on the wall and that others can see it, thus reassuring myself that it is real, and then appeal to a similar determination regarding the spot seen yesterday, as well as to certain assumptions about the careers of things such as spots on walls. But all of this requires further identity judgments. Suppose that I did not regard such true identity judgments and such a defense possible, that I thought it logically impossible for someone to have observed the spot during the intervening period. Would we have criteria, in the sense explained above, for regarding the identity judgment as true? By hypothesis, the criterion cannot consist in the sort of defense I have just described. Could it consist in our simply being clear about what it would be for the two spots to be identical? Could we have a conception of why this case should be a case of identity at all, of how it should differ from cases of exactly similar spots that are not identical? Could we have a clear grasp of the difference between a case of two such spots that are identical and a case of two such spots that are not identical? (Presumably we would not wish to *rule* that any two such spots are identical; if we did, we would be abusing, not applying, the concept of identity.) I think it obvious that we would have no such grasp, no such conception, no criteria of identity. But to conclude this is to conclude that in the case of nonexistent things the concept of identity is inapplicable precisely because the concept of indefinite identifiability is inapplicable.

But what is meant by the indefinite identifiability of an object? The answer is simple: there are, in the objectual but nonexistential sense of "there are" explained in our response to the fifth objection, an indefinite number of objects such that the object is identical with each of them. This answer may be equivalent to, but is conceptually prior to and far clearer than, the quasi-phenomenalist answer that what is meant is that were one to be in any one of an indefinite number of certain possible situations one would single out an object such that it is identical with the given object.

Yet further explanation is needed. Suppose that I imagine a certain nonexistent thing. Can I not remember it on an indefinite number of occasions, and thus is there not an indefinite number of objects each of which is identical with it, namely, all the objects of such rememberings? Yet the thing does not exist. Also, a hallucinatory thing can be remembered, and thus identified, on an indefinite number of occasions. Yet, surely, it remains hallucinatory. But it must be asked whether the identity statements corresponding to such rememberings ("The thing I remember is the same as the thing I imagined yesterday," "The thing I remember is the same as the thing I hallucinated yesterday") are really material identity statements. And it is clear that they are not, that they can only be formal identity statements. I cannot single out what the second subject term in each statement refers to differently from the way I single out what the first subject term refers to. To single out an object imagined or hallucinated in the past is to remember it. And to remember an imagined object is to remember imagining it, to remember a hallucinatory object is to remember hallucinating it. Memory is thus not an independent means of access to the nonexistent thing of the past; it does not reveal to us other objects with which the object of the past may be identical. (Commonsense holds that for a perceptual object to exist it is necessary that it can be perceived again, not that it can be remembered.)

Finally, one may ask whether our account of existence as indefinite identifiability is not really circular. To identify something one must perceive it, or single it out in some other way. We need not presuppose that what is perceived or singled out exists. But surely we must presuppose that the perceiving or the singling out itself exists, that it is actual, real? But this is not so. If we take the intentionality of consiousness seriously, we must say that a singling out of an object, whether in perception, or imagination, or thought, is nothing apart from its object. To use Sartrean terminology, it exhausts itself in its object. It is not itself an object, that is, something that might or might not exist. For it can be singled out only in terms of its object. For example, an imagined object may not exist, but what could be meant by saying that the imagining of it does not exist? Not that, although the object was singled out in imagination, no such imagining took place, for this would be self-contradictory. Not that the object was singled out in some other way, e.g., in perception, rather than in imagination, for then no imagining has been singled out that could exist or fail to exist; there is merely the general fact that the object was singled out but not in imagination. And not that, though the object was singled out in imagination, the imagining itself was unreal. For what could *this* mean? We could not mean that the imagining is not reidentifiable, since it can be reidentified only if its object can be reidentified (it cannot be singled out except through its object), and thus its alleged nonexistence would turn out to be merely the nonexistence of its object. Therefore, there can be no distinction between an existent and a nonexistent singling out, unless we mean by this, misleadingly, the distinction between a singling out of an existent object and a singling out of a nonexistent object.

CHAPTER FIVE

Essence

I

For something to be an entity, it must exist and be identifiable. But to exist and be identifiable, it must have a character, a content, properties, through which it could be identified and thus acknowledged as an existent. Absolutely bare things are absolutely incapable of identification and thus of existence.

Of course, we have allowed for properties of objects, especially those we called individuating. But we have provided no account of what it is for an object, and thus for an entity, to have a property, or of what it is for something to be a property, and to this extent our protometaphysics remains incomplete. Now the first task of any such account is to distinguish clearly between essential properties and accidental properties, in the traditional, Aristotelian senses of these terms, even if eventually it were to deny that one of the so distinguished classes has members. Initially, at least, the distinction may be stated as follows: An accidental property is distinguishable from that whose property it is, even if it belongs to it necessarily. An essential property, on the other hand, is not so distinguishable and for this reason may only be necessary; it is what we mention in stating what the thing is. Clearly, the difference between the two is enormous and perhaps better expressed if the phrase "essential property" were replaced with the word "essence," and the word "property" were reserved for accidental properties.

This chapter will be concerned with the elucidation of the distinction and especially with the clarification of the notion of essence. In chapter six we shall begin the account of the notion of an accidental property. If we describe our inquiry into identity and existence as concerned with the verb "to be" in its senses of identity and existence (illustrated traditionally by the statements "The Morning Star is the Evening Star" and "God is"), then we may describe our inquiry into essence and accident as concerned with the verb "to be" in its senses of essential and accidental predication (illustrated traditionally by the statements "Socrates is a man" and "Socrates is white"). It is in this latter part of the inquiry that the connection between protometaphysics and metaphysics becomes evident. The metaphysical question, what entities are there or at least are possible, is a question about essence, and the metaphysical question, what must entities be if they are to constitute a world, is a question about accidental properties, especially spatial and temporal relations.

We shall find that ultimately the notions of essence and accident are to be understood through the notion of identity, just as we have found that the notion of existence is to be so understood.

II

Philosophers have introduced the notion of essence in several, often not clearly connected ways. First, as the counterpart of the notion of existence.[1] If the existence of something is in any sense a property, then we must be able to speak of the thing in abstraction from its existence, and when we do so we would be speaking of its essence. Second, as "what the definition signifies."[2] Third, as the kind or sort ("secondary substance") of the thing—what is mentioned in answering the question "What is this?"[3] Fourth, as the property or set of properties that the thing has necessarily and that is unique to it.[4]

Introduced in the first way, the notion of essence coincides with our notion of an object, and I shall say nothing further about it. The second way is the classical one, and I shall consider it in detail in section III of this chapter. But the third, I believe, is both the philosophically most interesting and the most relevant to our purposes in this book; I shall develop it in detail in section IV. It is closely connected with the second. But in the present section I want to pay some attention to the fourth way of introducing the notion of essence, in view of its prominence in the recent literature.

Clearly, the key element in the fourth way of introducing the notion of essence is the idea of a necessary (or "essential") property, i.e., a property which the thing that has it has necessarily. There are two main questions to be raised regarding this idea. First, what is meant by saying that a certain property belongs to a thing necessarily? Second, are there such properties? I shall begin with the first.

The notion of necessity employed in describing a property of a thing as necessary has been called the notion of *de re* necessity, to be distinguished from the notion of *de dicto* necessity, which is applicable to statements. But it is not at all clear that such a distinction should be made. For what can be meant by saying that a certain thing has a certain property necessarily if not that it is necessarily true of it that it has that property? And how could this latter differ from saying that the statement ascribing the property to the thing is necessarily true? The supposition that there is a difference between *de re* and *de dicto* necessity rests not on any general considerations but on two quite specific and, at least on the surface, puzzling observations. First, there seems to be a difference between statements such as the following: "It is necessary that all bachelors are unmarried" and "All bachelors are necessarily unmarried." The truth of the former seems unquestionable, at least according to most reasonable theories of necessary truth. But it is not at all clear that the latter statement is true. Unless it is a carelessly stated version of the former, it seems to assert of each individual who is a bachelor that he could not have failed to be a bachelor, and this of course is false. Second, it seems misleading to speak, as I have done, of *the* statement ascribing to a certain thing a certain property. In some cases, there seem to be many statements satisfying this description, some of which indeed are necessarily true but others not. For example, "9 is greater than 8" and "The number of the planets is greater than 8" seem to be about the same thing and to ascribe to it the same property. But only the former, which is a mathematical statement, is unquestionably necessarily true. The latter seems to be a contingently true statement about our solar system.

If we are to become clear about the issue, we must make some distinctions. We must distinguish, first, necessarily true universal statements; second, the singular instantiations of such statements; and, third, singular statements that are *not* instantiations of necessarily true universal statements. And we must remember that for a statement to be genuinely, irreducibly singular its subject term, or at least one of its subject terms, must be an expression used referringly. I now suggest that to say that there is *de re* necessity is merely to say that there are necessarily true statements of the third kind, namely, necessarily true singular statements that are not instantiations of necessarily true universal statements. The distinction between *de dicto* and *de re* necessity is merely a confused way of making the distinction between necessarily true universal statements and their singular instantiations, on one hand, and necessarily true singular statements that are not instantiations of necessarily true universal statements, on the other hand.

If we say that "All bachelors are necessarily unmarried" is false, although "It is necessary that all bachelors are unmarried" is true, we may only mean that at least one genuinely singular statement about a particular bachelor that ascribes to him the property of being unmarried is only contingently true. Only if so interpreted would the former statement be really different from the latter. On the other hand, a statement such as "Socrates is self-identical" is merely an instantiation of a necessarily true universal statement, namely, "Everything is self-identical"; it derives its modal character entirely from the modal character of the latter; and thus, according to our suggestion, it should not be described as necessary *de re*. A similar remark may be made about a molecular singular statement such as "If Socrates is a bachelor then he is unmarried." If there are statements that should be described as necessary *de re*, they would be, according to our suggestion, necessarily true singular statements that are not instantiations of necessarily true universal statements. But to describe such statements thus would be grossly misleading. For it is not that a different notion of necessity is applicable to them but that they are a different sort of necessarily true statement. However, since they are *singular* statements, we may describe the properties expressed by their predicates as belonging to their subjects necessarily and justifiably inquire how such necessary ("essential") properties should be possible. But this would be merely to inquire how such necessarily true statements should be possible.

In fact, there is no general puzzle or doubt about there being such statements and thus about there being, in the above sense, necessary properties. For example, "9 is greater than 8" is a necessarily true singular statement that is not an instantiation of a necessarily true universal statement, and thus the number 9 has the property of being greater then 8 necessarily. Other examples would be "Crimson is darker than pink" and "Blue is a color." This has been denied, e.g., by Quine,[5] largely because the existence of necessary properties conflicts with the logico-linguistic theory of necessary truth, which can be stated most broadly, and perhaps redundantly, as holding that a necessarily true statement is one that is either a truth of logic, or synonymous with a truth of logic, or true solely in virtue of facts about language. Let us suppose that "9 is greater than 8" is true solely in virtue of facts about language. But does it not assert exactly what "The number of planets is greater than 8" asserts, even though there are no facts *about language* to which the truth of the latter statement could be solely due? Is the property of being greater than 8 then "essential" to the number 9, i.e., to the number of planets, or is it not? What answer we give would seem to depend on how we have described the number 9, but while this would be compatible with the logico-linguistic theory of necessary truth, it makes nonsense of the idea that the property belongs to the number necessarily and is incompatible with at least the spirit of existential generalization (if the number 9 has the property necessarily, then *something* has it necessarily, however it may be described).

If the logico-linguistic theory is rejected and replaced with an ontological theory, i.e., a theory that explicates the notion of necessary truth in terms of the nature of the entities constituting the subject matter of necessarily true statements, or, in the case of instantiations of universal necessarily true statements, the subject matter of these universal necessarily true statements, the above argument against necessary properties cannot even be stated.* In no case would the necessary truth of a statement be a function solely of the manner in which it is expressed. Of course, the puzzle regarding the seeming nonsubstitutivity of the coreferential expressions "9" and "the number of planets" would remain, but it can be dealt with in the way suggested in chapter three. Indeed, if the definite description "the number of the planets" is used referringly, it may single out exactly the same object that "9" singles out, and then the two expressions, as long

---

*I argue both for the rejection and for the replacement in *The Concept of Knowledge*, Part Two. Specifically, I argue there (pp. 157–66) that a necessarily true statement is one in which truth-sufficient reference is made only to entities that are unchangeable in the strongest sense of this term, namely, in the sense that they are not in time. It has been objected (by Ernest Sosa, in "The Nature of Knowledge and its Objects," *The Philosophical Review* 81 (1972): 364–71; and by Keith Lehrer in a review of *The Concept of Knowledge* in *The Journal of Philosophy* 69 (1972): 312–18) that the notion of truth-sufficient reference presupposes the notion of necessary truth and thus that the above account of necessary truth is circular. But this is not so. To say that in a given statement truth-sufficient reference is made to certain entities is to say that the *existence and nature* of these entities is sufficient to render the statement true. It is not to say that the statement is entailed by some other statement, and thus the notion of necessary truth is not presupposed through the use of the notion of entailment. The "sufficiency" in question is a feature not of a logical relationship between statements but of a relation between a statement and that in the world which renders it true.

as so used, would be intersubstitutible, the above two statements being in fact one and the same. If used nonreferringly, the statement would be best construed in accordance with Russell's theory of descriptions and the question of substitutivity would not even arise.*

Nevertheless, the real puzzle remains: granted that, as the ontological theory holds, nontemporal entities, e.g., universals such as numbers and colors, have necessary properties, do individual, spatiotemporal things have necessary properties? Indeed, they do have necessarily all properties the possession of which follows from necessarily true universal statements by instantiation (e.g., being formally self-identical), but do they have any other necessary properties, properties that some other individual things either do not have necessarily or do not have at all? For example, is Socrates necessarily human and this book necessarily made out of paper? To avoid the intrusion of considerations relevant only if one espouses the logico-linguistic theory of necessary truth, let us consider singular atomic statements about individual things with the demonstrative pronoun "this" as subject term. Our question then is, are any statements of the form "This is (an) F," where the logical subject is an individual thing and the predicate is not true necessarily of all individual things, necessarily true? According to the logico-linguistic theory, the answer of course should be "No." There are no facts about language that could render such a statement necessarily true, nor is it a truth of logic. But such would be the answer also of the ontological theory mentioned above. For, according to it, a necessarily true statement is one whose subject matter consists solely of nontem-

---

*In *The Nature of Necessity* Alvin Plantinga suggests that to say that a certain object (e.g., the number 12) has a certain property (e.g., being composite) essentially is to say that the object could not conceivably have lacked the property (p. 11, also p. 21), but also allows that some of the corresponding propositions (e.g., "The number of Apostles is composite") could be false (pp. 20–21). But, if such a proposition is understood as irreducibly singular, would its falsehood be conceivable? What would it be to conceive of this if not that the object in question does not have the property in question?

poral entities, or one that is an instantiation of a universal statement whose subject matter consists solely of nontemporal entities.

What can be said in favor of the contrary position? Unlike the logico-linguistic theory and the ontological theory, which at least purport to elucidate the notion of necessity, the contrary position seems to amount to a mere appeal to "intuitions." It appeals to the fact that some of the statements in question are such that their falsehood seems inconceivable (if no such appeal were made, then we would lose any sense of what is meant by describing them as necessary). But it does not offer an account of the possibility of the alleged necessary statements, or of the kind of connection between an individual thing and a property that may be described as necessary, or of the sense in which such a connection may be said to be necessary. The familiar suggestion that a is necessarily (an) F if and only if a exists only if it is (an) F can hardly count as such an account. The right side of this biconditional is only a trivial reformulation of the left side, since, of course, the suggestion does not presuppose that there are nonexistent things. (If it does presuppose this, then existence itself would be a necessary property; whatever exists would exist necessarily.) A second familiar suggestion, that a is necessarily (an) F if and only if "F" is a sortal that provides the criteria for individuating and tracing a, is, as we shall see, more promising, but can be taken seriously only if detailed independent accounts of identity, individuation, criteria, and essence are provided. A third suggestion, that a is necessarily (an) F if and only if it would be classified as (an) F in the true scientific theory at which the development of science supposedly aims, a theory that, among other things, would provide an adequate explanation of the behavior of a and of all its other properties,[6] seems to be either a stipulative definition of "necessarily (an) F," without discernible rationale, or, if the scientific theory in question is expected to include only classifications that are necessarily true, at best optimistic and in any case circular.

Yet there is a sense in which some statements of the form "This is (an) F" cannot be conceived to be false, even though they are not instantiations of necessarily true universal statements and even though their logical subjects are individual spatiotemporal things. Suppose we are referring to Socrates in the statement "This is a man." It seems conceivable that he should have been black rather than white, but not that he should have been, say, a number rather than a man.[7] Or if we are referring to this book in the statement "This is made of paper," it seems conceivable that it should have been in the bookcase rather than in one's hands, but not that it should have been made of ice rather than of paper.[8] If this is so, then either we must give up both the logico-linguistic theory and the ontological theory of necessary truth and allow for necessary properties of individual spatiotemporal things, or we must give up the conceivability criterion of necessary truth. But it is not so. Indeed, it does seem inconceivable, in the first case, that *this* should have been a number rather than a man, and, in the latter, that *this* should have been made of ice rather than of paper. But it seems so only because each of the above statements is quite naturally confused with a logically valid *argument*, the falsehood of the conditional statement corresponding to which is indeed inconceivable because it is an instantiation of the law of identity. I have in mind the arguments "Since this (Socrates) is human, it is human" and "Since this (book) is made of paper, it is made of paper," which in effect have the form "p, therefore p." The reason the confusion is natural in these but not in other cases is that our conception of the subject of the statement includes its having the property attributed to it. Our conception of Socrates is inseparable from our conception of him as a human being, and one's conception of this book may be inseparable from one's conception of it as made of paper (or at least as not made of ice!). This is a remark not about the meaning of proper names or definite descriptions but about the phenomenological fact responsible for the plausibility of the several theories that claim that both proper names and definite descriptions have descriptive content and that their reference is at least in part a function of their descriptive content. This is the fact that to refer to something in a genuine singular statement, as contrasted with merely uttering the sentence, one must understand what the statement is about, one must have a conception of what one is referring to and to have a conception of it one must do so in terms of certain of its properties. When we then attribute such a property to it, our attribution seems necessarily true and its falsehood inconceivable. But the reason for this is nothing more mysterious than that the attribution is confused with a logically valid argument. Let me explain.

The object we single out and refer to with the subject term of a statement may be regarded as an object or as a certain entity. If it is regarded as an *object*, then of course we cannot conceive of its failing to have the properties in terms of which it is so regarded, for they are the same as the properties in terms of which it is singled out, the properties it is perceived or imagined or thought of as having; it would not be (formally) the same object if it lacked any one of these properties. But the object *can* be conceived as being any entity (or kind of entity) the conception of which would be compatible with the properties in terms of which the object is singled out. For example, the object one singles out as the dark thing on the bench in the park can be conceived of as being a man, or a log, or a garment, or a box, since any such entity can be dark and on the bench in the park; but it cannot be conceived of as being a number, since a number cannot have a color or spatial location.

Once an object *is* conceived as being a certain entity (or kind of entity) among the various entities (or kinds of entities) it *can* be conceived to be, we are bound by that conception if our statement is to remain a statement about that (such an) entity, if it is to continue to be the statement we understand it to be, if it is to continue to be the statement it is. For the idea of reference to an entity as such, as we have seen, is unintelligible. What determines the entity (or kind of entity) the statement is about is only partially the object referred to. The determination is achieved chiefly by our conception of the entity, the sorts of other objects with which we would regard the object referred to as identical, the properties that guide us in singling out such other objects in our thought. (The employment of a uniquely satisfied description does not by itself fix such a conception of, let alone reference to, an entity, just as it does not do so in regard to an object. See above, pp. 26–35). And we cannot conceive the entity as failing to have these properties, the properties in terms of which we conceive it. Of course, there can be great variations among the entities we regard an object to be and therefore among the properties we cannot conceive of it as failing to have as an entity. These properties are a function of our interests, knowledge, and the context in which we single out the object. We may conceive of it as an entity that has a certain causal origin, or that is made of a certain stuff; i.e., we may include one or both of these properties in our conception of the entity, and then of course we could not conceive of that (formally) same entity as not having such a causal origin or as not being made of such stuff. It is more natural to conceive of an entity in terms of its sort, e.g., as a man or number, and this is why an entity's sort is usually a paradigm of a property it has necessarily, of one it cannot be conceived of as not having. This is more natural because the identification of an object regarded as an entity would be expressed in what I have called secondary identity judgments, i.e., judgments that would be logically complete only if they include a sortal. But in unusual cases we may include in our conception a "superficial" property such as that of being a professor, and then we can sincerely (though often only humorously) assert that we cannot conceive of the entity in question as being anything other than a professor.

But all these cases of our finding inconceivable something's failing to have a certain property F are in reality cases of our finding inconceivable that the argument "Since it is F, it is F," has a true premise but a false conclusion, that the corresponding instantiation of the law of identity is false. What I have tried to do is to explain why sometimes we are subject to such a confusion, not to suggest that there are genuine cases of necessarily true singular statements about individual spatiotemporal things that are not mere instantiations of necessarily true universal statements. If F is a property in terms of which *a* is conceived, then F is part of our conception of *a* and the inconceivability of its failing to be F is a species of the inconceivability of the falsehood of an instantiation of a necessarily true universal statement. If F is not such a property, then either *a* is conceived of in terms of some logically independent property (one that does not entail F), and we would not be inclined to suppose that *a* is F necessarily, or *a* is not conceived of in terms of any property, and then I suggest we have no conception of *a*, we do not know what entity "*a* is F" is about, we are not making a genuine singular statement about an entity with that sentence, and neither do we find *a*'s not being F conceivable nor do we find it inconceivable. In the latter case we may still be making a genuine statement if "*a*" is a definite description or a proper name explainable solely by means of a definite description. But then I suggest the statement is best understood as a general statement, namely as its Russellian paraphrase. We must not suppose that merely to know (or believe) that something has a unique property is to have a conception of it, let alone to be able to refer to it. There might indeed be a causal chain of an appropriate sort between *a* and the utterance of "*a*." But whether there is or there is not is irrelevant. My utterance of "*a*" is relevant only if it is part of the making of a statement; I can make a statement (as opposed to merely uttering a sentence) only if I understand the statement I am making; and to understand a genuinely singular statement I am making about *a* I must have a conception of *a*, whether or not I also enter in a causal relationship with it. I shall say more about what it is to have a conception of something shortly.*

*In "The De Re 'Must': A Note on the Logical Form of Essentialist Claims," in *Truth and Meaning*, ed. G. Evans and J. McDowell (Oxford: The Clarendon

III

According to the philosophical tradition, the essence of a thing is what is stated in the definition of the thing, a definition being understood as real rather than nominal (i.e., not as a stipulation of linguistic usage, or an abbreviation of another linguistic expression, or a report on, or consequence of, linguistic usage). Contrary to the usual philosophical opinion, there is no obvious general difficulty regarding the notion of a real definition. For a real definition may be thought of as a kind of necessary material identity statement, and there is no more reason for regarding such statements as being about language, or as true solely in virtue of facts about language, than there is for so regarding necessary statements in general.

Yet it is not appropriate to *define* a real definition as a necessary material identity statement. Not every such statement can be reasonably called a definition, whether real or nominal. For example, "The triangle is a (more properly, the) closed plane figure whose angles equal two right angles" has not ordinarily been regarded as a definition. One and the same object may be necessarily identical with any number of other objects; therefore, it may be the subject of any number of necessarily true material identity statements. But philosophers have tended to think of a real definition as unique; they have tended to think that a thing can have only one real definition.

Press, 1976), David Wiggins comes close to the above account (though with doubtful consistency with his other views). He says, beginning with a quotation from Quine, "'We in our maturity have come to look upon the child's mother as an integral body who, in an irregular closed orbit, revisits the child from time to time.' Question: Do we have any alternative but to see *the child's mother* in such a way? Or is it just that we had the choice of conceptualizing or not conceptualizing the world in such a way as to articulate such entities as women and their children? It may have been the purpose of some essentialists to deny that we had the second choice, but it is not my purpose. To confuse the two positions and try to transform a negative answer to the first into a negative answer to the second is to perpetuate one of the principal confusions which nourish the dispute between realism and idealism" (p. 286, note 2; the important italics are Wiggins's).

What guides us in our selection of the identity statements we are willing to call definitions? Why do we deny this title to the above statement about the triangle and prefer instead the statement "The triangle is a (the) plane closed three-sided figure"? I believe that we should answer these questions as follows: A definition is indeed a necessarily true material identity statement, but one whose second subject term (the definiens) is especially likely to be used referringly, to single out the thing it designates.* The importance of this necessary condition is great. It may be argued that we should speak only of what we understand, that to understand something is to know its *real* definition (i.e., to know a certain privileged material identity truth about it), and that to know its real definition is to be able to single it out, establish it, as an object before the mind by means of that definition. (This is why a real definition may be confused with a nominal definition, i.e., with a stipulation or explanation of the meaning of a word; the ideal such stipulation or explanation allows us to single out the thing to which the word applies.) The "definition" of the triangle mentioned in the previous paragraph is unacceptable because, and insofar as, it fails to meet this condition. "The triangle is a plane closed three-sided figure," on the other hand, does meet it.

But not every material identity statement that meets the above condition would be counted as a definition. For example, "The triangle is the figure of that road sign" might meet it, but certainly would not be a definition. What else is necessary? According to Aquinas, "the definition telling what a thing is signifies that by which a thing is located in its genus or species."[9] We may generalize this in the following way: a definition is a material identity statement that not only singles out the thing defined but also fixes, makes explicit, its place in conceptual space, in the correct classificatory system. And this immediately suggests that

*Cf. H. W. B. Joseph: "The essence of any species of figure includes so much as need be stated in order to set the figure as it were before us. . ." (*An Introduction to Logic*, Oxford: Clarendon Press, 1916), p. 96.

there are also material identity statements about individual things that serve an analogous purpose, a fact the importance of which we shall see shortly. The clue is again provided by Aquinas: designated matter, he says, "would enter into the definition of Socrates if Socrates could be defined."[10] If by "designated matter" we understand a particular parcel of matter, and if we agree with Aquinas that Socrates has an individual essence that differs from the essence of man precisely in including designated matter, while the essence of man includes undesignated matter,[11] then a material identity statement such as "Socrates is this man" or "Socrates is this human parcel of matter" would be *like* a definition in that it would serve to fix the place of Socrates in *physical or perceptual* space. One reason it would not be called a definition is precisely the unavoidable explicit or implicit occurrence in it of a demonstrative expression, the fact that it fixes the place of its logical subject in physical or perceptual space, not in conceptual space. But there is also a second reason. It is not clear that it is a necessary statement.

What lies behind the insistence that a real definition be a *necessary* statement? The answer is straightforward. A definition, in the traditional sense, is always a material identity statement about a property, not an individual thing. And on both the ontological theory and any standard version of the logico-linguistic theory of necessary truth, all statements that have solely properties as their subject matter, or are instantiations of universal statements that do so, are necessary. As to a statement such as "Socrates is this human parcel of matter," we must recall our discussion in section II. Insofar as our conception of Socrates includes the particular parcel of matter he is and the property of being a man, we find it inconceivable that he should have consisted of a different matter or to have not been a man, since the statement is in effect understood as an instantiation of the law of identity. But the statement is not explicitly such, it does not make explicit how its logical subject is conceived. Suppose its logical subject were conceived merely as this parcel of matter. It would be quite conceivable then that it should not have been "informed" by the property of being human.

IV

Does the notion of essence as understood in terms of the notion of a real definition help in the elucidation of essential predication? Let us call statements in which the verb "to be" occurs in its sense of essential predication essential statements. They are not definitions, even though they have an intimate connection with definitions. Our Aristotelian paradigms, "Socrates is a man" and "Socrates' color is white," are not definitions; they are not identity statements. This is obvious in the case of the first. But it is true also of the second. Even if "white" can be used to single out an object, it is not so used in this case. In no sense is one singling out two objects, Socrates' color and the color white, and then determining that they are one entity. In Fregean terminology, in no sense is one thing presented or given in two ways. How then are essential statements to be understood? On a superficial level, they could be taken to be mere tautologies, deducible from the corresponding "definitions," and then the traditional connection between the notion of definition and the notion of essential predication would be completely clear. For example, "Man is an animal" can be understood as a trivial deductive consequence of the definition of man as a rational animal, and "White is a color" as a trivial deductive consequence of the definition of white as the lightest color. Now if we "define" Socrates as this human parcel of matter then it follows trivially that Socrates is human, and if we "define" a certain color-object as "Socrates' white color" then it follows trivially that it is white. But if essential statements are to have the metaphysical significance ordinarily attributed to them, they cannot consist in such tautologies.

Our distinction between accidental and essential predication is intended to represent, though only very roughly, Aristotle's distinction between something's being *present in* a subject and something's being *predicable of* a subject.[12] Consider the statement "Socrates is white," which is a paradigm of accidental predication. (Let us refer to such statements as ordinary subject-predicate statements, to be contrasted with what I have called essential statements.) Surely, in reality it is a disguised conjunction, namely, "Socrates has this color, and this color is (the color) white." The first conjunct alone exemplifies accidental predication; it asserts a connection between two distinguishable, even if not independently identifiable things, namely, Socrates and, as Aristotle would say, a certain particular or individual quality, or, as we shall later say, a certain quality-object. Indeed, Socrates' color cannot be what it is independently of Socrates, for it is distinguishable from, say, Plato's color only by virtue of its being present in Socrates; this is why, I suggest, in the *Categories* Aristotle denies that it should be thought of as a *part* of Socrates.[13] Nevertheless, one can attend to Socrates without attending to his color, and to his color without attending to him. The second conjunct, however, exemplifies essential predication. It does not assert a connection between two distinguishable things, and therefore it does not assert a connection at all. We cannot distinguish between Socrates' color (assuming that it is white) and the color white; indeed, the latter cannot be singled out and referred to in itself at all, as distinct from, say, Socrates' color or Plato's color. The grammatical predicate of the essential statement "This color is white" cannot be used referringly, even if it were replaced with the noun-phrase "the color white." For, if it were used referringly, what object would it be used to single out? Not the object the subject term is used to single out, for then the statement would be equivalent to the trivial and uninformative formal identity statement "This color is this color," which it obviously is not. And not any other object, for then we would be able to distinguish between Socrates' (white) color and the color white, which we cannot. The fact is that we cannot single out the color white itself as an object, but only its instances, e.g., Socrates' color and Plato's color. Insofar as a Platonic Theory of Forms denies this, it is seriously defective.

That the statement "Socrates is white" is such a disguised conjunction is evident from the fact that there are two very different mistakes one can make when asserting it. Socrates may not really have the color one takes him to have; *this* color might not be his real color, one might be the victim of a perceptual illusion. Or, though he does really have the color one takes him to have (one is not the victim of a perceptual illusion) the color he does have might not be the color white; one might have made a mistake in recognition, or in classification, and thus be, so to speak, the victim of a conceptual illusion. The second sort of mistake is quite unlikely in the case of the color white, but common in the case of nonperceptual properties. Is a teaching assistant a student or a member of the faculty? One may be uncertain, indeed mistaken, about which is the more appropriate answer even if one knows exactly all of the person's relevant activities. A child or an uneducated person may know that a whale has mammalian characteristics but not know that it is not a fish.* Therefore, if a statement such as "Socrates is white" is our paradigm of a statement expressing accidental predication, of what I have called an ordinary subject-predicate statement, we may say that accidental predication presupposes essential predication. Aristotle insisted that "it is not in every case that something will be an accident of an accident. So there will be something which signifies as substance."[14]

An essential statement such as "This (Socrates') color is (the color) white" differs from an ordinary subject-predicate statement such as "Socrates is white" (i.e., "Socrates has this color, and this color is [the color] white") in that it is not, even in part, about two entities and therefore does not assert a connection between two entities. It differs from an identity statement in that

---

*And an educated person (e.g., Melville, in *Moby Dick*) may even offer reasonable arguments that it ought not to be classified as a fish.

only one of its (explicit or implicit) subject terms is used referringly, in contrast with, e.g., "Socrates' color is (the same as) Plato's color" or "Socrates' color is (the same as) Socrates' color." Significantly, this is also true of a statement such as "This is Socrates" when made to express immediate recognition. It is not an ordinary subject-predicate statement; it does not, even in part, assert a connection between two things, an individual and a property.* (Even if Socrates were a bundle of properties, *this* would not *have* that bundle, it would *be* that bundle.) But neither is it an identity statement. Even though in other statements the name "Socrates" may be used referringly, it is not so used in this statement; "this" alone is so used. For if the name were used referringly, what object would it be used to single out? Not the object "this" is used to single out, for then the statement would be equivalent to the trivial and uninformative formal identity statement "This is this," which it is not. And not any other object, presumably a *recollected* object that was Socrates, for in immediate recognition no such recollection occurs; moreover, if the statement were asserting the identity of *this* object with a certain recollected object, it could be made on the basis of an inference, without anything describable as recognition occurring. We have reason, therefore, to diverge from the tradition and regard also statements such as "This is Socrates" as essential, as expressing essential predication, in their philosophically most fundamental use, that of expressing immediate recognition.

But if essential statements are neither ordinary subject-predicate statements nor identity statements, then what are they? How should we understand them? We may say, initially, that an essential statement classifies what it is about, subsumes it under a concept, establishes its place in conceptual space. Yet, since it is not an ordinary subject-predicate statement, it does so not through the thing's possession of some property. (This is obvious

---

*Quine's "x pegasizes" is explained by him in terms of the "attribute of *being* Pegasus." See *From a Logical Point of View*, p. 8.

in the case of "The color of Socrates is white." The color of Socrates does not have the property of being white; it *is* that property.) Of course, ordinary subject-predicate statements are also classificatory. But the classificatory function of an essential statement is direct, while that of an ordinary subject-predicate statement is indirect. To say that Socrates is white is to classify him in the sense that it is to attribute to him a certain color that itself is classified as white. But to say that Socrates' color is white is to classify what the statement is about directly. And, as I shall shortly try to explain further, it is reasonable to stretch the ordinary use of "classify" by adding that also to say about a person one sees that he is Socrates is to classify what the statement is about. Clearly, essential statements so understood do play the fundamental role in knowledge they have been assigned by the philosophical tradition. We may say that while ordinary subject-predicate and material identity statements express information, essential statements express understanding. This is evident in respect to the most primitive sort of understanding, namely, recognition. Recognition is paradigmatically expressed in statements such as "This is Socrates" and "This color is (the color) white."

But in what does the direct classification performed by essential statements consist? Let us begin by noting that although essential statements are not identity statements, they are very much *like* identity statements. This and Socrates, if the statement "This is Socrates" is true, are literally one and the same entity, and so are the (generic) color of Socrates and the color white if the statement "Socrates' color is (the color) white" is true. This fact has encouraged the supposition that essential statements are linguistic in character, that "This is Socrates" means that this is called "Socrates" and that "Socrates' color is white" means that Socrates' color is called "white." The implausibility of this answer requires little discussion. Statements such as the above often express ordinary acts of immediate recognition. And it is absurd to suppose that recognition in general consists in, or even presupposes, knowing what to call the object recognized or, indeed, that it at all depends on the existence of language. It may occur even when we have no relevant vocabulary at our disposal. Surely at least some animals and languageless small children are capable of this most elementary intellectual act. But the supposition, however implausible, is excusable. For what else can an essential statement be? To say that it asserts a connection between a thing and its essence would be, at best, to confuse the essence of a thing with one or more of its properties, and thus to confuse essential statements with ordinary subject-predicate statements. To say, as I have done, that it subsumes a thing under a concept, or classifies it, is, in the absence of an independent characterization of concepts, obviously not enough.

It might be suggested that an essential statement asserts that the thing it is about is similar to certain other things, on the grounds that its most fundamental role is to express an act of recognition and that recognition consists in the judgment that the thing recognized resembles certain previously encountered things. This answer, when applied to properties, presupposes the resemblance theory of universals, which we shall consider in chapter seven. But even in the case of individual things it is simply false that the thing an essential statement is about is asserted to be similar to some particular thing or things. As I have already pointed out, to recognize something it is neither necessary nor sufficient that one recollect or single out in some other way any previously encountered thing. It is also false that the essential statement asserts that there is *some* thing in the past, whether or not recollected, that the thing the statement is about resembles; one may know such a general statement to be true, e.g., on the basis of others' testimony, even if one does not recognize the thing the statement is about and even if one cannot state what it is.

The nature of an essential statement, and thus of essential predication, can be understood, however, in terms of our distinction between objects and entities. An essential statement, I suggest, asserts of an *object* that it is a certain *entity*. It expresses the "relationship" between an object and the entity that object is. It is like an identity statement because, as we have seen, an object and the entity it is are not *two things*. Yet it is also unlike an identity statement because, as again we have seen, an entity cannot be referred to qua an entity, and thus only one expression in the statement is used referringly.

That this suggestion fits the examples of essential statements we have just discussed can be seen easily. "This is Socrates" and "This (Socrates') color is (the color) white" are, as we have seen, typical expressions of immediate acts of recognition. And what is immediate recognition if not the coming to know directly, noninferentially, about a certain object actually singled out before the mind that it is a certain familiar entity? To come to know this one need not recollect (single out in memory) another object with which the object recognized is materially identical, one need not remember having been confronted with the entity at an earlier time. To recognize this (person) as Socrates is to see him as being a certain familiar entity that can be encountered indefinitely by oneself or by others, i.e., we might add somewhat incautiously, to see him as an object belonging to a certain familiar class of objects, each of which is materially identical with every other. To recognize Socrates' color as white is to see it as an instance of a certain familiar color that can also be seen in Plato and at indefinitely many places, each instance of the color being an object formally distinct from, but materially identical with, every other instance of that color. We shall consider presently to what extent our suggestion fits other, more traditional examples of essential statements, as well as how we should understand what I have tried to express here by the term "familiar."

In chapter two I observed that the question, what is the nature of the relationship between an object and the entity it is? which we can now identify with the question of the nature of essential predication, is answered, if at all, by the whole of our inquiry.

For, in effect, it concerns the distinction between objects and
entities, and although I devoted chapter two to the explanation of
this distinction, ultimately it can be understood and appraised
only in terms of its several applications that constitute the subject
matter of this book. Obviously, the relationship between an object and the entity it is is *sui generis*; it belongs to no higher
genus in terms of which it can be defined and has no coordinate
species in terms of its similarities to which its nature may be
elucidated. On the other hand, we do not lack familiar linguistic
resources for expressing it. It is precisely what we express with
the verb "to be" in one of its ordinary senses. And if we mildly
regiment ordinary language by using "is identical with" or "is
the same as" instead of the "is" of identity, "exists" instead of the
"is" of existence, and "has the property" instead of the "is" of
accidental predication, we could reserve the verb "to be" for use
only in essential statements. We could then say, in not at all
unimportant conformity to ordinary usage and with considerable
richness of meaning, that the relationship asserted by an essential statement, the relationship between an object and the entity
it is, is that of *being*. Such a regimentation would not be merely
reasonable. Its very possibility is metaphysically significant. We
do have alternative ways of expressing what the "is" of identity,
the "is" of existence, and the "is" of accidental predication express. The sense of "is" that in ordinary English we may express
only by "is" is that of essential predication. We could then say, in
such a regimented language, that the unique relationship that
holds between objects and entities is *being*.

V

In chapter two I argued that we cannot refer to an entity qua an
entity, that we cannot single out an entity as such. But what sort
of consciousness does an essential statement then express? The
object it is about can, of course, be singled out and referred to.
But how can it be thought, judged, to be a certain entity if that

entity itself cannot be singled out or referred to? For example, in recognition, how can the entity the object is recognized as being, be *familiar*? I believe that there can be only one answer to this question. Either we should say that not all consciousness is intentional, that not all consciousness consists in the singling out of a thing, in the establishment of a thing as an object before the mind; or we should say that there is a kind of state very much like a state of consciousness but differing from the latter in that it is not intentional. I believe that there is only a verbal difference between these two alternatives, that they in fact constitute one answer. I shall adopt the first formulation in order to avoid the need for introducing a technical term for the states in question but also in order to reflect in the terminology to be employed their similarity to states of consciousness. Let us therefore say that there is a sense in which we are conscious of an entity as such, namely, that we know what it would be like for an object to be that entity, that we can recognize an object as being that entity, that we understand certain expressions as denoting that entity, even though we cannot single it out, be confronted with it in our consciousness, and even though therefore the expressions denoting it cannot be used referringly. And let us call such consciousness nonintentional (or nonreferential), to reflect the fact that it is not *directed* toward anything, that it has no accusative. Indeed, any particular case of it can be understood only as a consciousness *of* a certain particular thing, namely, of a certain entity. But the reason for this is not that it is directed toward, has as its accusative, that entity, but that its nature consists in being a necessary condition for the recognition of any objects that *are* that entity. It derives its identity, as expressed in saying of what it is a consciousness, from these objects; and the latter, of course, can be singled out—they can be accusatives of *intentional* consciousness.

The notion of nonintentional consciousness may be puzzling, but its application is not. *Pace* Plato, there is no such thing as singling out and referring to the color white as such, and *pace*

Aristotle, there is no such thing as singling out and referring to the person Socrates as such. We may only single out and refer to *objects* that are these entities, e.g., the color of Socrates or the person standing before me. But this does not mean that we have no consciousness of (that we do not know what it is to be, that we cannot recognize something as, that we do not know which entity is) the color white or the person Socrates.

The nonintentional character of our consciousness of an entity as such makes intelligible the fact that it may occur even if there were no entity of which it is consciousness. (Of course, the notion of there being a nonexistent entity is self-contradictory in our terminology. There are, in the nonexistential sense of "there are," objects that do not exist, objects that are not entities. In no sense of "there are" can it be true, however, that there are entities that do not exist.) Were the consciousness of an entity-as-such intentional, this would be impossible. Intentional consciousness must have an object, even if that object does not exist. But to grasp what is meant by saying that a certain consciousness is nonintentional is precisely to grasp that it need not have an object at all, whether existent or nonexistent. That one be able to recognize someone as Santa Claus, to understand what is meant by saying of someone, even though falsely, that he is Santa Claus, to know what it would be for an object that is Santa Claus to exist, does not require that there be such an entity as Santa Claus, nor does it of course consist in singling out any particular object. Therefore, strictly speaking, what an essential statement asserts is that a certain object is a certain entity if and only if it, the object, exists, i.e., the statement states what entity the object would be if there were such an entity, if the object existed. This is why there are true essential statements about objects even though it is false that these objects exist. An example might be a child's assertion about someone it has dreamed about that he is Santa Claus.

With the notion of nonintentional consciousness at our disposal, we can understand our inclination to say that an essential statement subsumes the thing the statement is about under a concept. The word "concept" as used by philosophers is, of course, a technical term. It is in need of clear and useful introduction, not elucidation. I believe that we would remain reasonably close to the way most philosophers have employed it if we say that a concept is a capacity for nonintentional consciousness of a certain entity qua an entity. To have a certain concept is to have the capacity for a certain such consciousness. One actualizes such a capacity when one recognizes an object as being a certain entity, or when one realizes what it would be like to single out an object that is that entity, or when one understands an essential statement about that entity. H. H. Price defined a concept as a capacity for recognition. Agreeing with his view that recognition is the most fundamental case in which a concept is actualized, I should rather say that a concept is a capacity for nonintentional consciousness of a certain entity, the occurrence of which consciousness is a necessary condition for the occurrence of recognition, the other necessary condition being the occurrence of intentional consciousness, a singling out, of the object that is recognized as being that entity.*

With the notion of nonintentional consciousness at our disposal, we can also understand the usual view that concepts are mental. Indeed, concepts are capacities for a certain kind of *consciousness*, and for this reason it is often better that we should call them *conceptions* (as we did in Section II of this chapter). We can understand why (conceptual) thought has been regarded as being quite different from perception. Perceptual consciousness is always intentional, it is always of an *object*, even if also of an entity, while the exercise of a concept is a case of nonintentional consciousness, it is never of an object, but only of an *entity*. We can understand the motivation behind the view that universals are concepts. Properties regarded as entities, e.g., the

*Compare Husserl's distinction between "empty" and "fulfilled" consciousness in *Logical Investigations*, Investigation VI.

color white as such, contrasted, say, with Socrates' color, are precisely what is meant by universals, and since we can have only nonintentional consciousness of them it is not surprising that some philosophers have confused in this case what we are conscious of with our (capacity for) consciousness of it. We can understand why it has sometimes been held that understanding consists in "seeing the universal in the particular." To understand an object is to subsume it under a concept, i.e., to see it as being a certain entity, and in the case of objects that are properties the entity in question would be a universal. We can understand why concepts, unlike mental images, have appeared to some philosophers ephemeral; not only are they mere capacities but they are capacities for *nonintentional* consciousness. We can understand why concepts have often been confused with words or uses or meanings of words; the linguistically competent person's capacity for nonintentional consciousness of a certain entity is usually and especially vividly exhibited by his calling objects that are that entity by the right name. And it is not unreasonable to say that his knowledge of the meaning of the name is nothing but that capacity and even that the meaning of the name is nothing but that entity qua an entity. Finally, we can understand why an essential statement is neither tautological nor trivially linguistic. That a certain object is a certain entity is neither a tautology nor a statement about language. The discovery of such a fact is, next to primary identity judgments, the most fundamental exercise of intelligence, both preceding the acquisition of language and constituting a necessary condition for it.

We can now, at last, answer the question this chapter began with, what is essence? The essence of an object, we can say, is simply the entity the object is, or, in order to allow for the application of the notion of essence to nonexistent things, the entity it would be if it were an entity. An essential statement states the essence of the object it is about. A concept is the capacity for nonintentional consciousness of a certain essence.

VI

The above notions of an essential statement and of essence can be extended so that they resemble more closely their traditional counterparts. To do so, in the case of properties, we must appeal to the distinction between specific and generic identity of property-objects. Let us say that the color of one thing and the color of another are *specifically* identical if they are exactly similar. But what shall we say if they are only inexactly similar? If we are to adopt an identity theory of universals, we must understand even inexact similarity as a sort of identity. But what sort? Not partial, i.e., consisting in the possession of a common part or element or property, for colors have no relevant parts or elements, and the properties with respect to which they differ (e.g., pink and crimson) are not distinguishable from the property they have in common (e.g., red).* Let us call the required sort of identity *generic*. The pink color of one book and the crimson color of another book are identical, but only generically. Insofar as generic identity is a case of material identity, we should also say that they are one generic property-entity, namely, the color red. But since each is also a certain specific property-entity, namely, respectively, the color pink and the color crimson, we may also say that these latter property-entities are themselves the color red, their specific differences being analogous to the formal nonidentity of two objects that are materially identical. And then we can extend our notions of essence and of an essential statement by saying that the color red is the essence of the color pink as well as of the color crimson (as the color crimson is the essence of the color of one crimson book as well as of the color of another crimson book), and that the statements "Pink is a red color" and "Crimson is a red color" are essential statements (as "The color

*W. E. Johnson expressed this by calling the specific shades of red determinates of the determinable red. Cf. his *Logic* (Cambridge: Cambridge University Press, 1921), Part 1, pp. 174–76. I discuss the distinction between specific and generic identity in detail in *Resemblance and Identity*, chapter 4.

of that book is pink" is an essential statement).* But, clearly, these would be extensions, indeed analogical uses, of our notions of essence and of an essential statement. For what I have called generic identity is only analogous to material identity, since the generic identicals are really, not only apparently, distinct. And the relationship between the color pink and the color red is only analogous to the relationship between an object and the entity it is, since both the color pink and the color red are understood only as entities when we say that the latter is the essence of the former.

Similar analogical extensions of our notions of essence and essential statement can be made in the case of individual things. And it is these extensions that bring us to, and throw light on, the notion of an individual kind or sort, which was the third notion of essence mentioned at the beginning of this chapter. I see someone whom I recognize as Peter. The *object* I see is the *entity* Peter. The *entity* is the essence of the *object*, and the assertion that the latter is the former is an essential statement. It presupposes statements of *individual* identity such as "The man I see now is the same as the man I met yesterday." But in addition to individual identity, which would correspond to what I called specific identity in the case of properties, we may speak analogically also of *sortal* identity in the case of individuals, which would correspond to what I called *generic* identity in the case of properties.[15] The man I see now would be *individually* identical with the man I met yesterday but *sortally* identical with every other man. Humanity would be the essence both of Peter and of John, because Peter and John, though distinct as individuals, are sortally identical, the sort being humanity (or Man). Each can be thought of as an *instance* of humanity, *just as* the color pink and the color crimson can be thought of as *species* of

---

*John Cook Wilson argued that a genus (generic quality) is with respect to its species (the subordinate specific qualities) as a moving body is to its manifestations at different places. Cf. *Statement and Inference* (Oxford: The Clarendon Press, 1926), vol. 2, p. 674.

the color red, which can be said to be identical only by analogy, but *only somewhat* as the color of one pink book and the color of another pink book can be thought of as *instances* of (i.e., in our terminology, objects that are the entity) pink, since these would be literally identical if colors are universals. Moreover, just as the color red and the color blue themselves may be thought of as having a common essence, namely, the property color, so for example, humanity and felinity can be thought of as having a common essence, namely, animality. The corresponding extension of the notion of an essential statement is now clear and in fact coincides with the usual examples of essential predication. "Peter is a man" and "Man is an animal" would be essential statements. And if we include in the latter a specification of what kind of animal man is, then we would obtain a paradigm of what has been regarded as a real definition, namely, "Man is a rational animal." But while we may be pleased that our account of the notions of essence and of an essential statement thus connects with, and I hope illuminates, the traditional applications of these notions, we must not forget that the latter can only be understood as analogical extensions of the former. Sortal identity is only analogous to identity, since the sortal identicals are really, not just apparently, distinct. And the relationship between Peter and humanity is only analogous to the relationship between the man I see now and Peter if both Peter and humanity are regarded only as entities when we say that Peter is a man.

I have explored such extensions of our notions of essence and of essential statement, themselves based on extensions of the notion of identity, not in order to defend them but in order to illuminate what I believe alone could be the justification of the traditional understanding of these notions. Elsewhere I have attempted a detailed defense of the notion of generic identity.[16] In the next chapter I shall argue that the ordinary notion of individual identity is seriously defective, and the argument will also apply, by implication, to the ordinary notion of sortal identity. But there is nothing fanciful about my claim that the traditional notions should be understood in the manner I have suggested. According to the philosophical tradition, a sort is not a property. Aristotle distinguishes sharply between what is present in its subject but not predicable of it (e.g., a certain whiteness) and what is predicable of its subject but not present in it (e.g., man).[17] And, as John Cook Wilson puts it, what I have called a sort covers or includes the whole of its subject, while a property covers or includes only an aspect of it.[18] He means by this that while the instances of a property such as the color white are, say, the color of Socrates and the color of Plato, the instances of a sort such as humanity are, say, Socrates and Plato themselves. Therefore, we cannot suppose that the connection between individuals and their sort is like the connection between individuals and their properties. We cannot distinguish between Socrates and his humanity in the way in which we can distinguish between Socrates and his white color. (This is why, I suggest, what is predicable of man, say, animal, is also predicable of Socrates, while what is predicable of white, say, color, is not predicable of Socrates.)[19] But then neither can we so distinguish between Plato and his humanity. And if we think of humanity as a universal, then we must conclude that Socrates' humanity is the same as Plato's humanity. Consequently, there must be a sense in which Socrates and Plato are one, are identical. (It is such identity that I have called sortal.) And it is just this conclusion that lay behind Abelard's *reductio ad absurdum* argument against universals, namely, that if "forms" such as Man and Animal were universals, then Socrates would be identical with Plato and, indeed, also with the ass.[20] If there are universals, if sorts are universals, and if we do not confuse the sort of an individual with a property of the individual, then individuals of the same sort must be regarded as identical, and their sort must be regarded as related to them in the way entities are related to objects. Such a reasoning depends on the failure to recognize that our use of the notion of identity when we speak of sortal identity, and thus our use of the notion of a universal when we describe sorts as universals, may only be analogical.

Let us summarize the results of our discussion in this chapter. After a criticism of the currently fashionable notion of an essential property, I attempted to elucidate the notions of essential predication, of essential statement, and of essence by following up their traditional connection with the notion of definition. I explored the respects in which a definition is like, and the respects in which it is unlike, a material identity statement. This exploration led us to explicate the above three notions, as well as that of a concept, in terms of the distinction between objects and entities. The essence of an *object* is the entity that the object would be if it were an entity. By analogical extension, the essence of an *entity* would be the generic (in the case of a property) or sortal (in the case of an individual) entity it is. An essential statement is one that states which entity the object it is about would be if the object existed, or, if about an entity, which generic or sortal entity it is. A concept is the capacity for nonintentional consciousness of an entity qua an entity; the entity may be an individual or a specific property, but it may also, though only analogically, be a sort of individuals or a generic property. We have a clear concept of an object only if we know what it is. We know this only if we know what entity it would be if it existed. And we know this latter only if we know what it would be for it to be materially identical, even if only generically or sortally, with other objects. Thus our account of the notions of essential predication, of an essential statement, and of essence is based on our account of the notion of identity. And this is as it should be, in view of the primacy of the notion of identity.

CHAPTER SIX

Substances

I

The unified account of identity, existence, and essential predication offered in the preceding chapters has been completely general, in keeping with the protometaphysical nature of our inquiry. I have used examples of people, colors, planets, and numbers in order to make this account clear, but I have taken no position on the question whether there are such entities, or even on the question whether we have intelligible concepts of them. These questions depend for their answers, at least in part, on the conclusions that protometaphysics reaches; therefore, protometaphysics must not presuppose any such answers.

But the nature of accidental predication cannot be discussed on an equally high level of generality. As we have seen, a typical example of an ordinary statement expressing accidental predication, such as "Socrates is white," must be regarded as a disguised conjunction, namely, "Socrates has this color [i.e., he does have the color we take him to have, the color he appears to have; we are not, for example, victims of a perceptual illusion], and this color is white." The second conjunct expresses essential predication. It is the first conjunct, rather than the whole statement or its abbreviated version "Socrates is white," that, strictly speaking, expresses accidental predication. And what it expresses is clearly a certain relationship between two things, namely, Socrates and his color, which are perfectly distinguishable, both in perception and in thought, even if the latter is not logically separable from the former. As we have seen, Aristotle described this relationship as that of being present in, and contrasted it sharply with that of being predicable of. I have called the latter essential predication, and this accords well with the tradition. To call the former accidental predication does not accord so well; the term "accident" is, of course, just the right term for one of the relata, but the relationship is not naturally describable as predication because it is not naturally describable with the verb "to be"; Socrates *has* this color, in no sense *is* he this color; indeed, we can say that he is white, but here the verb "to be" is usable precisely because what we mean is that he *has* a certain color, which *is* white.

Of course, it is unimportant whether or not we use the expression "accidental predication" or some other expression, e.g., "present in" or "inherence," for the relationship between Socrates and his color. What is important is that we recognize that it is a relationship between two distinct things, that it is quite different from essential predication or, of course, from identity or existence. To give an account of accidental predication is to give an account of this relationship. And such an account cannot be attempted in abstraction from the question of the nature of the relata of the relationship. We can hardly hope to understand a certain relation without understanding what sorts of things it relates. It is for this reason that our account of accidental predication cannot remain on the level of generality of our accounts of identity, existence, and essential predication. Unlike these latter, it cannot be purely protometaphysical. It must raise some questions about what sorts of entities there are or at least are possible.

The history of metaphysics has been concerned with two great categories of entities: material substances and qualities. And metaphysical theories fall into two main classes: those that allow for both material substances and qualities, and those that allow only for qualities. I shall refer to the former generally as the metaphysics of material substances, and to the latter as the metaphysics of qualities. A third possible theory, namely, one that acknowledges only substances and denies that there are qualities, has seldom if ever been held; as we shall see in chapter seven, the contemporary philosophers who appear to hold it are most charitably interpreted as really wishing to deny the existence of universals, not the existence of qualities. And a theory according to which individual things are systems, or "families," of sense-data, is really a variety of the metaphysics of qualities, since, presumably, it would hold that a sense-datum contains nothing but qualities.

Two explanatory comments are needed here. The first is terminological. In keeping with the terminology metaphysicians of qualities themselves employ, I have used the word "quality" rather than the word "property." Until now the latter has served us adequately. But it is often understood by contemporary philosophers as standing for whatever open sentences express. And the chief thesis of the metaphysics of qualities, namely, that an individual thing is a bundle of qualities, would be sheer nonsense if stated with the word "property" so understood. Indeed, even if not needed in other contexts (as it was not, for example, in our discussion in chapter three of the relation between the substitutivity of coreferential expressions and the indiscernibility of identicals), a sharp distinction between properties and what, if anything, is expressed by open sentences must be made, at least provisionally, in any clear discussion of accidental predication. For it is required by the more fundamental distinction between predication and that which is predicated. Even if this distinction is eventually to be rejected,* our terminology must allow us to state and discuss it. And surely "property" is the natural term for the predicated, not for the predication-*cum*-the predicated. The natural view is that, for example, it is not "x is white," but rather just the word "white" in it, that stands for a property; for the

---

*I shall discuss the Fregean reason for rejecting it in chapter eight. For a discussion of the distinction between properties and what open sentences express see Reinhardt Grossmann, *Ontological Reduction* (Bloomington and London: Indiana University Press, 1973), pp. 116–22.

natural view is that the property in question is the color white, and surely it is the word "white" in any sentence of that form that stands for the color white. And, regarding more complicated open sentences, such as "x is not white now but will be white tomorrow," the suggestion that they stand for properties strikes us as a philosophical monstrosity. Surely, a sentence of this form does not say of its logical subject that it has a certain property, but, on the contrary, denies that it does and affirms only that it will have that property tomorrow. Indeed, we often find useful such locutions as "the property of being white" and eschew locutions such as "the property white" and especially the ungrammatical "the property triangular." But this need not be anything more than a matter of style and surface grammar. To avoid misunderstandings, however, it is better, when it matters, that we avoid the term "property." The term "quality" is an obvious traditional substitute for it, especially in any discussion of the metaphysics of qualities, and has the virtue of being almost untouched by current philosophical usage. Even if one were inclined to say that a thing's being white, rather than its white color, is a property of it, one would hardly be inclined to say that the thing's being white, rather than its white color, is a quality of it.

The second comment that needs to be made is not terminological. It may seem that the category of material substances is too specific, and that the more general category is that of an individual thing. But many metaphysicians have acknowledged that there are individual things but also have claimed that an individual thing is nothing but a bundle* or, better, cluster of qualities and have denied that there are material substances; it would be misleading to say that such philosophers have allowed for two categories of entities: individual things and qualities. It may also seem that the notion of a material substance is only a specifica-

*For example, Bertrand Russell so describes individual things in *An Inquiry into Meaning and Truth*, p. 97.

tion of the more general notion of a substance, and that the latter is the one to be contrasted with the notion of a quality. But even though many metaphysicians have claimed that there are immaterial substances, such as God, angels, and perhaps human souls, there can be little doubt that the application of the notion of substance to such entities can be understood only insofar as there is some analogy between them and material substances. Purely formal definitions of substance in general, e.g., Aristotle's "what is neither predicable of nor present in something else," or Spinoza's "what exists in itself and is conceived through itself," employ notions that can hardly be understood independently of the notions of substance and quality.

According to the metaphysics of material substances, accidental predication is a relation that holds between a quality and a material substance. According to the metaphysics of qualities, it is a relation between a quality and an individual thing that in some sense consists only of qualities; therefore, according to it, the more fundamental relation, in terms of which we must understand accidental predication, is the relation holding between two or more qualities when these qualities are "together" in, or "constitute," one and the same individual thing. In this chapter I shall argue that the metaphysics of material substances must be rejected; therefore, so must be its account of accidental predication. In chapters seven and eight I shall try to offer an adequate account of accidental predication in terms of the metaphysics of qualities. Such an account must include a theory of the nature of qualities (are they universals?), as well as a theory of the nature of the clusters of qualities the metaphysics of qualities claims individual things to be (how are such clusters held together?). But in all these metaphysical discussions I shall try to be guided solely by the protometaphysical conclusions already reached.

II

The world emerges as a result of the application of the concepts of identity and existence. This fact constitutes the subject matter of protometaphysics. The kind of world that can so emerge is the subject matter of metaphysics. We may think of protometaphysics as the prolegomenon to any legitimate metaphysics. Metaphysics is concerned with the kinds of entities that are possible (logically, but in the broad sense of this word) and with the manner in which they are connected. It is concerned with the constitution and structure of all possible worlds and therefore also, but only indirectly, with the *most general* constitution and structure of the actual world. Metaphysics as such cannot inquire directly into the characteristics of the actual world. Such an inquiry, insofar as it is philosophical and not scientific, would be primarily epistemological in nature. For example, whether material substances are possible is a purely metaphysical question; whether, given that they are possible, they exist, is mainly a problem of epistemology, namely, the problem of our knowledge of "the external world," the problem of perception.

Superficially considered, our protometaphysical conclusions seem to provide no guidance regarding the metaphysics we should adopt. Indeed, for something to be an entity, it must have an essence and be identifiable and thus exist. This ought to be acknowledged by any metaphysics. But are the entities that can satisfy this condition, that are possible, only material substances, or material substances and qualities, or only qualities? Protometaphysics appears to suggest no answers to such questions. But this appearance is deceptive.

The essence of an object is the entity it would be if the object existed. The concept of that entity is the capacity for nonintentional consciousness of it. Whether the object *does* exist depends on whether there is an indefinite number of other objects with which it is materially identical. But whether the object *can* exist, whether there are such an essence and such a concept, depends on whether it *can* (logically) be identified with an indefinite number of other objects. Yet there are no objects that cannot exist. Such an object would be necessarily nonexistent. And how could what necessarily does not exist be a genuine object of thought or perception, how could it be singled out? If it could, what would we substitute for thinkability or conceivability as our ultimate criterion of logical possibility?

But while, strictly speaking, there can be no question whether something is a genuine object or not and thus whether a certain entity is possible, there can be another, closely related question. It is the question (usually philosophical) whether certain *ostensible* concepts (ordinarily their ostensibility consists in the presence in everyday usage of certain words) are *genuine* concepts. Such a question can be stated in at least two seemingly very different yet equivalent ways. (1) Can we single out in thought or perception objects corresponding to such an ostensible concept? If we can, then there also can be an entity corresponding to the concept, since every object is a possible existent, a possible entity. This is the classical empiricist and contemporary phenomenological version of the question. (2) If an object corresponding to the ostensible concept were singled out, would it be capable of indefinite identification, would we understand what it would be like for it to be identical with other objects, would there be *criteria* for its identity with other objects? I believe that this second version of the question is philosophically the deeper one. The first version suggests that the question is to be answered by bare phenomenological appeals and makes incomprehensible the fact of philosophical disagreement about it.

I have already offered an explanation of what I mean by a criterion (see above, pp. 114–17). A criterion for the applicability of the concept F to x is a certain kind of logically sufficient condition for the applicability of the concept F to x. This is why what I mean by a criterion should not be confused with Wittgenstein's use of the term, although I believe that some of his motives for introducing it were similar to mine. To say that if a concept is genuine then there must be criteria for its application is to say that it must be possible for one to be clear about the difference between the cases to which the concept is applicable and the cases to which it is not, to have a firm grasp of what it is for one thing to fall under the concept and for another not to fall under it. It need not be the case that one should be able to *express* informatively, nontrivially, or even nontautologically, the criteria for the application of the concept, that one should be able to distinguish the criteria from the fact of the applicability of the concept, for a case to which the concept is applicable may be a paradigm of its applicability. Nor is it necessary that one be able to know, to determine, to *verify* that the concept is or that it is not applicable in a given case; it suffices that one understand what it would be for it to be applicable or to be inapplicable in that case. But it is necessary that if the criteria are present then the concept is applicable (in the case of a paradigm this conditional would be a tautology). For what would one understand by the *in*applicability of the concept in a case in which the criteria, in our sense of the term, are present?

III

There are no material substances because there are no criteria for the identity of material substances. And there are no criteria for the identity of material substances because there is nothing about a material substance to which we can conceivably appeal that is a logically sufficient (or indeed even necessary) condition of its identity. Therefore, we do not really understand what it would be for a material substance to be identifiable and thus what it would be for an entity to be a material substance.

More specifically, I shall argue that there are no criteria for the identity of material substances through time. For the possibility of such identity is a necessary feature of material substances.* Of

---

*"It seems most distinctive of substance that what is numerically one and the same is able to receive contraries. . . . For example, an individual man—one and the same—becomes pale at one time and dark at another, and hot and cold, and

course, we do have criteria for the truth of judgments such as "The chair to your left is the same as the chair to my right"; and chairs are ordinarily regarded as material substances. But there are these criteria only because it is not essential to the truth of such a judgment that what it is about be a material substance. Our criterion for it is spatial coincidence and qualitative identity, and the judgment would be true regardless of whether the chair is supposed to be a material substance or a cluster of qualities.

The natural or commonsense metaphysics is the metaphysics of persistent material substances, of chairs, rivers, mountains, planets, plants, animals, and men, and of the various stuffs that constitute them, as these are ordinarily understood. It is also the metaphysics of contemporary science, with the possible exception of the most fundamental branches of physics, as well as of most of contemporary Anglo-American philosophy. We look to Aristotle and Aquinas, of course, for the classical and most developed versions of this metaphysics. We shall find our account of the notion of essence in chapter five useful in attempting to understand them, but I shall not engage in exegesis of Aristotle's or Aquinas's actual views.

What is a material substance? Let us not choose as our example an artifact, such as a chair. For we are inclined, perhaps rightly so, to ignore the most distinctive features of such a thing, e.g., a chair's shape and function, and if asked to say what it is, to answer, e.g., that it is wood. For the same reason we should not take as our example a quantity of a stuff, e.g., the water contained in a glass; if asked to say what it is, we are inclined to answer, e.g., that it is water, and to ignore those of its features, in particular its location and shape, in virtue of which it is a distinct individual thing. Nor should we take stuffs as such, e.g., wood and water, as our examples, for they exhibit a pseudouniversality that makes them difficult, if not impossible, to regard as individual things.

bad and good. No thing like this is to be seen in any other case." Aristotle, *Categories* 4a 10–21, trans. J. L. Ackrill.

Let us follow Aristotle and Aquinas and take as our example an individual man, say, Socrates.

Pointing at Socrates, one may ask, what is this? (Not, what is Socrates?, for, as we saw in chapter five, the very use of the name "Socrates" may presuppose an answer to the question.) What is the most obviously appropriate answer? Clearly, as the discussion in chapter five has shown, that this is a man, not that there is humanity in it, nor that it has a certain connection to humanity, whether we call this participation or exemplification, but that it *is* a man, that *what it is* is *a man*. We might also say that this is white in response to the question, what is this? But if we do, the reason would be that we regard the question as elliptical for "What color is this?" or, more fully, for "What is the color of this?" while the question that calls for the answer "It is a man" is not elliptical at all. This becomes evident when we note, as Aristotle did, that though Socrates is white, he is not a color even though white is a color; but, given that Socrates is a man, it follows that he is an animal, since man is an animal. Socrates *has* a white color, he *is not* a white color. But he does not *have* humanity, he *is* human, a man. If we regard humanity and the color white as universals, then, as I suggested earlier, the distinction would be made quite clear by saying that it is Socrates' *color* that is an instance of the color white, and not Socrates himself, while *Socrates* himself is an instance of humanity. Humanity, to use Cook Wilson's illuminating terminology, covers Socrates' whole being, just as the color white covers the whole being of his color, i.e., of his whiteness. But, obviously, the color white does not cover Socrates' whole being. Socrates is much more than a white thing, and his additional elements need not even be connected with his being white. On the other hand, we should say either that there is nothing that Socrates is in addition to being a man, or, if there is (e.g., a philosopher or white), that he is that only if he is a man or something that being a man involves, e.g., having an intellect or a body. It is in this sense that we may say that Socrates' being a man constitutes what he *is;* that it is his nature or essence. His white color, on the other hand, is merely *in* him; it is a mere quality or accident of him, something he *has*. This is why Socrates can have contrary qualities over time; it is merely a special case of one thing bearing the same relation to different things. But he cannot be human at one time and not human at another.

But what then is it for Socrates to be a man? Let us suppose that to say that Socrates is a man is to say that he is a rational animal. But to say that he is an animal is to say, in part, that he has flesh and bones. In other words, his matter is *part* of what he is, of his essence. This is why, while we *ought* not to say when asked "What is Socrates?" that he is flesh and bones (or nitrogen, hydrogen, carbon, etc.), we *could* say this and in a way we would be right. For Socrates' matter corresponds to the genus in the definition of his essence,[1] namely, to animal, and the genus is predicable of Socrates just as the specific difference (i.e., rational) is predicable of him. Yet, obviously, what Socrates is, is not just flesh and bones. He is also a man. Are we to conclude then that he is a composite of these two, of his matter and his being a man? But to conclude this would be to disguise the difference between Socrates' being a man and his being, say, white, the difference between essential and accidental predication, and to suggest that Socrates' being a man is something distinguishable from his flesh and bones. In reality his being a man necessarily involves his having flesh and bones, for having flesh and bones is part of what it is to be a man. We may add also that his being *this* particular man necessarily involves his having *these* particular flesh and bones. The matter of a material substance is part of what the substance is, of its essence.*

---

*"This kind of matter [i.e., "designated matter," which is matter "considered under determined dimensions" and is "the principle of individuation"] is not part of the definition of man as man, but it would enter into the definition of Socrates if Socrates could be defined. The definition of man, on the contrary, does include undesignated matter. In this definition we do not put this particular bone and this particular flesh, but bone and flesh absolutely, which are the undesig-

The above sort of analysis of what Socrates is, is also applicable
to his flesh and bones. For these are only his so-called proximate
matter and may themselves be understood as material substances
that have their own matter (e.g., protoplasm). The analysis can
then be applied to the latter, and regardless of whether we think
that the ultimate elements are earth, air, fire, and water, or the
elementary particles of contemporary physics, we are inevitably
led either into an infinite regress or to the level of ultimate,
prime matter, of mere stuff. (To suppose that the ultimate elements themselves need not involve matter would be to suppose
that they are not material substances and, presumably, to accept
the metaphysics of qualities. To suppose that they are material
but not analyzable into matter and form would be to use the term
"material" vacuously and to make nonsense of the hylomorphic
analysis to which the metaphysics of material substances is
committed.)

Now, on neither alternative can we identify through time the
ultimate matter of which the essence of a material substance in
part consists; on the former because there is no such ultimate
matter; on the latter because the ultimate matter has no essence
of its own, is by definition characterless.[2] But a material substance is essentially a parcel of its proximate matter. To identify
it through time and thus be able to think of it as an entity requires
the identification of its proximate matter through at least brief
intervals of time, even if the substance need not consist of the
same matter throughout its existence.[3] Yet no identification of the
proximate matter of a substance is possible, either because such

nated matter of man" (Aquinas, p. 37). I should add that Aristotle's, if not
Aquinas's, view of the relationship between a material substance and its matter is
inseparable from, indeed ultimately based on, his distinction between actuality
and potentiality. The matter of Socrates and his form are not two parts of his
essence, of what he is. Rather, in a sense they are one and the same, the matter
being potentially what the form is actually (*Metaphysics* 1045b 17–19). But the
distinction between actuality and potentiality does not shed light upon, but
rather presupposes, the identity of a material substance through time, and thus is
useless for our purposes.

an identification would involve the completion of an infinite process or because the matter on which the ultimate identification of any proximate matter would depend is itself in principle unidentifiable. The supposition that there is content to the distinction between the ultimate matter of a substance remaining numerically the same through an interval of time and its being replaced by "another" ultimate matter is obviously absurd.[4] Therefore, given the dependence of the identity of a material substance through time on the identity of at least some of its matter, through at least some intervals of time, it follows that no identification of material substances through time is possible.

Moreover, if we are to acknowledge obvious everyday and scientific facts, we must allow, as I have done above, that at least at some level of proximity the matter of any material substance is constantly changing. But how is this compatible with the identity of the substance?[5] Indeed, we regard only gradual or partial sudden changes in the material constitution of a substance as compatible with its identity, not sudden complete or even major partial changes, e.g., the sudden replacement of all the molecules of this table, or even all the molecules of its top and three of its four legs, with numerically different even though qualitively the same molecules. (This may not be true of a person, but only if we suppose that a person is not merely a material substance.) How slow, or how minor must a change be to remain compatible with identity? The fact is that we have no clear, determinate answer to this question.

According to P. T. Geach, "Tibbles himself consists at a given moment, of a 'soul' existing in a given parcel of matter; but his 'essence' or 'nature' consists of that 'soul' plus *matter*, not: plus a given parcel of matter; but Tibbles remains a cat, and the same cat, in spite of a thoroughgoing metabolism, and his 'essence' is precisely that in virtue of which this continues to hold true of him."[6] Geach is aware of the objection: "How can there be flesh and bones that are not *this* flesh and *these* bones or matter that is not *this* matter?" (p. 84). He correctly points out that "matter" here should not be understood as a general term, applicable to particular pieces of matter such as *this* matter. A sufficient reason for this would be that Tibbles's matter could not then be a *part* of his essence; matter-in-general may be a part of cat-in-general, but not of an individual cat—of what it is to be a cat, but not of what it is to be Tibbles. But the reason Geach does give is that "This matter is matter individuated in this way; and for Aquinas the same matter may now be individuated in this way and now not individuated at all . . . '*this* flesh' here means '*this* matter, possessed of the attributes of flesh'; and if *this* matter is no part of the essence of Tibbles, neither is *this* flesh. . . . But if matter exists under Tibbles' individualized cat-form, this requires that some of the matter shall possess the attributes of flesh and bones . . ." (p. 84). And this seems to me to be no reason at all. If the same matter can be now this flesh in Tibbles and later that flesh, then it can still be true that Tibbles's essence contains the same matter, though not the same flesh, throughout his existence. But if Tibbles's essence includes matter only in the sense that it requires that Tibbles have, at any one time, *some* matter, then we are understanding "matter" as a general term. The only intelligible supposition is that the essence of a material substance includes the particular matter it has. If (perhaps because of metabolism) it does not have the same particular matter at all times of its existence, then it does not have the same essence at all times of its existence and thus there is no one, identical thing at those times. But the thesis I wish to defend is not that a material substance cannot endure through time because its matter does not *in fact* so endure. The thesis I wish to defend is that the very idea of matter, which is essential to the idea of a material substance, is such that there can be no criteria for its enduring through time and therefore also no criteria for its failing to endure through time.*

*In *The Persistence of Matter,* Eli Hirsh acknowledges that "for the case of the persistence of matter I think we can draw no . . . distinction between [observational] criteria and evidence of identity; here, in a sense, we have only evi-

Indeed, the abandonment of the metaphysics of material substances in the seventeenth and eighteenth centuries was motivated precisely by the unintelligibility of the notion of (prime) matter. Contrary to appearances, it had little to do with purely epistemological considerations. For example, Hume's argument against material substance is mainly that we have no idea of such an entity, not just that we cannot know it because we cannot perceive it. Of course, for him, the two considerations are related. And it is plausible to suppose that we find the notion of prime matter unintelligible because we cannot even imagine what it would be to perceive prime matter, the ultimate formless substrate. We can perceive the surfaces of what are supposed to be material substances and thus, in a sense not compatible with the Aristotelian notion of prime matter, the boundaries of their prime matter. But we cannot perceive the matter itself, as such. (Proximate matter would be perceivable if material substances are perceivable but only because it is itself a complex of material substances.) And, of course, even if there are entities of which we can have only a purely intellectual, not perceptual, awareness, matter can hardly be supposed to be such an entity. Thus the recognition of the unperceivability of matter led to the recognition of the unintelligibility of the notion of matter, and the latter led to the recognition of the unintelligibility of the notion of a material substance. Therefore, even if the argument I have presented against the metaphysics of material substances is novel, the more fundamental considerations behind it are not. A material substance is essentially, though not solely, a parcel of matter, and it is intelligible only if its matter is intelligible. Its

---

dence and no criteria" (p. 48), and argues that "the identity of matter is determined by theoretical considerations, and is ultimately clarified by the laws of science" (p. 54; see also "Physical Identity," p. 386). But we can have no evidence for what we can have no criteria; to have no criteria for the identity of matter is to fail to attach clear content to the idea of such identity, and so no theoretical considerations or explanations could be understood as being concerned with *the identity of matter*.

identity requires the identity of its matter, at least in some of its parts and through some segments of its history. Both the classical and the modern philosophers held that matter as such is unintelligible, the former on the grounds of its indefinability, and the latter on the grounds of its unobservability. And for the identity of what is unintelligible there can be no criteria.

IV

It may seem that my argument against the metaphysics of material substances is directed only against its Aristotelian variety. But this is not so. As I have already observed, both common sense and virtually all of science conceive of individual things, sometimes explicitly but always at least implicitly, as being material substances. And so do almost all current philosophical writers on the essence and identity of individual things. It is not surprising, therefore, that the application of the concept of identity to individual things, as these are ordinarily understood, has been found to be notoriously obscure, even when no explicit assumption is made that they are material substances.

The only possible criterion for the identity through time of an individual thing as it is ordinarily understood would be some degree or kind of qualitative similarity and at least some approximation to spatiotemporal continuity.* And the least questionable case would be that of a thing, say a chair, a rock, or an animal, continually observed from, say, t_1 to t_3, that remains perfectly unaltered qualitatively and motionless during that period of

---

*A representative statement of such a criterion is the following: "If one locates each of the particulars a and b [under covering concept or concepts] and, where appropriate, *sc.* in the case of 'identity through time,' traces a and b through space and time [under covering concepts], one must find that a and b coincide [under some covering concept]." Wiggins, *Identity and Spatio-Temporal Continuity*, p. 35. Cf. also his "The Individuation of Things and Places," *Aristotelian Society Suppl Vol.* 38 (1963): 176, and "On Being in the Same Place at the Same Time," *Philosophical Review* 77 (1968): 93; and Richard Swinburne, *Space and Time* (New York: St. Martin's Press, 1968), pp. 22–23.

time. If anything could be a case of identity of such a thing through time, this would be one. But that the thing observed at t_1 and the thing observed at t_3 have exactly the same qualities, occupy exactly the same place, and are temporally continuous does not constitute a logically sufficient condition for their being identical. The reason is simple and familiar from, though of course independent of, the doctrine of continual Divine re-creation of the world from moment to moment.* The former thing may have ceased to exist at t_2 and immediately thereupon the latter thing may have begun to exist.† They would not be identical, even though qualitatively completely indistinguishable and spatiotemporally perfectly continuous. Therefore, even complete qualitative indistinguishability and perfect spatiotemporal continuity fail to be logically sufficient conditions of identity through time for an individual thing as ordinarily understood. Even *they* are not a criterion of such identity, in the sense of "criterion" I have defended earlier. But then nothing else could be such a criterion. Therefore, there are no criteria for the identity of individual things through time, as such things are ordinarily understood.‡

*See, for example, Descartes, *Meditation* III. R. M. Chisholm refers to, and discusses, Jonathan Edwards' version of this doctrine in "Identity Through Time," note 4, in *Language, Belief, and Metaphysics*, ed. Howard E. Kiefer and Milton K. Munitz (Albany: State University of New York Press, 1970), also in *Person and Object* (LaSalle: Open Court Publishing Company, 1976), pp. 138–40. Compare Whitehead's view that, if time is "taken seriously," actual entities must be regarded as "perpetually perishing." ("Time," *Proceedings of the Sixth International Congress of Philosophy* [New York: Longmans, Green and Co., 1927]; also *Process and Reality* [New York: The Social Science Book Store, 1929], pp. 43, 222–23.)

†What is meant here by "immediately thereupon"? The notion expressed is a species of the general notion another species of which is that of a change taking place at a certain time, e.g., of a thing's beginning to move or changing its velocity at a certain time.

‡There is an analogy here between individual things and sounds. Unless we appeal to the identity of the physical source of a sound, we have no criteria for distinguishing between the case of a sound persisting through an interval of time and the case of a sound ceasing to exist at some moment during that interval and

That such instantaneous replacement is conceivable seems to me obvious. Indeed, any philosopher who has claimed that individual things should be understood as spatiotemporal "worms," or as continuous series of "time-slices," has in effect claimed that such instantaneous replacement is not only a possibility but true of all individual things at all times (at least at all times of phenomenologically minimal duration). One time-slice replaces the preceding time-slice; it is no more identical with it than one spatial part ("spatial slice") of a thing is identical with another, even though adjacent, spatial part of the thing, and so a spatiotemporal worm no more involves something remaining identical at all times during its duration than a spatial thing's occupancy of each part of the region it occupies involves there being something identical in each such part.

There is no difficulty in conceiving of a thing's suddenly vanishing. Nor is there any difficulty in conceiving of a thing's suddenly coming into existence. And that two things existing at different times should be qualitatively indistinguishable is also perfectly conceivable. All this does not entail that the case of instantaneous replacement I have described is conceivable. But it does substantiate the claim that such a case is conceivable, in the absence of any reasons to the contrary. Indeed, instantaneous replacement without qualitative change is not *imaginable, visualizable*, in the literal senses of these terms, but only because such an instantaneous replacement is not the sort of thing that could be *perceived*, not because, though it is the *sort* of thing that could be perceived, it cannot be imagined. The unimaginability in question is trivial, like the unimaginability of a tree that no one, not even the imaginer, perceives. Imagination is imaginary perception, and it is trivially true that what cannot be perceived cannot be imagined and therefore that one cannot imagine something unless one imagines it as perceived. Unimaginability in

being immediately succeeded by another qualitatively indistinguishable sound. The analogy was suggested to me by Richard Gale, *Negation and Nonbeing* (American Philosophical Quarterly Monograph Series, 10, 1976), p. 84.

this sense ought not to be regarded as a criterion of impossibility.[7] But if it is, then the nonexistence of individual things as they are ordinarily understood, of material substances, containing much that is unperceived and existing even when not perceived, would follow directly from the application of that criterion, as Berkeley and Hume in fact argued.

If someone finds such instantaneous replacement inconceivable, he is likely to be thinking of the thing observed at t_1 and the thing observed at t_3 not as substances but as "clusters" of qualities. If so, he may well be right. (I shall consider this question in chapter eight.) The identity of a cluster of qualities is presumably determined by the identity of its constituents and of their order. And by hypothesis the qualities of the things, including their spatial relations, as well as the order of these, are identical. (Their temporal relations would not be identical, of course. If these are included in the clusters, then it becomes trivially true that clusters of qualities cannot endure. But we shall see that there are reasons against such an inclusion. Moreover, if in general we regard the temporal location of an enduring individual thing as one of its properties, then we must say, in my view incoherently, that mere endurance constitutes a change.)

Not only does nothing seem to be a logically *sufficient* condition for the identity of an individual thing through time; nothing seems to be even a logically *necessary* condition. The recent literature has made this abundantly clear. I shall only mention here a number of plausible counterexamples to the view that spatiotemporal continuity and some degree or kind of qualitative similarity are necessary conditions of such identity. Of course, my purpose is not to show that they are genuine counterexamples, i.e., that they are cases of identity even though a certain allegedly necessary condition is not satisfied; my purpose is to show that the concept of identity has no clear application to individual things as they are ordinarily understood, and the plausibility of the counterexamples contributes to showing this. For if nothing is a necessary condition of individual identity through time then this strengthens the thesis that nothing also is a sufficient condition, insofar as it is plausible to believe that any such sufficient condition would be the conjunction of the necessary conditions.

Counterexamples to the requirement of qualitative similarity are plentiful. There is the Proteus case. In the *Odyssey* we are told the following story " . . . the Old man did not forget the subtlety of his arts. First he turned into a great bearded lion, and then to a serpent, then to a leopard, then to a great boar, and he turned into fluid water, to a tree with towering branches, but we held stiffly on to him with enduring spirit."[8] The transformation of a tadpole into a frog is an actual such counterexample. So are an indefinite number of other, less extreme cases. When does the remodeling of a house (e.g., the addition of new wings, stories, etc.) become a case of building a new house? When is a philosophical paper just a revision of an old paper and when is it a new paper? The fact is that we do not know what to say. For practical (especially legal) reasons we may stipulate an answer, but the very need for a *stipulation* shows that the concept of identity has no clear application to such cases.

Counterexamples to the requirement of spatiotemporal continuity also abound.[9] There is the case of temporary disassembly. A bicycle is taken apart, but shortly afterwards the pieces are put back together. Surely, we would say, the so-obtained bicycle is the same as the old one. But there was a time during which it did not exist. There are the cases of fission: an amoeba divides into two, and is spatiotemporally continuous with both. Which, if either, is it, since it cannot be both? I am looking at my cat, which, in keeping with philosophical tradition, is lying calmly on the mat. Suddenly it disappears from the mat and immediately thereupon appears lying, just as calmly, on the chair, with the same characteristics it had in the past. Is this logically impossible? Or my cat suddenly vanishes from the mat, is nowhere to be found for an hour, and then suddenly is again lying on the mat. Is this logically impossible?

It is generally assumed that the requirement of spatiotemporal continuity is intimately connected with the principle that two bodies cannot occupy the same place at the same time.[10] The reasons behind the assumption are not always clear, but the following may be suggested. It seems plausible to suppose that if two bodies (e.g., billiard balls) can occupy the same place at some time, they can do so without ever being separate. But then we would never have criteria for judging that what we take to be one body is really one. (Weighing the body would not be such a criterion; some billiard balls may weigh twice as much as others.) And surely the notion of identity loses any significance as applied to bodies if we have no criteria even for *counting* contemporaneous bodies. Yet there seems to be no obvious unintelligibility in the description of two moving bodies (e.g., billiard balls) whose paths cross and that come to occupy simultaneously even though temporarily the place of their crossing.*

There are other, no less familiar, puzzles that arise because of the obscurity and indeterminacy of the application of the concept of identity to individual things as they are ordinarily understood. Strawson has pointed out that "the identification and distinction of places turn on the identification and distinction of things; and the identification and distinction of things turn, in part, on the identification and distinction of places."[11] To determine that an individual thing satisfies the requirement of spatiotemporal continuity, we must determine that certain identity judgments about places (and also times!) are true. But this latter determination is possible only on the basis of true identity judgments about things. Swinburne suggests that the paradox may be avoided if we allow for "provisional" identity judgments that are based only on the satisfaction of the requirement of qualitative similar-

---

*I am not denying here the general principle that no two things of the same kind that are in space can occupy the same place at the same time. Rather, I am pointing out that insofar as material substances may be imagined to violate it, they are not an intelligible category of entity. The principle is not open to such imaginary counterexamples from the categories of qualities, e.g., colors.

ity. Surely he is right, but his qualification that such judgments may only be provisional, by which he means that they are subject to confirmation by other identity judgments, themselves in part based on the satisfaction of the requirement of spatiotemporal continuity, is unacceptable: the problem is precisely where to reach logical rock bottom in our understanding of the identity of substances, and the multiplication of putative bits of indirect evidence can have no value as a solution of that problem. It would seem, therefore, that the requirement of qualitative similarity is primary. But the admission that this is so makes even more glaring the absence of a logically sufficient condition for the identity of individual things through time. Clearly, no mere qualitative similarity, however complete, is such a condition.

There are also the examples of nonidentical individual things that nevertheless supposedly possess the same (proximate) matter. A jug is broken into pieces and then the pieces are put together so that they make a coffeepot.[12] It seems obvious that the coffeepot is not identical with the jug, even though it also seems obvious that its matter is identical with that of the jug. Yet we are inclined to say that the jug and its matter, i.e., the aggregate of its parts, are one and the same thing, and so are the coffeepot and the aggregate of its parts. Wiggins attempts to avoid the paradox by appealing to what he calls the "constitutive" sense of "is," which, he insists, is different from the identity sense of "is."[13] But our discussion above casts doubt on the existence of such a sense. No clear distinction between a material substance and the aggregate of its parts, or its matter, is possible, because the notion of a material substance includes that of its matter. It is simply a fact about our language that the "is" in "That heap of fragments is the jug you saw yesterday" is most naturally understood as the "is" of identity, and only philosophical argument might lead us to understand it otherwise.

Certain other cases are the mirror image of those just described. They are cases in which an individual thing seems to remain identical through a drastic, even complete, change in its proximate matter. Theseus's ship is completely rebuilt, each of its parts being replaced by a new one. We want to say that it is still the same ship. But, as soon as we reflect upon the case, we are also inclined to deny that it is the same ship. The possibility that the old planks have been used for the construction of another ship, thus facing us with the question which of the two ships is identical with the original one, merely dramatizes the failure of the concept of identity to have a clear application to the case; it is not the root of the paradox. A less fanciful example is the following. A bicycle has one of its wheels replaced but, presumably, is still the same bicycle. Later it also has the other wheel replaced. Suppose we say that the replacement of one wheel is compatible with the bicycle's remaining the same, but the replacement of two wheels is not. Do we then have here a case of identity failing to be transitive?[14]

V

My purpose in this chapter has been to show that the concept of identity has no clear application to material substances, to individual things as they are ordinarily understood; more specifically, that there are no criteria, in the sense explained earlier, for their identity through time. And the demand here for clarity, for criteria, is not exorbitant. A concept has a genuine application to a certain domain only insofar as it can divide it into at least some cases to which it is clearly applicable and at least some cases to which it is clearly not applicable, even if there could be borderline cases that fall into neither category (a possibility I shall deny shortly). The *word* associated with the concept may have application; for some purposes it may be useful, indeed indispensable. But we must not confuse a concept with the word associated with it. The application of words such as "identical" or "same" to what are supposed to be material substances is a feature of ordinary discourse that is indeed pervasive but nonetheless conceptually vacuous. If asked how it is possible that there should be such a feature, that we should have such a *use* for these words yet no *concept* behind the use, I should reply that it is possible in the way we have a standard use of words for causal, objectively necessary connection and yet, if Hume is right, no genuine concept, no genuine understanding of such a connection. Another example would be the *ordinary* use of the words "knowledge" and "evidence."* I shall have more to say on this question in chapter eight.

My argument must not be confused with the sceptic's claim that we can never know whether a material substance remains the same if our observation of it is interrupted. What I have argued is that we do not *understand* what it would be for a substance to remain the same, whether observed or not, and whether uninterruptedly observed or not. Indeed, it is common usage to apply the word "same" to such cases. But such usage constitutes the employment of a *concept* only if it is governed by a criterion. And my point has been that it is not so governed, since there is no such criterion.

Strawson argues that the view that nothing can be known to be identical with something previously observed is incoherent.[15] I do not believe that his argument is sound. But what matters for my purposes here is that the view Strawson considers is not the one I have been defending. My view is not epistemological at all. A comparison with the attribution to another person of having a toothache may make this clear. A sceptic denies the possibility of knowing that another person has a toothache, on the grounds that nothing can serve as adequate evidence for this. Strawson offers an argument against this sort of scepticism too. But there is a crucial difference between substantial identity and other persons' having toothaches. Even if I cannot know that another person has a toothache, I can know, at least according to the sceptic, what it is to have a toothache from my own case. But the identity of material substances through time is not only something that *I*

*I discuss this latter case in *The Concept of Knowledge*, pp. 54–61.

cannot know. It is something that *cannot* be known, in any circumstances, by anyone, because it is something we do not understand. We do not know *what* it would be for material substances to remain identical through time, not just *that* some do.

The topic of the identity of material substances through time thus resembles, as I have already suggested, the topic of causality rather than that of other minds. Hume argued that we have no idea of objective necessary connection and, insofar as such a connection is part of what we mean by causal connection, that we do not have an idea of causal connection. His argument may be reformulated as follows: All that *could* serve as criteria for saying that this A is the cause of this B is their spatiotemporal contiguity, the fact that this A precedes this B in time, and the fact that in the past A's and B's have been constantly so conjoined. But these cannot be criteria for the presence of a causal connection, since we can easily suppose that they are satisfied even though this A is not the cause of this B, i.e., even though their conjunction, indeed perhaps the conjunction of all past A's with B's, is *accidental*, not *necessary*. If such an argument is called sceptical, then we should distinguish this sort of scepticism from that regarding, for example, the possibility of knowledge of other minds.

The *general* motive behind Strawson's argument for the identifiability of individual things is his conviction that the concept of identity is the very backbone of thought and discourse and therefore that it must have application if thought and discourse are to be possible. I share this conviction and argued for it in chapter two. But the rejection of individual identity through time does not deprive us of an applicable concept of identity. There is also qualitative identity, i.e., the identity of qualities, which is both more fundamental than and independent of individual identity.[16] That qualitative identity suffices as the backbone of thought and discourse is made plausible by the fact that it holds also through time and thus can ground the reapplicability of our concepts. Universal qualities may not be *in* space and time, but they are identifiable *through* space and *through* time. Thus they provide us with the stable, indefinitely identifiable subject matter that thought and discourse indeed do require. I shall, of course, return to this topic.

VI

The conclusion that there are no *enduring* material substances does not entail that there are no individual things, such as chairs, rocks, and animals, or indeed even that such things are not material. For individual things might be understood in some other way that is not affected by our reasoning. For example, they might be understood as systems of sense-data. (Cf. H. H. Price's detailed account of "families" of sense-data.)[17] They might also be understood as temporal series of momentary *material* things.* Whether the first alternative is acceptable is largely a question for the philosophy of perception, which I shall not consider in this book beyond what I said about it in chapter four. Regarding the second alternative, it suffices to point out that the materiality of momentary material things could play no role in our thought, in our singling out and identification, of them. The notion of matter is needed for our understanding of enduring individual things, not of momentary things.† The latter's qualities (including spatial and temporal relations) are completely adequate criteria for their identity. Therefore, the status of such things as

---

*This seems to be the view of philosophers such as Quine (see, for example, *The Methods of Logic*, 3d ed. [New York: Holt, Rinehart and Winston, 1972], p. 222), who speak of material things as having temporal parts. See also Nelson Goodman, *The Structure of Appearance* (Indianapolis: The Bobbs-Merrill Co., 1966), p. 128. It could be regarded also as the view of Gustav Bergmann insofar as his momentary bare particulars are best understood as momentary bits of matter. (For references to Bergmann, see chapter seven, note 13.)

†According to Aristotle, individual things must contain matter if their identity through change is to be possible. See, for example, *Metaphysics*, 1044b 22–28, *Physics*, 1, 7. Bergmann's argument for bare particulars from the demands of the problem of individuation will be considered in chapter seven.

entities would be independent of their being material. Therefore, an adequate metaphysical account of them ought not to attribute to them the possession of matter, and so they ought not to be regarded as material. Indeed, on either of these two alternatives there would be clear criteria for the identity of individual things through time. A judgment of such identity would assert that the temporal series, or the family of sense-data, to which a certain momentary material thing, or a certain sense-datum, belongs, is identical with the temporal series, or family of sense-data, to which a certain other momentary material thing, or sense-datum, belongs. And the criteria of identity for temporal series or for families of sense-data are quite perspicuous, being largely, though not wholly, the criteria of identity for classes.

It may be worth mentioning that the second alternative, the view that an individual thing is really a temporal series of momentary material things, a spatiotemporal "worm" divisible into "time-slices," is in no way a defense of the identity of individual things through time as they are understood by commonsense; it is a rejection of it.[18] The appeal a proponent of the view usually makes to the analogy between space and time leads precisely to the conclusion that there are no enduring things. To say that a certain individual thing is identical through the place it occupies is merely to say that its parts, each of which occupies its own place and is not identical with any other part, are so related (e.g., are spatially contiguous or move together, etc.) that we regard them as parts of one thing; it is not to say that the thing itself, as a whole, is at each place occupied by one of its parts. According to commonsense, however, the individual thing itself, the whole of it, is at each moment during its existence. To destroy a spatial part of a thing is to destroy the thing partially; to destroy a "temporal part" of a thing would be, according to commonsense, to destroy the thing completely. An enduring thing can change; a series of momentary things cannot, it is eternally fixed. If there is a spatial analogue to identity through time, that would be the identity of a quality through space, i.e., its presence in many places *as a whole*, its being a universal quality.

Eli Hirsch has argued[19] that what he calls the scheme of persistent objects and the scheme of (certain kinds of) sequences of momentary objects are equivalent, that whatever can be said in one can be said in the other, that there can be no empirical evidence in favor of one rather than the other. This is an application to a new subject of a metaphilosophical view that used to be in some vogue. (We may recall Ayer's view of realism and of the sense-datum theory as alternative languages.) As in its other applications, it ignores the sense, indeed the only sense, in which competing philosophical theories, which by hypothesis are not scientific, may be not equivalent. They convey different pictures of the world, suggest different analogies, enforce different ways of seeing the same subject matter. And one such picture, or analogy, or way of seeing, may be more adequate to the nature of that subject matter than any of its alternatives. But Hirsch also seems to suggest that what we *mean* by "the same object" in a diachronic context is the same as what we mean by "the same sequence of momentary objects." If so, he is surely mistaken. To say that a certain object at t_1 is the same as a certain object at t_2 entails that whatever is true of one is also true of the other; if one is F at t_1, then the other is also F at t_1. To say that, although not the same object, they are members of some appropriate sequence, whatever it may be, would not license such enforcement of indiscernibility; it would license the assertion that whatever is true of the series to which the one belongs is true of the series to which the other belongs, but not that whatever is true of the one member of the series is true of the other. On the first alternative we can say, for example, that one and the same thing is F at t_1 and not F at t_2. On the other alternative we cannot say this; it would not be true of any member of the sequence, and it might not be true of the sequence itself if "F" is a predicate not applicable to such things as sequences.

But in addition to the sense-datum and the momentary-material-thing views of individual identity, there is a third. An individual thing may be understood as a cluster of qualities, or at least as a temporal series of clusters of qualities. This view includes the defensible features of the second. (It need make no pretensions to agreement with commonsense.) It also includes whatever metaphysical content the first has; a sense-datum is certainly a cluster of qualities, if anything is such. Thus the rejection of the metaphysics of material substances leads to what I have called the metaphysics of qualities. Of course, the latter cannot consist in a mere assertion that there are only qualities and their clusters. The notion of a cluster of qualities is quite obscure, especially when distinguished, as of course it must be, from the notion of a mere collection or set of qualities. And, obviously, we cannot even begin to elucidate it without a prior account of the nature of qualities. The crucial question such an account must answer is whether qualities are universal or particular. Clusters of universal qualities would be quite different from clusters of particular qualities. And we shall find that the nature of the spatiotemporal structure of a world of clusters of qualities also depends on whether qualities are universal or particular.

The account of the nature of clusters of qualities, and of the nature of the spatiotemporal structure in which such clusters are embedded, is in effect an account of accidental predication as the latter would be understood in the metaphysics of qualities. What is asserted by the ordinary statement that Socrates is white is, in effect, that Socrates has a certain color and that this color is white. We have seen that the statement expresses accidental predication only in virtue of its first implicit conjunct, the second being a statement of essential predication. According to the metaphysics of qualities, Socrates may only be a cluster of qualities or a temporal series of clusters of qualities. His having a certain color may only be the inclusion of that color in that cluster, or in some or all clusters in that series. An account of accidental predication, in the metaphysics of qualities, would consist in an account of what it is for a quality to be included in a cluster.

But is not the metaphysics of qualities, to which I have said the rejection of the metaphysics of material substances leads us, also open to our general objection to the latter? Are there clear criteria of identity for qualities? I shall consider this question, usually raised when contrasting qualities with classes, with respect to the most fundamental case, the identity of a quality of one individual thing and a quality of another individual thing, in the next chapter. Regarding the opinion that, unlike attributes, "classes raise no perplexities over identity, being identical if and only if their members are identical,"[20] it should suffice here to remark that, on the basis of this opinion itself, the identity of classes would not be perplexing only if the identity of their members were not perplexing. And the latter would not be perplexing, if the members are individual things, only if the identity of attributes were not perplexing, since we have no criteria for the identity of individual things that do not include the identity of at least some of their attributes. If the members are attributes, then the dependence of the identity of the classes on the identity of attributes is direct.[21]

CHAPTER SEVEN

Qualities

I

The task before us in this and the next chapter is to develop the rudiments of a pure metaphysics of qualities, under the guidance of the protometaphysics developed earlier. As we have seen, a crucial part of this task is to provide an account of the nature of clusters of qualities. Such an account would be in effect an account of accidental predication.

I shall begin by clearing up two likely misunderstandings. First, I do indeed take for granted that there are qualities, but not that qualities are universals. If there are not material substances, how could there also not be qualities, assuming that there is anything at all? Some philosophers have attempted to avoid ontological commitment to qualities by arguing that abstract singular terms are eliminable and that general terms need not be understood as standing for entities.[1] But surely they have done so only because of their belief that qualities may only be universals (and therefore, in a never adequately explained sense, abstract and otherworldly), a belief encouraged by the absence from both ordinary language and standard logical notation of singular simple predicates, i.e., of simple predicates logically applicable to only one thing and thus capable of being regarded as standing for particular qualities. But to deny that there are qualities at all would be metaphysical madness. The shape of an individual thing is at least as obviously in the world as the individual thing itself, indeed more obviously so, if our critique of the metaphysics of material substances has been adequate. Its observability is quite unquestionable, and absolutely necessary for the observability of the individual thing.

Suppose that qualities are particular, i.e., that no two individual things can, logically, have numerically the same quality.* Abstract singular terms could then be understood as names of classes of such particular qualities, not as names of classes of the individual things that have the qualities, and so we would avoid both the motives for, and the difficulties of, the elimination of such terms. For example, to say that blue is a color would be to say that a certain class of particular qualities (namely, those called blue) is included in a certain other class of particular qualities (namely, those called colors). And the use of general terms could be understood as serving to express membership of an individual thing's particular quality in a class of particular qualities. For example, to say that *a* is blue would be to say that *a* has a particular quality that is a member of a certain class of particular qualities, namely, those called blue. If there are difficulties with this analysis, they arise out of the supposition that qualities are particular, not out of the acceptance of the existence of qualities. One special difficulty, pointed out by Nicholas Wolterstorff,[2] namely, that all uninstantiated qualities would then be identical, since each would be identical with the null class, is in reality a difficulty for the supposition that there are *uninstantiated* particular qualities. This supposition is hardly intelligible and in any case has no plausibility whatever, even though the supposition that there are uninstantiated *universal* qualities is, I believe, both intelligible and defensible.†

---

*If we do not wish to employ the notion of an individual thing in explaining what is meant by "a particular quality," and if we count places and times as qualities, then we can say that a quality is particular if it cannot, logically, be together with two or more qualities belonging to the same category; e.g., a color would be particular if it cannot be together with two shapes, or two places, or two times, etc., and a time (place) would be particular if it cannot be together with two places (times), or two colors, or two shapes, etc. Cf. Nelson Goodman, *The Structure of Appearance*, pp. 249–50.

†I defend it in *Resemblance and Identity*, pp. 183–97.

The second likely misunderstanding is that when we ask whether qualities are universal or particular we are asking for an account of the meaning of general terms.[3] But we are not. We may agree that the ordinary use of a general term, though not arbitrary, is governed by what Wittgenstein called family re- semblances rather than by association with a universal quality or with a class of particular qualities all of which resemble each other in the same way. But to ask whether qualities are universal or particular is to ask whether a quality of one individual thing and a quality of another individual thing can be identical, and this is not a question about general words or about language at all. Indeed, in many cases (e.g., those involving unusual shapes), we can ask this question and answer it even if we do not possess a sufficiently specific general word for the qualities.

It may be remarked in this connection that the greater is the extent to which general terms are used in accordance with family resemblances, the wider is the gap between thought and lan- guage. For, even if our uses of words can, our *concepts* cannot be understood in terms of family resemblances, assuming that by a concept we mean a principle of recognition or, generally, of classification. An indeterminate network of family resemblances cannot constitute such a principle. This is why the more obvious it is that a certain word (e.g., "game") is used in accordance with family resemblances, the less willing we are to speak of a con- cept (e.g., of the concept of game), to use the word for serious classificatory purposes, to speak of *recognizing* something as an object of the application of the word (e.g., as a game). Similar remarks may be made regarding so-called vague and inexact predicates, the existence of which is sometimes taken to be a reason for denying the law of excluded middle.[4] Words (or their uses) may be vague or inexact, and sometimes the application of a word to something may be neither correct nor incorrect. But there can be no vague or inexact concepts, and the subsumption of something under a given concept is either correct or incorrect. For example, that the application of the word "blue" to a certain peculiar shade is neither correct nor incorrect does not entail that we have a certain color-concept such that the shade is neither subsumable nor not subsumable under that concept. Any concept relevant to this case would be one in terms of which we can recognize shades of color. And there is no such thing as our neither recognizing nor failing to recognize a certain shade, although there is such a thing as a word that neither clearly applies nor clearly fails to apply to a certain shade. If there are cases in which the application of the word "blue" is indeterminate, this shows that there is no one concept expressed by the word, not that there is an indeterminate concept. Unlike a word, a concept must either clearly apply to a given thing or clearly fail to apply to it; just as a property must either belong to a given thing or fail to belong to it, even though the corresponding predicate may, in some cases, neither clearly apply nor clearly fail to apply. We must not lose sight of the enormous difference between language, on one hand, and thought and the world, on the other.*

II

Ordinarily we have no doubt that the concept of identity is applicable to qualities of distinct individual things. We feel no hesitation in speaking of things having, for example, the same

---

*My distinction between a word (or the use of a word) and a concept is parallel to, though hardly the same as, Gilbert Ryle's important and still insufficiently appreciated distinction between the *usage* of a word and the *use* of the word. (See his "Ordinary Language," *The Philosophical Review* 62 [1953], reprinted in *Ordinary Language*, ed. V. C. Chappell [Englewood Cliffs: Prentice-Hall, 1964]). He writes, "[. . . the] appeal to prevalence is philosophically pointless, besides being philologically risky. What is wanted is, perhaps, the extraction of the logical rules implicitly governing a concept, i.e., a way of operating with an expression (or any other expression that does the same work)" (p. 33 in Chappell). Earlier, Ryle points out that "A usage is a custom, practice, fashion or vogue" (p. 31), which, in the case of words, is of interest to philologists, and that a use is "a way of operating with something" (p. 31). I discuss the notion of the use of an expression, as distinguished from its usage, in *Resemblance and Identity*, pp. 87–94.

shape or the same color. Of course, this is not enough. There must also be criteria, in the sense of logically sufficient conditions, for the correctness of such speech. Indeed, it often happens, especially in the case of perceptible qualities, that the criteria cannot be stated nontautologically (even if the empirical evidence for their satisfaction can be). For example, to say that the color of this page is (exactly) the same as the color of the next page if and only if they do not differ as qualities would be to utter a tautology. So would be to offer as a criterion in the case of chromatic colors the fact that they have the same hue and degrees of saturation and brightness; and even such a tautology seems unavailable regarding judgments of the identity of the hues or degrees themselves. In this respect, the identity of at least some qualities of distinct individual things is like an experience's being a pain. There are criteria for the application of the word "pain" to an experience, but they cannot be stated nontautologically (even though, at least in the case of other persons, the evidence for their satisfaction can be). As I have observed earlier, in such cases it is better to speak of something's being a paradigm of the application of a concept, rather than of its satisfying the criteria for such an application. We may say that in these cases the criterion for the application of the concept to a certain thing is the thing (e.g., the identity, or the property of being a pain) itself. There can be no question that there are such criteria; if there were not, thought and language would be impossible.

That there are criteria, in our broad but exacting sense of this term, for the application of the concept of identity to qualities of diverse individual things is evident. We can attach no sense to the supposition that even though certain qualities of some diverse things are as we perceive them to be, they are not identical. Again, a likely example would be the color of this page and the color of the next page. The idea that although they are as we perceive them to be (i.e., we are not victims of a perceptual illusion) they are not identical has no content. There is nothing here that is analogous to the possibility of the annihilation of one material substance and the creation of another, qualitatively indistinguishable and spatiotemporally continuous substance. It makes no sense to suppose that even God can make the color of this page and the color of the next page nonidentical, as long as they are as we perceive them to be. But it makes perfectly good sense to suppose that the page I now see is not identical with the page I saw a moment ago, even if we take for granted that they are exactly as they are perceived.

The unquestionable existence of genuine criteria of identity for at least some qualities is the source of the strength of the metaphysics of qualities. And it is but an aspect of what originally attracted the seventeenth- and eighteenth-century philosophers to the metaphysics of qualities: the fact that, unlike material substances, at least some qualities are completely transparent intellectually, contain nothing hidden, possess a character that is wholly open to us.

But the above should not be regarded as a sufficient argument for the view that qualities are universals. Although the application of the concept of identity to qualities of diverse individual things often satisfies genuine criteria and sometimes is even paradigmatic, there is a *philosophical* reason for rejecting it. Let me explain.

x satisfies the (a) criterion for being F only if, given that it is as we take it to be (e.g., we are not misled by perceptual appearances), it follows logically necessarily that it is F, we cannot conceive of it as not being F, we cannot intelligibly suppose that it is not F. But the inconceivability of x's not being F must not be confused with the inconceivability of a *philosophical* reason for denying that it is F. For such a reason may be systematic and revisionist in nature. It may be the belief, perhaps motivated by the existence of conflicts between the application of the concept F to x and the application to x of other concepts regarded as incompatible with F, that a different concept, or even a different conceptual scheme, is preferable.

Of course, a philosopher may deny that x satisfies the (a) criterion for being F without (explicitly or implicitly) proposing a revision of the concept F. He may simply claim that x's not being F is in fact quite conceivable. This he would do presumably by providing counterexamples to the applicability of the concept F to x, i.e., by imagining and describing in detail cases in which we would not apply the concept F to x, in which we would not regard x as F, even though no revision of the concept is proposed or covertly performed.

This is why the appeal to criteria in philosophy, though ultimately decisive and unavoidable, is not a simple matter. First, we must distinguish the question whether x satisfies the (a) criterion for the application of the concept F from the question whether the word "F" is standardly applied to x. A word may be standardly applied to something even though its applicability is far from being logically necessary, even though it is perfectly conceivable that its application should be false. Second, we must distinguish the question whether we are denying that it is inconceivable that x should be not F from the question whether, admitting that this is inconceivable, we are denying the adequacy of the conceptual scheme, or at least of the concept F, in terms of which it is inconceivable.

We must keep these two distinctions in mind when we consider whether there are criteria for the identity of certain alleged entities, even whether certain situations involving these entities constitute paradigms of identity. Indeed, as we shall see in Appendix B, there can be no question regarding the adequacy of the general concept of identity (and, derivatively, of that of existence). But from this it does not follow that it is in fact applicable to certain situations in which it is standardly applied, or that there cannot be philosophical reasons for denying its applicability even to certain paradigmatic situations to which it is applied.

In the case of the application of the concept of identity to qualities of diverse individual things there are such philosophical reasons. Such identity seems to conflict with the most fundamental necessary condition for the application of that concept, namely, the indiscernibility of identicals. This is why there is a philosophical problem of universals. This is why most philosophers have denied that qualities are universals, even though such a denial involves a major conceptual revision.

The conflict is explicitly the hub of the controversy between G. F. Stout and G. E. Moore regarding the existence of universals.[5] Stout argued that the qualities of individual things have location in space, namely, the location of the individual things that exemplify them. Since diverse contemporaneous individual things have diverse spatial locations, the location of the qualities of one individual thing is diverse from the location of the qualities of any other contemporaneous individual thing. And, if we assume that it is logically possible for noncontemporaneous things to have been contemporaneous, it seems to follow by an immediate application of the principle of the indiscernibility of identicals that no qualities of diverse individual things can be identical, and thus, by definition, that no qualities are universals. Moore, on the other hand, argued that qualities do not, strictly speaking, have location in space; to say that a quality has a certain location is only to say that it is exemplified by an individual thing that has that location. He concluded, in effect, that since the only respect in which it can be plausibly held that every quality of one individual thing is discernible from each quality of every other individual thing is in fact not a genuine respect of discernibility, there are no grounds for denying that qualities of diverse individual things can be identical, and thus for denying that qualities are universals.

It should be remarked that while the issue arises in a particularly sharp form with respect to the qualities of *spatial* things, it is not limited to these. The apparent distinctness, and thus the apparent discernibility,* of the qualities of diverse spatial things is striking, especially in the case of shape and color, because the

---

*I hope the reader will recall the account of the connection between the notions of identity and indiscernibility in chapter three.

real distinctness of spatial things is striking—and the latter is striking because it consists primarily in their possession of distinct spatial locations. The apparent distinctness of the qualities of (whether real or imaginary) nonspatial individual things, e.g., angels, is not striking, because the real distinctness of such individual things is not striking, and this is not striking because our conception of them as individual things is unclear.* In any case, if the qualities of spatial individuals are universals, there would be no reason for denying that the qualities of nonspatial individuals are also universals. On the other hand, if the qualities of spatial individuals are not universals, then there would be no reason for supposing that the qualities of nonspatial individuals are universals. We shall follow Stout and Moore, therefore, and limit our discussion to the qualities of spatial individuals.

The issue also arises particularly clearly with respect to the *perceptible* qualities of individual things, but, again, it is not limited to them. It applies to any qualities of any individual things of which we can form a clear conception. For example, the unobservable particles of physics, insofar as we have a clear conception of them, are presumably individual things possessing qualities. Whether they are to be understood as mere clusters of their qualities and whether their qualities are universals are questions that differ from the corresponding questions about perceptible individual things and their perceptible qualities only in having a far less clear, far less intuitive subject matter.†

---

*Aquinas held that angels can differ as individuals only if they differ in species.

†Hilary Putnam has argued ("On Properties," in *Essays in Honor of Carl G. Hempel*, ed. N. Rescher [Dordrecht: Reidel, 1969]) that quantification over *properties* is indispensable in science. But, as we have seen, it follows from this that science is committed to the existence of *universals* only if the logically prior and quite independent philosophical question whether properties (qualities) are universals, rather than particulars, has been given an affirmative answer. In "The Elements of Being," *The Review of Metaphysics* 6 (1953): 3–18, 171–93, Donald C. Williams describes three lollipops, each of which is "partially similar to each other and partially different from it," and adds: "If we can give a good account of this circumstance in this affair we shall have the instrument to expose the anatomy of everything, from an electron or an apple to archangels and the World

I should also remark that there is no impropriety in stating the problem of universals as a question about the qualities of individual things without providing a prior account of the nature of an individual thing. The fact about the perceptible qualities of spatial individual things that gives rise to the problem, namely, their apparent spatial discernibility even when apparently identical, remains a fact regardless of what account of individual things we eventually offer. The metaphysics of material substances and the metaphysics of qualities, in all of their varieties, face essentially the same problem of universals. But, as we shall see, how the problem is solved does affect directly the specific account the metaphysics of qualities would offer of the nature of individual things.

III

Was Stout or Moore right? It seems clear to me that Stout's fundamental premise, that the qualities of spatial individual things have spatial location, namely, the location of the things whose qualities they are, is true. Indeed, as he observed, if it were not true then the localizability of individual things themselves would be impossible. For how can we tell where a certain individual thing is if not by where we perceive (or in some other manner detect) its qualities? Moreover, the premise is phenomenologically obvious. We perceive qualities as being at certain places even if we do not perceive them as being qualities of certain individual things. For example, especially if we are painters or interior decorators, we can see red here and blue there even if we completely ignore the fact that there is a red individual thing here and a blue individual thing there. Therefore, clearly, Moore was wrong if he meant that to say that a

All" (p. 4). On the previous page he had remarked that " . . . one example ought for our present theme to be as good as another," and stated his view that "First philosophy, according to the traditional schedule, is analytic ontology, examining the traits necessary to whatever is, in this or any other possible world."

quality has a certain location is to say that a certain individual thing that has the quality has that location. On the other hand, if he meant that since qualities are universals and therefore capable of multiple location it would be appropriate to deny them location in space at all, on the grounds that what has multiple location would be more properly described as not having location at all, then he might have been right but would have begged the question against Stout. He should first have shown that qualities are universals, and met Stout's argument for the opposite conclusion in some other way.

But while Stout's fundamental premise seems obviously true, his conclusion does not follow. (Conversely, I shall in effect argue, Moore's fundamental premise is false, but the conclusion is true.) A quality may have spatial location and, moreover, be located wherever it is exemplified, but its location may be *multiple*, namely at all places where the diverse individual things exemplifying it are located. Indeed, *individual things* cannot have multiple spatial location at the same time. But why should we suppose that this is true also of their qualities?* I suggest that there is no satisfactory reason to be given in support of this supposition and therefore that Stout's argument fails, even though his fundamental premise is true. He could, of course, have not simply appealed to the fact that qualities have spatial location but also claimed that the qualities of diverse individual things have *diverse* spatial locations. But this now would have begged the question against Moore. If the color of *a* is identical with the color of *b*, then of course it is located both where *a* is and where *b* is.

The fact is that Stout's general reason for denying that there are universals was nothing more than what I have called the apparent distinctness of those qualities of diverse individuals that we ordinarily describe as identical, the fact that to say that the one is

---

*This supposition has played a crucial role in philosophy ever since Plato's *Parmenides*.

identical with the other is not to say that it is identical with itself, that for the one to be at a certain place is not quite the same as for the other to be at that place, that seeing the one is not quite the same as seeing the other, that naming the one is not quite the same as naming the other, that believing something about the one is not quite the same as believing it about the other, i.e., all the facts about the qualities in question that would require us to say that even though identical they appear distinct. But, as we have seen, this is true of *all* cases of material identity. It is because of the apparent distinctness of such qualities that there can be a *problem* of universals, that one can intelligibly even if wrongly suppose that they do have diverse spatial locations and thus that they are not identical. And it is this apparent distinctness that a view such as Moore's ignores by in effect analyzing the relationship between such qualities as a case of *formal* identity, thus rendering the existence of philosophical disagreement about universals incomprehensible. But just as from the identity of two qualities it does not follow that they do not appear to be distinct, so from the apparent distinctness of two qualities it does not follow that they are really distinct. Unlike both Moore and Stout, we must seek the solution of the problem of universals in considerations that do not purport to make the solution, whether Moore's or Stout's, self-evidently true. Our account of material identity in chapters one and two makes such a solution possible.

The problem of universals is the question whether a quality of one individual thing can (logically) be the same entity as a quality of another individual thing. Let us label the sort of fact about certain qualities that, rightly or wrongly, we may be inclined to (and in ordinary discourse usually do) describe as sameness or identity, "recurrence of qualities." Now a philosopher who denies that there are universals may not merely appeal to the apparent distinctness of recurrent qualities. He must also provide an account of the fact of the recurrence of qualities, an account that is a genuine alternative to that given in terms of identity. Obviously, he must regard the recurrence of qualities as a sort of relation between distinct, particular qualities; no other logical possibility is open to one who holds that qualities are particulars and yet acknowledges the fact of the recurrence of some, but not other, qualities. And he also must hold that the relation in question is that expressed in ordinary language by the verb "resemble" or its synonyms (such as "is like," "is similar to," "matches"), i.e., that it is the relation of resemblance; ordinary thought contains no other suitable concept for the required relation, and on such fundamental topics we must, at least initially, employ only concepts we already possess. If the Resemblance Theory, i.e., the account of the recurrence of qualities in terms of a relation of resemblance, is unacceptable, then there would seem to be no alternative to the Identity Theory, to the account in terms of identity, to the view that qualities are universals. For, as we have seen, the chief argument against the latter, namely, the apparent distinctness of the qualities it holds to be identical, is not conclusive, and the theory derives ample independent support from the fact that in ordinary discourse the recurrence of qualities is a *paradigm* of identity.

IV

Bertrand Russell argued that the Resemblance Theory is not a genuine alternative to the Identity Theory because, if it is to avoid an infinite regress, it must allow for the existence of at least one universal, namely, the relation of resemblance; and once the possibility of universals is in this way granted no reason seems to remain for denying that all qualities are universals.[6]

But must the Resemblance Theory really allow that the relation of resemblance is itself a universal? Its appeal to this relation may be understood in three ways. First, it serves the purely ontological function of providing an account of the recurrence of qualities. For example, the recurrence of blue color in the individual things A and B would be accounted for as the presence of a particular relation of resemblance between the particular color of A, say, a, and the particular color of B, say, b. To be sure, this relation would itself be related by a particular resemblance relation to every other particular resemblance relation. If we use "R" as short for "resemblance" and add to it superscripts to signify orders of resemblance relations (i.e., to distinguish between resemblances between qualities, resemblances between resemblances between qualities, resemblances between resemblances between resemblances between qualities, etc.) and subscripts to designate particular relations of resemblance within the same order, then we can call two particular first-order resemblance relations R_1^1 and R_2^1, and their resemblance R_1^2. If we allow for cross-resemblances, i.e., resemblances between resemblances of different orders, then we may designate, for example, the relation between R_1^1 and R_1^2, as $R_1^{(1,2)}$. Now, it would follow that there is an infinite number of particular relations of resemblance from either one of the following assumptions: (1) there is an infinite number of resembling monadic qualities, and (2) there are at least two first-order resemblances, there is no highest order of relations of resemblance, and there are no restrictions on cross-resemblances.

If only the first assumption is granted, an infinite number of particular relations of resemblance would be no more paradoxical than an infinite number of individual things in space. If the second assumption is granted, the infinite number of particular relations of resemblance would be as puzzling or intellectually discomfiting as the infinite divisibility of space. On neither of the assumptions would the Resemblance Theory be involved in a *vicious* infinite regress.

Second, the appeal to a relation of resemblance may be understood as part of an account of the meaning of general terms. (This is, in fact, how Russell seems to have understood it.) To say that a is F, it would be held, is correct only if a resembles (to a specifiable degree or in a specific way) b (or $b, c, d \ldots$ at least as closely as these resemble each other[7]), where b (or also $c, d \ldots$) is a paradigm of the application of the term "F," e.g., is F by "ostensive definition." Since "resemble" is itself a general term, a similar condition would be necessary for *its* correct application, *if it were to be applied.* For example, to say that $R_i^1(a,b)$ would be correct only if R_i^1 resembles (let us call this particular resemblance R_i^2) R_2^1, R_2^1 being a paradigm of the application of the term "resemble." And if we were to say that $R_i^2(R_1^1, R_2^1)$, then this would be correct only if R_i^2 resembles (let us call this particular resemblance R_i^3) R_2^2, R_2^2 being a paradigm of second-order resemblance. We are faced with an infinite regress. But, again, there is nothing vicious about it. At worst, it too is like the infinite divisibility of space, and certainly is only potential. For one may say correctly that *a* is F even if one does not say (perhaps cannot say, because of limitations of one's vocabulary) that *a* resembles *b*. And certainly one can use "resemble" to assert that there are certain two first-order resemblances without also asserting that there is a second-order resemblance between these first-order resemblances. The correct application of a general term may presuppose, have as a necessary condition, that a certain resemblance holds, but it neither constitutes an assertion to the effect that this resemblance holds nor requires that such an assertion be made, or even be capable of being made with our actual vocabulary.

Third, the appeal to a relation of resemblance may be epistemological in nature. It may be part of the justification one must be able to provide for one's application of a general term, including the term "resemble," in any particular case, if one is to know (or at least rationally believe) that the term is applicable in that particular case. To know that *a* is F would require, in part, that one know, say, that $R_i^1(a,b)$; to know that $R_i^1(a,b)$ would require, in part, that one know, say, that $R_i^2(R_1^1, R_2^1)$, etc. It would seem that now a vicious infinite regress is unavoidable. But in fact the argument depends on equivocation. Knowing what something is, is not the same as knowing what to call it. If one knows that *a* is F one may, but need not, also know that the *word* "F" is applicable to *a*. A dog may know that someone is his master, and a child may know that lemons are unpleasant tasting, without the possession of a relevant, or indeed any, vocabulary. One's knowing that a certain surface is octagonal may be *accompanied* by knowing that the word "octagonal" is the correct word for its shape, but *consists* only in knowing how many sides the shape has, perhaps on the basis of having counted the sides correctly. Now a person may know that *a* is F, even if he does not know that *a* resembles *b*, *b* being the paradigm for the application of "F," for to know that *a* is F he need not know that "F" is the correct word for *a*. And he may know that "F" is the correct word for *a* because he knows that *a* resembles *b* and that *b* is the paradigm for the application of "F," even if he does not know that "resemble" is the right word for the relation between *a* and *b* that legitimizes his application of "F" to *a*. And in the case of higher-order resemblances he would almost certainly not express his grounds for knowledge in language, if for no other reason than that he would lack the required vocabulary.

I conclude that Russell's argument against the Resemblance Theory is unsuccessful.* I shall now state what I believe is a successful argument against it.[8]

V

The Identity Theory requires no explanation, but only defense, since it uses a well-established concept, governed by paradigms in a variety of both qualitative and nonqualitative contexts, and simply endorses what we ordinarily take for granted, that this concept is applicable to some qualities of distinct indi-

---

*Infinite regress arguments, analogous to those we have discussed, may also be offered against the Identity Theory, and my response to them would parallel that made to such arguments against the Resemblance Theory. In his "Infinite Regress Arguments and the Problem of Universals," *Australasian Journal of Philosophy* 52 (1974): 191–201, D. M. Armstrong charges that all theories of universals are involved in one sort or another of an infinite regress, but offers, as far as I can see, no defense of his claim that these regresses are in fact vicious.

vidual things. Not so with the Resemblance Theory. The concept of resemblance has nonderivative application only to such qualities. (A so-called resemblance between individual things is nothing but a resemblance between some of their qualities.) Before it is defended, the Resemblance Theory must be explained. What exactly does it assert, if not, although in different words, the same as what the Identity Theory asserts? How does resemblance of qualities differ from identity of qualities? The explanation cannot be guided by the application of the concept of resemblance in nonqualitative contexts, as an explanation of the identity of qualities could be guided by the application of the concept of identity in nonqualitative contexts. For, unlike the concept of identity, the concept of resemblance has no such application. What other alternative is there? I suggest that the only alternative left is to show that the concept of resemblance, though applicable only in qualitative contexts, is a species of a more general and already quite unquestionable concept that is both different from and incompatible with the concept of identity. Indeed, as we have seen, the Resemblance Theory does adopt this alternative. The more general concept it appeals to is that of a relation, and it answers our question by claiming that resemblance is a relation. Thus, the Resemblance Theory does not merely deny the existence of universals. It purports, as it must, to offer an *account* of the recurrence of qualities; if it did not do so, it would not be a philosophical theory but a mere reformulation, a blind terminological stipulation. It offers such an account in terms of a relation of resemblance. To be successful, (1) this account must be logically coherent and perspicuous, and (2) its description of a case of recurrence of qualities must be a genuine alternative to the description of the case in terms of qualitative identity, it must not be reducible to or in any other way dependent on the account in terms of universals. I shall argue that necessary condition (1) can be satisfied only if necessary condition (2) is not satisfied.

Initially, the Resemblance Theory may be taken as claiming

simply that a case of the recurrence of qualities is an ordinary dyadic relational fact, adequately describable in statements of the form R(x,y), e.g., "The color of this page resembles the color of the next page." But this claim is easily seen to be false. The fact is that resemblance statements of that form are logically incomplete (even though the contexts in which they are made often disguise this fact), in the precise sense that as they stand they have no determinate truth-value, that there are no sufficient or necessary conditions for their truth. For example, for the color of this page and the color of the next page to resemble each other, must they resemble exactly, or almost exactly, or just in that both are white, or just in that both are colors, rather than say a color and a shape, or perhaps even just in that both are qualities, rather than say a quality and an individual thing? The fact that since the subject terms of the statement are definite descriptions including the word "color" some of these possibilities are foreclosed merely suggests how the Resemblance Theory should be revised and does not constitute a defense of it. To be adequate, the theory must be capable of offering logically complete descriptions of the recurrence of qualities in which only proper names or demonstratives occur as subject terms. It must be capable of determining the truth-conditions of a statement such as "*a* resembles *b*" when "*a*" and "*b*" are introduced ostensively as proper names of, respectively, the color of this page and the color of the next page.

The difficulty may seem avoidable by the inclusion in the resemblance statement of a specification of the resemblance. Russell, for example, suggested that this be done by means of such verbs as "color-resemble" (and presumably even verbs such as "this-specific-shade-of-color-resemble"). He might have said, for example, that *a* color-resembles *b*. An equivalent and more familiar way of achieving the needed specification would be to say that *a* and *b* resemble in respect of color. Such resemblance statements are, of course, logically coherent and complete. But they fail to be genuine, clear alternatives to the corresponding identity statements. For are they not merely verbose rewordings of "*a* and *b* are the same color"? (*a* and *b*, we must not forget, are the colors of the two pages, not the pages themselves.) Of course, the resemblance theorist would claim that the specification, whether achieved in Russell's or in the usual way, does not involve reference to a universal, to a qualitative identity, but only makes explicit the specific kind of resemblance relation that is asserted, somewhat as someone's family relation to another person may be specified by describing it as the relation of being his brother or first cousin. But, clearly, even if there are species of the relation of resemblance, the specification in question does not specify the relation itself, but rather the *terms* between which it holds. It is like the specification of a relation of being a sibling as the relation of being a brother, rather than like the specification of a relation of being a cousin as the relation of being a first cousin. We do not have independent notions of specific kinds of a relation of resemblance; what we do have is independent notions of specific kinds of the relata such a relation may have, e.g., colors. Perhaps the Resemblance Theory so modified does not presuppose the Identity Theory, but neither does it offer a clear alternative to it.

But logically complete resemblance statements are possible without the above sort of specification. They have the form "x resembles y more than w resembles z." (If $x = w$, then the statement would usually be abbreviated to one of the form "x resembles y more than z.")[9] On the assumption that the resemblance asserted is not derivative from more fundamental resemblances, such statements are logically complete. (By more fundamental resemblances here I mean resemblances between various components of x, y, w, and z, or resemblances between certain relations of x, y, w, and z to some other things. The assumption eliminates cases such as x's resembling y more than z in that the hue of x resembles the hue of y more than the hue of z, even though x resembles z more than y in that x's degree of brightness resembles z's degree of brightness more than y's degree of brightness; or cases such as crimson's resembling green more than pink in that crimson and green, but not pink, are among Mary's favorite colors.)

But while such statements are logically complete, they are puzzling. They are not direct assertions of the holding of a relation of resemblance; rather, they are assertions of the holding of a relation of difference in degree between two instances of resemblance. If *a* resembles *b* more than *c* resembles *d*, a relation of resemblance may be coherently supposed to hold only between *a* and *b*, and again between *c* and *d*, not among all four as a genuine tetradic relation might. But we have seen that it cannot be supposed to hold between *a* and *b*, or between *c* and *d*, because if it could, the statements "*a* resembles *b*" and "*c* resembles *d*" would themselves be logically complete, which they are not. Yet it must be capable of holding between *a* and *b*, and again between *c* and *d*, if the statement "*a* resembles *b* more than *c* resembles *d*" is to be both logically coherent and understood in accordance with the Resemblance Theory. For this statement presupposes or entails that its two component propositional clauses ("*a* resembles *b*" and "*c* resembles *d*") *are* true, and would be logically coherent only if they *could* be true, if they have a truth-value. This means that if it is logically coherent this statement cannot be asserting the holding of a relation of difference in degree between two instances of the relation of resemblance. But there is nothing else it could be asserting that involves a relation of resemblance, that would accord with the Resemblance Theory. Therefore, its content must be understood as drastically different from what the Resemblance Theory claims it to be.

Let me explain this with two comparisons. What the resemblance theorist would wish is that a statement such as "*a* resembles *b* more than *c* resembles *d*" be understood as similar to a statement such as "*a* loves *b* more than *c* loves *d*." But the two statements are fundamentally dissimilar. Indeed, the latter does assert a relation of difference in degree, namely, one holding between two instances of the relation of loving, rather than directly a relation of loving. (The relation of loving holds between a and b, and again between c and d, not among all four as if it were a tetradic relation.) But the component propositional clauses, which the statement presupposes or entails and which therefore must be capable of being true, of having a truth-value, if the statement is to be logically coherent, are logically complete, perfectly capable of being true, very much in possession of a truth-value. And in this crucial respect they are totally unlike the component propositional clauses of the resemblance statement.

In fact the statement "a resembles b more than c resembles d" is similar not to "a loves b more than c loves d" but to "a is farther from b than c is from d" (i.e., "a is far from b more than c is far from d"). Statements of the form "x is far from y" are logically incomplete, just like statements of the form "x resembles y." They have no determinate truth-value; there are no sufficient or necessary conditions for their truth. (How far must x be from y in order to be far from y?) We would hardly suppose that they assert the holding of a relation of being-far-from between x and y. And to be rendered complete they must be expanded into statements of the form "x is farther from y than w is from z" (or "x is farther from y than from z," if $x = w$). But it is clear that neither do statements of this latter form assert the holding of a relation of difference in degree between two instances of a relation of being-far-from. What they assert is quite different: that the *distance* between x and y (whether short or long, and whether understood as the straight line connecting x and y or in some other way) is greater than the distance between w and z. Once this is understood, the phantom of a relation of being-far-from disappears and what replaces it is two distances and a relation between them.

Now what would be the analogous replacement of the alleged relation of resemblance? The Identity Theorist would suggest that we cannot even think of a serious alternative to the following answer. To say that two qualities resemble each other is to say that they are identical, whether specifically or generically, that they are the same universal, whether specific (determinate) or generic (determinable). And to say that they resemble more than certain other two qualities resemble would be to say that the universal they are is of lesser generality than the universal the latter are.

It may seem that this suggestion gains us nothing. Is not "*a* and *b* are the same universal" logically incomplete just as "*a* and *b* resemble each other" is, and for the same reason? May not the universal in question be as specific as a certain shade of white and as general as being-a-quality? But there is a fundamental difference between the two cases. "*a* and *b* are the same universal" can be completed in a way entirely consonant with the Identity Theory by simply naming the universal, by adding, e.g., that it is this specific shade of white or that it is the (generic) color white. But, as we have seen, a similar completion of the resemblance statement (e.g., "*a* resembles *b* in that both are white" or "*a* color-resembles *b*") either presupposes, or at least does not issue in a clear alternative to, the Identity Theory.

It may be suggested that resemblance statements of the form "*x* resembles *y* more than *z*" can be understood in terms of quality-orders.[10] Certain qualities, e.g., colors, can be ordered in series, whether discrete or continuous, and thus we can speak of one quality being between two other qualities; the ordering relation can be darker-than, higher-in-pitch-than, warmer-than, etc. It may seem plausible now that to say that a quality *a* resembles a quality *b* more than a third quality *c* is to say that *b* is between *a* and *c* in a certain quality order. Indeed, it seems just false that every resemblance statement of the above form presupposes an appropriate quality-order. In saying that a certain shade of pink resembles a certain other shade of pink more than a certain shade of green, neither is one ordinarily appealing to the positions of the three shades in some order of colors nor need one be even aware of the possibility of such an order. And in comparing gustatory or olfactory qualities we ordinarily do not appeal to orders: usually it would be doubtful that there is a relevant order at all. Nevertheless, such observations cannot be a decisive refutation of the suggestion. What does refute it, I believe, is the fact that the ordinary terminology of resemblances is applicable to the elements of a quality-order not because of the relation of qualitative betweenness, but because the dyadic ordering relation, e.g., darker-than, that generates the order in terms of which the relation of betweenness would be defined, *recurs* and thus constitutes just the sort of fact that in ordinary language would be described with the terminology of resemblance or, alternatively, with that of qualitative identity. Let us consider an order of shades in which *a* is darker than *b*, *b* is darker than *c*, and *b* therefore can be said to be between *a* and *c*. It would be natural to say also that *a* resembles *b* more than *c*. Why? I suggest that the reason is that *a* and *b* have something in common that *a* and *c* do not have, namely, the relation of being darker than *c*, and not simply and directly because of any betweenness relation among *a*, *b*, and *c*. Indeed, there is such a relation of betweenness in a quality-order. But it is the recurrence of the generating relation, not the consequent betweenness, that is appropriately described as resemblance. And if there is not a relation of resemblance, then, I suggest, such recurrence could only be the presence in several quality pairs of one and the same relational universal.

The conclusion I believe we should reach is that the Resemblance Theory either presupposes the Identity Theory or fails to offer a clear alternative to it, or is forced to appeal to logically incomplete or logically incoherent statements. I believe also that this means that we ought to accept the Identity Theory, that we ought to hold that the qualities of individual things are universals.

VI

We sought a solution of the problem of universals not for its own sake but in order to determine the fundamental nature of the world, the nature it would share with all possible worlds. Is the world then a mere collection or set of universals, given that it consists ultimately only of qualities and that all qualities are universals? Surely not. Even a world of Platonic Forms would not be a mere collection of Forms. The Forms would mix, as Plato points out in the *Sophist*, and this is why it would make sense to speak of them as constituting a world. Presumably, the mixing in question would constitute what contemporary philosophers call states of affairs or facts. This is why there is a point to saying that a world is a totality of facts, not of things, even though a fact consists of things and therefore so does the world. It is this mixing of its ultimate constituents that would provide such a world with structure, with unity, and thus distinguish it from a mere collection of Forms.

But a world of Platonic Forms would consist only of entities as such, not of objects. Neither it nor any of its constituents would be a possible object of perception or imagination or thought. Such a world is inconceivable. In fact, the only sort of world we find conceivable is one that results from the mixture of qualities that enter in the fabric of space and time, the sort of mixture that produces individual things, even though these must be understood as mere mixtures, or as we have called them clusters, of qualities, rather than as the things of commonsense. For it is only as constituents of individual things that qualities can be singled out in perception, imagination, or thought, i.e., can be objects and not merely entities.

Consequently, the general question before us now is, how can universal qualities constitute a spatiotemporal world of individual things? And there are three specific questions. First, can individual things really consist only of qualities, can they be mere clusters of qualities, as the metaphysics of qualities requires? Second, what is the nature of this clustering, or, as it has sometimes been called, togetherness, of qualities? Third, are space and time themselves qualities (presumably, relations)? If they are, how exactly are they to be understood, what is the nature of *their* clustering, or togetherness, with individual things, and how can they have the unity that is rightly emphasized by the absolutist conception of space and time? If they are not, does this not require that we abandon the metaphysics of qualities? I shall argue that these questions can be answered adequately only on the basis of the distinction between objects and entities. I shall consider them in the above order, the first in this chapter, the second and third in the next.

But before I do so I want to stress that the above three questions, especially the second, arise even for the view according to which qualities are particular, not universal. As long as particular qualities are regarded as entities (if they are not, if they are "particular" only qua objects, then the view becomes indistinguishable from that according to which they are universal), their togetherness in an individual thing must also be accounted for. Mere appeal to their having the same spatial and temporal relations, or to their entering in some special relation with each other, would be insufficient. Relations are presumably themselves together with their relata, and thus this togetherness must itself be accounted for. Indeed, G. F. Stout argued that "A sneeze is certainly particular. . . . But it is also a character predicable of something else, the particular man who sneezes. It has its being only in its concrescence with the other qualities and relations of the concrete individual while he is sneezing. The sneeze cannot continue to exist in however altered a form apart from the sneezer, as a hand or eye may when severed from the body."[11] Essentially the same view has recently been defended by D. C. Long, who argues that since a particular quality can be identified only by reference to its owner, it is logically impossible for it to have another owner, and thus that the question of its togetherness with its owner's other qualities does not arise.[12] But if so, the question that does then arise concerns the sense, if any, in which the quality is an *entity* at all, the sense in which *it* is identifiable, even if not independently of its owner.

Now, to the first question. It has been argued by Gustav Bergmann[13] that the individuation of numerically distinct individual things requires that they contain, in addition to their universal qualities, a nonqualitative element, namely, a bare particular. Such an element is described as bare in order to signify that it is not a quality ("has no nature"), and as a particular in order to signify that no two individual things can share it. The argument for the existence of bare particulars may be stated as follows: Suppose that there are two momentary individual things existing at the same time, such as two spots, a and b, which have exactly the same monadic qualities. By hypothesis, they do not differ in respect to any monadic quality. But since they are nonidentical, there must be a respect in which they do differ; they must satisfy the principle of the identity of indiscernibles, there must be a ground of their individuation. Therefore, they must contain some nonqualitative elements in respect to which to differ; these elements would be called bare particulars, in accordance with the above explanation of this term, each spot containing a unique bare particular.

Clearly, if so stated, the argument for bare particulars is inadequate. Individual things may differ in respect to their relational qualities, not only in respect to their monadic qualities.[14] For example, spot a may be to the left of spot b, while spot b is of course not to the left of itself. Indeed, since such a difference must involve irreflexive relations (if, e.g., spot b might also be to the left of spot b, then it would not be distinguishable from spot a in this respect), it cannot be present, the relation cannot hold, unless the spots are numerically diverse. But surely this is what we want: that the respect of difference between the two spots entail their nonidentity! If it did not, it would not be sufficient for their individuation. Russell argued that this entailment cannot be formal—that it is not a logical truth, in the narrow sense of this term, that for example the relation to-the-left-of is irreflexive—and thought that the individuation of individual things should not depend on what is at best a synthetic a priori necessary truth.[15] But this is a confusion. If by the individuation of individual things is meant their being discernible in at least one respect (if this is not what is meant, it becomes completely obscure what is meant and why individuation should be supposed to require particulars), then we do not *want* the difference to be such that it logically (in the narrow sense) entails their nonidentity. For the principle of the identity of indiscernibles is not a truth of logic, although it can, trivially, be made analytic by a stipulative definition of identity as indiscernibility. To be true, the principle of the identity of indiscernibles requires only that in fact any two nonidentical things differ in some respect. To be necessarily true, it requires that it be impossible that nonidentical things should differ in no respect. Of course, the principle is of philosophical interest only if necessary. But its necessity need not be that of a truth of logic. It could be synthetic a priori, which would not mean that it is somehow "less necessary." Indeed, it is not at all clear that the *necessity* of the truths of logic (e.g., of the principle of noncontradiction) differs from the *necessity* of the usual examples of synthetic a priori truths.[16]

But the argument for bare particulars can be given a deeper and more defensible version. It can be understood as a response to the question, what must individual things be in order to be capable of entering in individuating, presumably spatial and temporal, relations?[17] It would then be based on the premise that such relations cannot hold between universal qualities, and would conclude that in order to enter into such relations individual things must be more than mere clusters of qualities, that they must contain unique nonqualitative elements, namely, bare particulars. And the argument for the premise would be that, first, the supposition that universals (e.g., colors and shapes) can enter in spatial or temporal relations is absurd, and, second, that even if they could, any spatial or temporal relation between two spots that share the same monadic qualities would be reflexive (since the two spots would contain the same qualities), a consequence both intrinsically absurd and incompatible with the *individuating* role of such relations.

On the surface, this version of the argument seems hardly worth discussing. Indeed, if individual things may only be mere sets, or collections, of universal qualities unless there are bare particulars, then the argument is successful. Neither universal qualities nor sets of such qualities can be intelligibly supposed to enter in spatial or temporal relations. But surely individual things are not mere sets, whether of qualities only or of qualities plus bare particulars. At the very least, they consist of their qualities in the sense that their qualities are their parts. This is the minimal meaning of calling them "clusters" or "bundles." And a thing that has parts may have qualities, both relational and nonrelational, that neither any of its parts nor the mere set of all of its parts can have. For example, one person may be the father of another even though no part of him nor the set of all of his parts can be intelligibly described as a father. Therefore, individual things may consist only of universal qualities and yet enter in individuating spatial and temporal relations.

But when considered more deeply, the second version of the argument is seen to have power. Its defender may grant everything I have said and still ask the rhetorical question, if an individual thing consists of nothing but universal qualities, even though it is more than the mere set of these qualities, *how* can it enter in spatial and temporal relations? We need not suppose that the thing is the mere set of its qualities in order to perceive the philosophical difficulty. How can something all of whose parts are universals enter in spatial or temporal relations? Or, equivalently, how can *universals* constitute something spatiotemporal? It seems unintelligible to suppose that they can. And, indeed, it is unintelligible. But, I suggest, the reason is that it is quite insufficient to say merely that individual things consist of their universal qualities, or that the latter are parts of the former. It is also necessary to give an account of the manner in which they so consist, of the clustering, or togetherness, of the qualities of an individual thing, of the sense, if any, in which the qualities of an individual thing may be said to be parts of it. It is not surprising that without such an account we cannot see how individual things can enter in spatial and temporal relations if they consist of nothing but universal qualities.

CHAPTER EIGHT

Accidental Connections

I

The problem of the clustering, togetherness, of the qualities of an individual thing is an application in the metaphysics of qualities of the general problem of how to understand complexity, be it the complexity of an Aristotelian substance, or the complexity of a state of affairs, or the complexity of a cluster of qualities. It is the problem of how to understand the *unity* of a complex. The attempt to solve it led to Frege's chief metaphysical innovation, the distinction between concepts and objects and, more generally, between unsaturated and saturated things. The despair over it was at least one of the reasons for Bradley's metaphysical monism in *Appearance and Reality*. The struggle with it characterized Russell's early philosophical work and constituted the topic of an instructive debate between him and Bradley. And one of the major metaphysical theses in Wittgenstein's *Tractatus*, that objects hang one in another like the links in a chain, is a proposed solution of that problem.

Russell described the source of the puzzle regarding complexity as follows: "A complex differs from the mere aggregate of its constituents, since it is one, not many, and the relation which is one of its constituents enters into it as an actually relating relation, and not merely as one member of the aggregate."[1] And the puzzle itself can be stated as follows: Let a complex W (whether it be a cluster of qualities, or a material substance, or a state of affairs) have as its constituents *a* and *b*. Clearly, it is not the same as the set, or aggregate, of its constituents, for there would be that

212

set even if there were not such a complex as W. (E.g., a certain rectangular white spot cannot be the set whose members are the shape rectangularity and the color white, for there would be that set even if there were not that rectangular white spot.) Have we perhaps omitted another, third, constituent of W, which accounts for the difference between W and the set (*a*,*b*)? Let us call such a third constituent *c*. Presumably, it would be some sort of relation or connection between *a* and *b*. But whatever *c* is, W is also not identical with the set (*a*,*b*,*c*). Obviously, we would reach the same result if we proceeded to find in W still other constituents, however special and abstruse we supposed their metaphysical character to be. Russell recognized that if *c* is responsible for the unity of W, by being let us say a relation between *a* and *b*, it is so not in virtue of merely being a constituent of W but in virtue of being a constituent that *does* something, namely, actually relates *a* and *b*. He called such constituents verbs (not to be confused with the words that stand for them): "The capacity for combining terms into a single complex is the defining characteristic of what I call *verbs*."[2] This view was held by Russell as early as *The Principles of Mathematics*, although there he was willing to acknowledge its obscurity: "The verb, when used as a verb, embodies the unity of the proposition, and is thus distinguishable from the verb considered as a term, though I do not know how to give a clear account of the precise nature of the distinction."[3]

A very similar view had been held a decade earlier by Frege. His defense of his distinction between concepts and objects, which led him to deny that, for example, the concept *horse* is a concept, ends, revealingly, with the passage:

> Somebody may think that this is an artificially created difficulty; that there is no need at all to take account of such an unmanageable thing as what I call a concept; that one might, like Kerry, regard an object's falling under a concept as a relation, in which the same thing could occur now as object, now as concept. The words "object" and "concept" would then serve only to indicate the different positions in the relation. This may be done; but any-

> body who thinks that the difficulty is avoided this way is very much mistaken; it is only shifted. For not all the parts of a thought can be complete; at least one must be "unsaturated," or predicative; otherwise they would not hold together.*

He means, of course, that the shift consists in regarding now the relation of falling under a concept, instead of the concept itself, as the constituent responsible for the togetherness of the parts of the thought. The puzzle about the concept *horse* not being a concept is the same as Russell's puzzle about the distinction between a relation considered as a constituent of a complex and the relation considered as actually relating. If we reserve the term "relation" only for the latter case, then we could say, e.g., that the relation being-larger-than, as it might be listed in an inventory of the constituents of the state of affairs A's-being-larger-than-B, is not a relation.

The inadequacy of Russell's, and by implication Frege's, solution of the problem of the unity of complexes was pointed out sufficiently by F. H. Bradley: ". . . my difficulty as to 'unities' remains. Is there anything, I ask, in a unity beside its 'constituents,' i.e., the terms and the relation, and, if there is anything more, in what does this 'more' consist? . . . What is the difference between a relation which relates in fact and one which does not so relate?"[4] Bradley's criticism applies even if the relation in question is a special one, such as what Frege called the relation of falling under a concept, or what Russell called the relation of predication,[5] or the primative relation of togetherness that Nelson Goodman postulates,[6] or what Bergmann calls the tie of exemplification as well as the "relation" he supposes to hold between a complex (a fact) and the mode of actuality or the mode of potentiality (possibility).[7] The point of Bradley's criticism is not that there are no such relations, or that there is no distinction to be made between such a relation as a constituent of a complex

---

*"On Concept and Object," in *Translations*, pp. 54–55. By "thought" Frege meant the sense of a sentence and denied that it is anything mental or subjective.

and its actually relating the remaining constituents. The point is that the postulation of any such relations fails to achieve its purpose, namely, the elucidation of the nature of the togetherness of the constituents of a complex, the nature of the unity of the complex, precisely because it must be supplemented with that distinction. For the notion of a relation's actually relating the constituents of the complex is no clearer than, perhaps not even different from, the notion of the togetherness of these constituents.

It may be added here that Frege's description of what he calls concepts (i.e., properties) as "unsaturated" or "incomplete" may seem to answer the question why a concept and the object falling under it need no third thing to relate them only as long as we fail to note that it presupposes and does not even attempt to elucidate the above distinction. How are we to understand the difference between an object's actually falling under a certain concept and its not falling under that concept? To say that the former is to be understood as analogous to the filling of an empty place in an open sentence with a constant would be a case of *ignoratio elenchi*; in the latter case there *is* something third, namely, the spatial relation of the constant to the sentence, the occupancy by the former of a place in the latter. To say that it is to be understood in terms of the fact that the thought (in Frege's sense of "thought") corresponding to it has as its reference the object he called the True, would be a case of *obscurum per obscurius*, and moreover it would still be to appeal to the *actual* holding of a relation, namely, the relation, whatever it may be, between the thought and the True.

II

The moral to be drawn from the failure of the above-mentioned attempts to give an account of the unity of a complex, and thus, by implication, of the clustering of the qualities of an individual thing, is not that such an account is impossible, nor that the proposed accounts must contain some simple mistake in reasoning. Their inadequacy has a deep root. It is the result of a wrong conception of the sense in which the constituents of a complex thing are parts of it, and this conception itself results from a wrong view of material identity, from the failure to make a distinction such as ours between objects and entities.

If we do not allow for some difference between the white color of one spot and the white color of another spot when, in accordance with the Identity Theory of Universals, we conclude that they are the same entity, i.e., the universal color white, then we cannot suppose that the color of a spot bears a *necessary* relationship to the other qualities of the spot. They must be taken merely to happen to be together, and their togetherness must be understood as something additional to, even if categorially different from, the qualities that are together. Yet, if the togetherness is understood as something additional, then *its* togetherness with the qualities would be equally in need of acknowledgment, and thus an infinite regress, so eloquently described by Bradley, arises.[8] If not understood as something additional, then it becomes quite unclear how the appeal to it can serve a philosophical function, indeed what such an appeal would amount to.

Similar observations can be made regarding the theory according to which an individual thing is a cluster of *particular* qualities and the theory according to which an individual thing consists of its universal qualities plus a bare particular, as long as the thing's constituents are regarded by the theory as entities and not also as objects. Either such constituent entities are only contingently together in the thing, and then an appeal to something else must be made in elucidating their togetherness, an infinite regress thus immediately arising. Or they are necessarily together, and then we face the mystery of how spatiotemporal particulars, whether particular qualities or bare particulars, can enter in such a necessary relationship, how they can be the subject matter of necessarily true statements. (That they can would be denied both by all versions of the linguistic theory of necessary truth and by what I have called the ontological theory; and even what has recently been called essentialism would deny what the second alternative implies, namely, that individual things have *only* essential properties.)

I do not mean that if the togetherness of the constituents of a complex could be understood as necessary then we would not need an account of it. The togetherness of the numbers 9 and 2 and the relation of being-greater-than in the state of affairs we express by saying that 9 is greater than 2 is necessary, yet we certainly demand an explanation of its nature. In this case, however, such an explanation is readily forthcoming. It makes no appeal to further constituents of the state of affairs. Instead, it appeals to the general fact about a necessarily true statement that the identity of each of the constituents of its subject matter, or the identity of each of the concepts employed in it, is a function of the identities of the remaining constituents, or of the identities of the remaining concepts; e.g., that either 9 or 2 or the relation of being-greater-than would not be what it is if 9 were not greater than 2, or that either the concept of 9 or the concept of 2 or the concept of being-greater-than would not be what it is if the statement were false. All theories of necessary truth agree on this *general* fact; they differ in their specific accounts of it, e.g., on whether the account in terms of subject matter or the account in terms of concepts is true, and, if the latter, on whether concepts should be understood as psychological entities or as rule-governed uses of words or in some third way.

If the togetherness of the constituents of a cluster of qualities is contingent, then the Bradleyan infinite regress is unavoidable. But why have philosophers generally assumed that it is contingent? In particular, since we have already rejected on independent grounds the theory that an individual thing consists of particular qualities, as well as the theory that it consists of universal qualities plus a bare particular, why have philosophers generally assumed that the universals constituting an individual thing do so contingently, are together in it contingently? I have already suggested that the reason is that, because of their general conception of material identity, they have also shared a certain conception of what it is for qualities of distinct individual things to be identical, of what it is for qualities to be universals. According to this conception, the white color of one spot is in no sense distinguishable from the white color of another spot. The two spots merely happen to exemplify one color, and this joint exemplification is understood, often with the help of Russell's theory of descriptions, as analogous to two persons having the same father. Universal qualities are understood as mere entities. And as mere entities their togetherness in some cases and non-togetherness in other cases are indeed quite contingent. There is nothing about the color white as such that requires it to be the color of this page and thus to be together with the shape rectangularity as such. On this conception, universal qualities are self-contained entities that merely happen to be exemplified by some but not other individual things, somewhat like balloons tied to pegs, sometimes to one peg only, sometimes to many. The white color of one spot and the white color of another spot are no more distinguishable than a balloon tied by two strings each leading to a separate peg would be distinguishable into two balloons. The color of a spot can have no special, unique, and necessary connection to the spot, just as a balloon has no such connection to any peg to which it is tied.

But the qualities of individual things are not mere entities. They are also objects. A quality of one thing and a quality of another thing may be identical as entities but still they would be distinguishable as objects, and they would be so distinguishable precisely because of their togetherness with different other quality-objects. The balloon theory of universals is a gross misrepresentation of the facts, but merely a special case of the misrepresentation of the facts of material identity in general, to which we devoted the first two chapters of this book. The togetherness of the qualities of an individual thing considered as entities is indeed contingent, and in need not of a philosophical but of a causal account. However, their togetherness as objects is necessary, in the very strong sense that each is the object it is only because the others are the objects they are, that the formal identity of each is a function of the formal identities of the others. Such a togetherness requires neither a causal account nor a philosophical account in terms of additional constituents, but philosophical understanding. It is like the togetherness of the numbers 9 and 2 and the relation of being-greater-than, which we explain neither causally nor through additional constituents, and unlike it only in that it is a togetherness of objects qua objects, while the latter is also a togetherness of objects qua entities. But it is entirely unlike the togetherness of the parts of a clock or of the bricks in a wall. Individual things are not clusters of quality-entities, i.e., universals, as such; they are clusters of quality-objects, even though these are also entities.

A quality-entity, i.e., a universal, instantiated by an individual thing need not be instantiated by it, it need not be together with the other qualities of the individual thing. But a quality-object must. It is the object it is only because it is in the individual thing in which it is. But this individual thing is not a material substance or a bare particular, nor the mere set of quality-entities that ordinarily would be attributed to it. It is a cluster of quality-*objects* and the object is a constituent of that cluster. Nothing holds, or is needed for holding, the constituents of the cluster together, for it is essential to each that it be together with the others in the same cluster. The question "What holds the qualities of an individual thing together?" makes sense only if it would make sense to suppose that the qualities in question might not have been together, that they could have been the qualities they are even if they had not been together. Indeed, if the qualities are considered as entities, then this does make sense. But if they are considered as objects, it does not. And what quality-entities an individual thing contains depends entirely on what quality-objects it contains.

Consider a rectangular white spot. We may distinguish its

color, its shape, perhaps its surface. If considered as *entities,* as universals, the shape and the color of the spot need not have been together; there need not have been this or any other rectangular white spot. And if the surface can be thought of as a distinct entity at all, which I shall deny shortly, then it need not have been rectangular and white; certainly a surface considered as an entity can be supposed to change color and perhaps even its shape. But let us consider the shape, color, and surface of the spot as *objects,* as things that cannot be singled out twice, cannot change, cannot be reidentified. Clearly, then, the color of the spot would be logically inseparable from the surface. But the surface would be logically inseparable from the shape. From this it follows, though it can also be seen directly, that the color is logically inseparable from the shape, even if one could be singled out when the other is not. For to say that one object is logically inseparable from another, that the formal identity of the one depends on the formal identity of the other, is not to say that to single out the one we must also single out the other, that to notice the one requires that we also notice the other, although this is often the case. It is to say that we could not single out or notice both and yet understand what it would be for them not to be together. In Fregean terminology, though not meaning, each is an unsaturated thing in itself and is saturated by the other. In Wittgenstein's Tractarian terminology, the two hang one in another like the links of a chain, with no intermediary needed or possible. But, contrary to both Frege and Wittgenstein, they hang together necessarily.

Indeed, we may imagine the spot as having a different color yet the same shape, but here by "same shape" we could only mean same *shape-entity,* not same *shape-object;* a change in the color entails a replacement of the *shape-object* by another *shape-object,* even if they are the same *shape-entity.* It would now be, e.g., the shape of the blue spot, not the shape of the white spot, even if they are the same shape, and the spots the same spot, as entities. An analogous remark may be made regarding the imaginability of the spot as having a different shape but the same color.

I have spoken of the surface of the spot in order to make the inseparability of the constituents of the spot more obvious. In fact, however, there is no basis for supposing that the surface (not to be confused with the size) of the spot is something additional to its qualities. If by the shape of an individual thing we mean a quality that involves both geometrical figure and size (just as by a chromatic color we understand a quality that involves hue, saturation, and brightness), then the surface-object in the spot is indistinguishable from the shape-object. Whatever we wish to say about the surface-object can be adequately conveyed by a statement about the shape-object, about the latter's geometrical figure and especially size, or about what other objects are its fellow-constituents of the cluster. It is worth noting that while the color and the shape of the spot are logically independent when considered as entities (one could have been present without the other), the surface, even if considered as an entity, cannot strictly speaking have a different shape, it can only be a part of, or contain as a part, or overlap with, a surface that has that different shape; while the shape, of course, can be the shape also of another surface.

Our conclusion that the togetherness of the constituents of a cluster of qualities qua *objects* is necessary is not incompatible with the contingency of ordinary accidental predications about individual things. Accidental predications are ordinarily about things considered as entities, even if also as objects, and the togetherness of the constituents of a cluster of qualities qua *entities* is indeed contingent. The quality-entities constituting the cluster need not have constituted it. In necessary accidental predications, the constituents of the complex (which presumably is a state of affairs, not an individual thing) are necessarily together also qua entities, not only qua objects, the criterion for this being the inconceivability of *any* corresponding objects that are not together in the requisite manner. The rectangular shape-object and the white color-object of this page cannot be conceived as not being together, but another rectangular shape-object and another white color-object that are not together are perfectly conceivable. On the other hand, it is not only inconceivable that a certain crimson color-object might not have been darker than a certain pink color-object; this is also inconceivable regarding any other crimson color-object and pink color-object. This is why we consider the statement that crimson is darker than pink to be necessarily true.

III

The above account of the togetherness of the qualities of an individual thing suggests also a solution of the third main problem the metaphysics of qualities faces, namely, how are the spatial and temporal relations of individual things to be understood, how can individual things enter in such relations if they consist only of qualities, what is the nature of their togetherness with their spatial and temporal relations, how can the latter possess the sort of unity, wholeness, that is rightly emphasized by the absolutist theory of space and time? The problem must receive a solution, not just for the sake of the completeness of a metaphysics of qualities but also for a very specific reason. The only conceivable world, I have argued, is a spatiotemporal world, a world consisting of spatiotemporal individual things, in a broad sense of "individual thing" in which even color spots count as individual things. And I have also argued that the first problem facing the metaphysics of qualities, namely, whether individual things can indeed be coherently supposed to consist only of qualities, or whether they must also contain a nonqualitative constituent such as a bare particular, is ultimately a problem about the spatiotemporality of an individual thing. We saw that the deeper and only plausible argument for bare particulars is that they alone can be coherently regarded as the primary relata of spatial and temporal relations, individual things being such relata only in a secondary, derivative way.

Can an individual thing, such as our rectangular white spot, enter in spatial relations if it consists only of qualities and if qualities are universals? It is now evident that it can, since an individual thing is not only a cluster of universals, of quality-entities, but also a cluster of quality-objects, one of which, namely the shape-object, is just the sort of thing that does enter in such relations. What accounts for the togetherness of a spatial relation and the individual thing which enters in it? Nothing but the formal identity of the shape-object that is the true relatum of the relation, the fact that it would not be the object it is, even if it might still be the entity it is, if it were not a relatum of that relation. And why is space given to us in perception as a unity, as a whole, rather than as a network of relations? The reason is that shape-objects are not discrete things, capable of being connected only by certain additional things, namely, spatial relations, but rather things each of which is partially coincident, partially formally identical, with its neighbors; it is their very nature to constitute a whole, to possess a unity, to *be* space. Let me explain.

The shape-objects of individual things, for example those singled out in a single visual field, fit one in another even more intimately than the color-object and shape-object of a single individual thing fit one in another. They do so by partially coinciding, namely, by sharing sides or parts, as illustrated in the figure
$\boxed{a\,|\,b}$. Such a coincidence is a case of formal identity; the right side of a does not even appear distinct from the left side of b. And no shape-object fails to partially coincide, in this manner, with at least one other shape-object even if some shape-objects are not closed. For example, the shape-object of a partially coincides with the shape-object of b, but also with the shape-object whose outer side coincides with the rectangular shape-object of this page and whose inner side coincides with the shape-object of a. Perhaps we can say that it also coincides with the inner side of the shape-object whose outer side is the oblong of the visual field, and, if singled out by a divine eye and if space is infinite, also with the shape-object which has the same inner side but no outer side at all. Thus the space in which we single out objects is

fundamentally the mesh of shape-objects, a mesh entirely constituted by formal identities of parts of distinct shape-objects, rather than by the presence among shape-objects of peculiar, stringlike additional things such as spatial relations, even if we acknowledge, for other reasons, that there also are spatial relations. Clearly, a similar view may be held of time, with what may be called duration-objects (e.g., the present moment) being the analogue to shape-objects, and a one-dimensional sequence of partially coinciding duration-objects being the analogue to the two- or three-dimensional mesh of shape-objects. And since qualities qua entities, i.e., universals, are nonspatiotemporal and enter in space and time only qua objects, and space and time are constituted by objects, not by entities as such, there is a sense in which the spatiotemporal world may be said to be a shadow of the world of entities, something that has no reality of its own. This would be a conclusion not unlike the one Plato reached.

Not only do the partial formal identities of shape-objects account for the unity of space; they are also constitutive of at least some spatial relations *insofar as these are regarded as holding between objects*. This can be seen particularly clearly in the case of the crucial relation of betweenness. Consider the figure $\boxed{a\,|\,b\,|\,c}$. Square b is between square a and square c. Need we suppose that in addition to the monadic qualities of the whole rectangle and of its three parts there is a "polyadic" quality, namely, the three-term relation of spatial betweenness, holding between squares a, b, and c? We need not. The fact about the above figure that we describe by saying that b is between a and c consists entirely in the fact that a certain part of the shape-object of a is coincident, formally identical, with a certain part of the shape-object of b, a certain part of the shape-object of b is coincident with a certain part of the shape-object of c, and no part of the shape-object of a is coincident with a part of the shape-object of c.* These coincidences are perfectly observable and no more

*To say this is not, of course, to offer a definition of spatial betweenness *in general*. It is to say that this is what b's being between a and c consists in. The

puzzling than any other case of formal identity. (Such as, for example, in the figure $\boxed{\text{a} \cdot \text{b}}$, the formal identity of the point to the right of *a* and the point to the left of *b* [see above,p. 23].) And if the spatial betweenness in this particular case is reducible to partial coincidences, so would be also all other relations that could be understood in terms of it. Similar conclusions can be reached regarding temporal betweenness and the temporal relations that can be understood in terms of temporal betweenness, as long as they are taken to have objects qua objects as their relata.

I have engaged in this excursion into the philosophy of space and time in order to make clearer the view of individual things as clusters of qualities. We think of such a cluster as consisting only of monadic qualities but also recognize that it has spatial and temporal characteristics. And we face the despair-inducing question of the nature of the togetherness of *these* characteristics, especially if regarded as relations, with the individual things they characterize (even if we have understood the nature of the togetherness of the monadic qualities of an individual thing), as well as the awesome question of how space and time as unities, as wholes, can be constituted by such characteristics of individual things. Thus the recognition of the fact of the partial formal identities of shape-objects and of duration-objects, though not required for the account of the togetherness of the constituents of a cluster of monadic qualities, complements that account, and the two together constitute the rudiments of a metaphysical theory of the nature of an individual thing and of the spatiotemporal world that is its home. The development of this theory in detail, however, lies beyond the bounds of this book. We have been concerned with it only insofar as it is needed by the protometaphysical account of accidental predication.

---

spatial betweenness in other cases *involving shape-objects* would still consist in partial coincidences, but these latter might be more complicated and indirect, as for example in the figures $\boxed{\text{a} \mid \text{b} \mid \boxed{\text{c}}}$ and $\boxed{\boxed{\text{a} \mid \text{b} \mid \text{c}}}$ (I owe these examples to Albert Casullo and Evan Fales).

IV

The application of the distinction between objects and entities to qualities yields an obvious solution to the problem of individuation. We saw that in its simpler form this problem can be solved by an appeal to differences in spatiotemporal relations, but that it also has a deeper form, namely, the question, how can clusters of universal qualities enter in such relations since neither their constituents nor the sets of their constituents can do so? As long as we think of the constituents of a cluster merely as universal qualities, i.e., as quality-entities, we are incapable of understanding the difference between a cluster of qualities and a mere set of qualities, and thus incapable of finding an answer. But clusters consist not only of quality-entities but also of quality-objects; indeed, the togetherness of their qualities can only be the togetherness of the corresponding quality-objects. Now two clusters consisting of the same quality-entities would still be distinguishable insofar as they consist of different quality-objects. And while no quality-entities, i.e., universals, can as such be intelligibly described as entering in spatiotemporal relations, some quality-objects can. The shape of one rectangular white spot, qua an object, can be literally to the left of the shape of another rectangular white spot, again qua an object. Of course, by hypothesis, they are one and the same shape considered as an entity. But to infer from this that the shape-*entity* is to the left of itself would be no more reasonable than to infer from the identity of the Evening Star and the Morning Star that the Evening Star, since it appears in the sky, say, twelve hours later than the Morning Star, appears twelve hours later than itself.

Nor would it be reasonable to infer that the two contemporaneous spots themselves differ only qua objects, that they are one and the same entity. Even though the shape-objects of the spots are materially identical, the spatial relations and, more fundamentally, the *locations* of the shape-objects and thus of the spots in the mesh of shape-objects, are not. Of course, we could *enforce* the indiscernibility of the two spots and disallow that qua entities they really differ in respect of location, as in fact we would do so regarding the shape-objects. We could acknowledge that the locations are really different but insist that one and the same spot has both locations, that, though an individual thing, it has *multiple* location (see above, pp. 66–67 and pp. 193–95). But, as we have seen, such enforcement of indiscernibility can be grounded only in a prior judgment of identity. And no criteria of identity would legitimize a judgment that the spots are identical; the situation is totally unlike any paradigm of identity. Therefore, the two spots really differ in respect of their locations. They do not merely appear to do so. And this suffices for their individuation. But our appeal to difference in location involves no divergence from the metaphysics of qualities. As we have seen, the mesh of shape-objects and the locations of shape-objects in it consist entirely in partial coincidences of shape-objects, of certain qualities. But if the two shape-objects in the spots are materially identical and therefore we enforce their indiscernibility with respect to location, and if the spots have location only in virtue of their shape-objects, how can the spots have different locations? The answer is that the shape-object of a spot is a constituent of the spot; it is together with the other qualities not qua an entity but qua an object. Therefore, the spot derives its location from the location of its shape-object only insofar as the latter is an object. And qua an object it does have a different location from that of the shape-object of the other spot. Objects, qua objects, have the qualities they are singled out as having.

In chapter six I remarked that even if there are not material substances the general requirement of coherent thought and discourse that there be things identical through time would be satisfied by the fact that *qualities* are reidentifiable through time. May we now add that the individual things of commonsense, insofar as they can be understood as clusters of qualities, are also capable of identity through time, and thus that even the often suggested (e.g., by Strawson) specific requirement that thought and discourse be grounded in reidentifiable *individual* things is satisfied? Can we preserve some of the most important ordinary applications of the concept of identity, namely those having to do with the identity of individual things through time, and thus weaken (though not eliminate) the strongly revisionist character of our denial that the individual things of commonsense are capable of such identity? Does our account yield criteria of identity for clusters that would allow us to vindicate at least partially the commonsense conception of an individual thing?

Superficially considered, these questions may seem to deserve affirmative answers. To say that a cluster consists of quality-objects is not to say that it does not consist also of quality-entities, for the quality-objects in it *are* also entities and thus subjects of true material identity judgments. And on the basis of such judgments about its constituents, true material identity judgments can also be made about the cluster itself. This is why we must not suppose that since the constituents of a cluster are together only qua objects, not qua entities, that a cluster can itself only be an object, and not also an entity, which would entail that no individual things can exist. The spatiotemporal world may have no reality of its own, but from this it does not follow that it has no reality. Whether a cluster exists depends only on whether it is indefinitely identifiable. Whether it *can* exist depends only on whether it can be indefinitely identifiable, on whether there are genuine criteria of identity for it.

In fact it is only to individual things, to clusters, that the concept of existence is ordinarily applied, not to their qualitative constituents. We regard a single instance of a universal quality (even if in an imaginary or hallucinatory thing) as a guarantee of the existence of the universal quality, of its indefinite identifiability. Universals are necessary existents. The reason for this is that, as we saw in chapter four, nonexistent objects literally have the qualities they are singled out as having. A universal quality therefore can be identified in nonexistent as well as in existent things. To determine that there is a certain universal quality it suffices to imagine a thing that exemplifies it; for if one is imaginable then so are an indefinite number of such things. And while we have no criteria for the identity of imaginary individual things, we do have criteria for the identity of their qualities. They are the same as the criteria of identity for qualities of existent things, since the qualities themselves are the same. Hence the usual view that the criterion for the existence of a universal is the logical possibility of its being instantiated. It is the existence of clusters that is a contingent matter and thus likely to be ordinarily of interest. One may single out a certain cluster-object even though there is no other cluster-object with which it is identical. While there can be no serious question about the existence of the white color and rectangular shape that constitute it, there can be a very serious question about the existence of a certain rectangular white spot; for example, it could be hallucinatory, or an after-image.

Now, what would be the criterion of identity for clusters? The answer may seem obvious: identity of constitution. For, as I pointed out earlier, material identity judgments about clusters may only be based on material identity judgments about their constituents. But it is the wrong answer. That this is so can be seen immediately from the fact that according to such a criterion a rectangular white spot would be identical with every other rectangular white spot of exactly the same shape and color, and the entity the criterion would legitimize would not be an individual thing but a *sort* of an individual thing, a complex universal, the universal of being a rectangular white spot. The proposed criterion is in fact the criterion of identity for sets; but a cluster of qualities is not a mere set, whether of quality-entities or quality-objects. To capture the individuality of a cluster an adequate criterion of identity must take into account also the *location* of the cluster in space and time. As we have seen, this can be understood in terms of the partial coincidences of shape-objects and of duration-objects. To say that a certain cluster at t_1 and a certain cluster at t_2 have the same location in space is to say that their shape-objects enter in partial coincidences with the (materially) same shape-objects surrounding them, and these latter enter in partial coincidences with the (materially) same shape-objects that surround *them*, etc. The account of what it is for two clusters to have the same location in time, i.e., to be contemporaneous, would be analogous. Of course, these are accounts of *relative* location. But they ought to be such. Whether space and time are absolute or relational, we can have a criterion of identity only for relative location. The two accounts also presuppose, respectively, that there can be only one space and only one time. I believe that this presupposition is necessarily true but shall not attempt to defend it here.

May we now say that the criterion of identity for clusters is sameness of constitution *and* of spatial and temporal location? There is no doubt that such a criterion would be a perfectly clear logically sufficient condition of identity. That there is such a criterion guarantees that clusters of qualities are identifiable, that they can be the subject matter of true material identity judgments, and thus that they can be entities, that they can exist. But it makes possible only the identity and existence of *momentary* clusters. It cannot be a criterion of identity through time. A cluster at t_1 and a cluster at t_2 have different locations in time.

To allow for the identity of a cluster through time, the criterion of identity for clusters would need to be revised. Such identity would be possible only if the duration-object of a cluster is not regarded as being one of its constituents. For two clusters have different locations in time only in the sense that their duration-objects have different locations in time. And these different locations are constitutive of the formal identities of the duration-objects; therefore, they cannot be regarded as irrelevant to the identities of the clusters unless the duration-objects are so regarded. But to regard the duration-object of a cluster as irrelevant to its identity is in effect to regard it as not being a constituent of the cluster. Such an exclusion of the duration from the constitution of a cluster would in fact conform to commonsense, which does not recognize the notion of a temporal part of an individual thing as it does recognize the notion of a spatial part. To some extent this is due to our greater interest in the remaining constituents of clusters and in *their* togetherness.* But perhaps it is also due to the fact that the duration of a cluster is (at least ordinarily) apprehended only if a change in some other constituent (whether monadic or relational) is apprehended. A third, more fundamental, though related, reason may be that time does not appear to commonsense to be a *thing*, as space of course does.†

But what could be meant by "excluding" from a cluster its duration, when obviously every cluster that we would regard as a spatiotemporal individual thing does include duration? Even though a cluster does include its duration as a constituent, and each of its constituents, including its duration, is necessarily connected with every other, we ordinarily attend not to the whole cluster but to what may be called subclusters of it, i.e., to parts of the cluster that are themselves clusters of qualities, and we are concerned only with the identity of these subclusters through time. An individual thing is a cluster of all the qualities that would be truly attributed to it. But just as we can be interested in, attend to, and identify through time (and space) one of its qualities without also identifying any of its other qualities, so we can be interested in, attend to, and identify through time not the whole cluster but some one of its subclusters, without concern for its remaining constituents. Therefore, what would correspond in our account to an individual thing of commonsense would not be a complete cluster (i.e., the cluster of all the qualities that would be truly attributed to the thing) but at most a

*Anthony Quinton points out that a substantive concept determines the spatial characteristics of the things falling under it, but not their temporal characteristics. *The Nature of Things* (London: Routledge and Kegan Paul, 1973), pp. 70, 77.

†According to Spinoza, extension is an attribute of God (*Ethics*, Part Two, Prop. II), but time is not, duration being defined simply as the indefinite continuation of existence (*Ethics*, Part Two, Def. V).

certain subcluster, one that does not include duration among its constituents.

With this revision of the criterion, we are able to claim that at least one kind of situation is an entirely clear and unquestionable case of the identity of a cluster of qualities through time. Let us imagine a cluster at t_1 and a cluster at t_3 such that they share exactly the same quality-entities but neither is regarded as including duration, have the same location in space, and are temporally continuous. Can we conceive of the first cluster ceasing to exist at t_2 and the second cluster immediately thereupon beginning to exist, as we did in chapter six regarding the parallel case of a material substance? No, we cannot. The reason is that the identity of such a cluster of qualities is entirely a function of the identities of its constituents and their spatial location, and these by hypothesis the clusters share. They contain nothing with respect to which they could be conceived to differ. And there are clear criteria for the identity of their constituents and of their spatial locations. The criterion for the latter we have already stated; the criteria for the former are the criteria of identity for qualities. Contrast this with the case of a material substance. A material substance is not a cluster of qualities, it does not consist merely of qualities, it is mainly a parcel of matter. This is why it is possible for us to conceive that a substance at t_1 and a substance at t_3, although they have exactly the same qualities and the same spatial location and are 'temporally continuous, are nevertheless not identical. Even if we were to suppose (as we usually do, without justification) that their identity would not require the identity of *all* the matter they contain, and throughout their existence, we must, as indeed we do, regard *some* identity truths regarding the matter as essential to the identity of the substance. (For example, sudden and complete replacement of the matter would not be compatible with the identity of the substance.) But, as we have seen, any criteria for the identity of matter must rest, ultimately, on criteria for the identity of prime matter; and we have no such criteria; the notion of prime matter has no intelligible content.

But while the situation described above would be an entirely clear and unquestionable case of the identity of a cluster through time, and thus vindicates the commonsense belief that there are enduring individual things, the criterion of identity I have stated hardly suffices for the vindication of most of the commonsense applications of the concept of identity. It is too liberal in some respects and too strict in others. Indeed, it guarantees that the case we have considered is one of identity. But it would do so even if the clusters were not temporally continuous. To be at all compatible with commonsense, it must include some condition of temporal continuity, even though this would make it difficult to understand how the clusters could still be regarded as excluding temporal duration. On the other hand, it disallows the identity of clusters that differ in spatial location and, even if ever so slightly, in their constituent qualities. It requires us to regard any change, whether locomotion or alteration, as incompatible with identity through time. To conform to commonsense, our criterion would need therefore to be revised further. We would need either to allow that identical clusters may be really, not just apparently, discernible with respect to spatial location, or to exclude also the shape-object, as we excluded the duration-object, from the constitution of a cluster, although presumably still to insist that the clusters do have spatial locations and moreover that the latter are members of a continuous series. (But see above, p. 173). We would also need either to allow for various differences in constitution, namely, all those involving qualities with respect to which commonsense would regard change as compatible with identity, or to exclude such qualities from the constitution of a cluster.

I shall not attempt to state the criterion that would emerge after such revisions. As long as it has to do only with qualities and spatial and temporal locations, it would be a clear criterion. But either it would not deserve to be called a criterion of *identity* or that for the identity of which it is a criterion would at best be a subcluster bearing only remote resemblance to what commonsense regards as an individual thing. Neither our primitive concept of identity nor any philosophical considerations could justify us in regarding as identical clusters that are really discernible, that differ in constitution. On the other hand, the subclusters that would really be identical would be so impoverished (they would consist only of qualities with respect to which an individual thing cannot change) that they could hardly be said to be *individual* things. To suppose, therefore, that the required revisions would vindicate the commonsense notion of an individual thing would be disingenuous. Of course, we could say that an individual thing is a certain kind of spatiotemporal series of clusters of qualities and that the identity of an individual thing at t_1 with an individual thing at t_2 consists not in the identity of a certain cluster of qualities at t_1 with a certain cluster of qualities at t_2 but in the identity of a certain series of clusters of which one member is at t_1 with a certain series of which one member is at t_2. But this would not be even remotely what commonsense regards as the identity of an individual thing through time (see above, pp. 180–81).

Our conclusion should not be surprising. We have explained what a criterion of identity for clusters must be if it is to render the identity of clusters through time similar to the identity through time that commonsense ascribes to individual things. But this ascription is governed chiefly by pragmatic considerations, rather than by the concept of identity or by philosophical considerations. For practical purposes, many cases that do not satisfy the concept of identity, or at least do not do so clearly and unquestionably, are regarded as if they were cases of identity. We have practical reasons for enforcing greater simplification upon the world than the concept of identity legitimizes. If faced with the question of a ship like Theseus's, a court of law may need to *rule* that one of the two ships is Theseus's, even if it has no conceptual justification for such a ruling. The fact that the notion of identity does have such pragmatically motivated applications does not render these applications conceptually clear, it does not show that they are governed by genuine criteria of identity. A stipulation, however justified pragmatically, is not a judgment of truth. In this respect, the concept of identity is not unique. There are, for example, similarly unclear, and justified only by expediency, applications of the concepts of knowledge, white, and circularity; respectively, to some mere true rational beliefs, to some shades of gray, and to some ellipses; but this fact constitutes no argument that these are genuine cases of knowledge, whiteness, or circularity.[9] The pragmatic justifiability of some divergences from the criteria we do have for the application of our concepts is no reason for supposing either that these are not divergences but rather applications of the same concepts legitimized by some other criteria, or that the criteria we do have are much more liberal than we suppose.[10]

Let me summarize. Our account of the nature of the togetherness of the constituents of a cluster of qualities has in effect been an account of accidental predication and thus completes our inquiry into being qua being. In chapters one, two, and three I was concerned with what is expressed by the use of the verb "to be" in its sense of identity; a major claim of this book has been that this is its philosophically fundamental sense, the others being comprehensible only through it. In chapter four I was concerned with what is expressed by the verb "to be" in its sense of existence, in chapter five with what is expressed by it in its sense of essential predication, and in the present chapter with what is expressed by it in its sense of accidental predication.

The standard examples of accidental predication, statements such as "Socrates is white," are not, of course, to be understood as directly asserting that a certain cluster of qualities contains a certain quality as a constituent, even though what they do assert, insofar as understandable at all, may only be understood ultimately in terms of such containment. The name "Socrates," like any other ordinary name, has no clear, determinate reference. We have no clear idea of what cluster or subcluster of qualities is Socrates and is supposed to remain identical throughout

Socrates' existence, since we have no clear idea of what changes are supposed to be compatible with Socrates' identity. This is only to be expected, given the pragmatic nature of our ordinary applications of the concept of identity and, consequently, the pragmatic nature of our assignment and employment of proper names. Our inquiry in this chapter does lead, however, to the conclusion that Socrates is, if anything at all, either a cluster of qualities or a subcluster of such a cluster, or a temporal series of such clusters or subclusters, and that his being white consists in the inclusion of a white color-object in such a cluster or subcluster, or in at least one member of a series of such clusters or subclusters.

IV

In my exposition of the metaphysics of qualities I have used as examples individual things such as color spots, monadic qualities such as colors and shapes, relations such as to-the-left-of and (spatial or temporal) betweenness. My choice of these examples, together with my rejection of the metaphysics of material substances, may appear to constitute a commitment to a phenomenalist, perhaps sense-datum, metaphysics. Is this so? The answer is not simple.

It would be negative, if the question is interpreted as asking whether a metaphysics of qualities must be phenomenalist. My argument against material substances in chapter six had nothing to do with the philosophy of perception, which is the home of phenomenalism; its commitment to a mild verificationism, though an epistemological feature, is one that, I believe, every philosophical theory must make. And that individual things may only be clusters of qualities does not entail that they are sense-data or families of sense-data. Even the particles the physicist tells us about would be clusters of qualities (it would be surprising if the thoughtful physicist would disagree), but they certainly would not be sense-data (see above, p. 192).

But the answer would be qualifiedly affirmative if the question is interpreted as asking whether a metaphysics of qualities must acknowledge that what may be called phenomenal individual things and phenomenal qualities have philosophical primacy, both epistemological and metaphysical. By phenomenal individual things and qualities I mean those that can be objects of consciousness, whether of perception, or of imagination, or of pure thought, and that can be *wholly* objects of consciousness; I thus exclude things or qualities only parts or aspects of which can actually be objects of consciousness, the rest needing to be inferred. I call them phenomenal since, in the case of perception, they are what has often been described as the directly observable, the given. Now my reason for an affirmative answer to the question is to be found in the protometaphysics developed in the earlier parts of this book, not in the usual epistemological considerations. Only insofar as something can be an object of consciousness can it also be singled out and serve as the logical subject of a genuine singular judgment. Only such a thing, therefore, can be identified and regarded as existent. Indeed, we do make general statements (often disguised in singular sentences) about things that cannot be objects of consciousness, but such general statements, being incapable of instantiation in genuine singular statements, may only be accorded a derivative status. If science is capable only of such general statements then it does not have either the epistemological or the metaphysical primacy that thought, discourse, and knowledge about what can be singled out do have.

It is only in this sense and for these reasons that an adequate metaphysics is phenomenalist or, to use a term that can now be seen to be more appropriate, phenomenological. It is mainly concerned with the most general nature of that which must be known if anything is to be known; with the most general nature of the objects of primary, direct, noninferential knowledge, both a posteriori and a priori. For such knowledge is possible only of objects of consciousness. As I have pointed out before, metaphysical questions are not separable from epistemological considerations. We may suppose the world to be only what we can understand it to be, we can understand it to be only what we can know it to be, and we can know it only if we can single out some parts or aspects of it. What is epistemologically primary is therefore also metaphysically primary.

APPENDIX A

Relations

In these appendixes I shall consider briefly two important topics closely connected with the main tenets of this book, but an adequate investigation of which cannot be attempted here.

Formally, accidental predication on the most fundamental level, that of monadic predication regarding a single cluster, would be represented in statements of the form "x is a constituent of cluster y." No relations are mentioned in such statements, since clusterhood and constituency in a cluster are to be understood entirely in terms of the notion of (formal) identity, as explained in chapter eight. But what about relational accidental predications?

It has been usual for twentieth-century philosophers to regard relations as a category of qualities, differing from the category that includes, e.g., colors and shapes, only in the number of individuals the instantiation of its members requires. It has also been usual to introduce the notion of a state of affairs for that which is described by a statement of relational predication; and in the absence of an account of cluster-constituency such as that offered in chapter eight, to regard even what statements of monadic predication describe as relational states of affairs, the alleged relation being that of predication, or exemplification, or falling under a concept.

Our account of monadic accidental predication in chapter eight can be easily generalized so that it would accommodate relational accidental predication as the latter is usually understood. For example, the statement "*a* is larger than *b*" could be taken to stand for a complex thing consisting of the shape-objects in *a* and *b* and a certain relation-object, very much as the sort of cluster we regard as an individual thing consists of monadic quality-objects. But since this complex thing would ordinarily be expressed in language with a declarative sentence, not with a name or a definite description as would an ordinary cluster, it would be appropriate to mark the difference by calling it a state of affairs. The unity of its constituents would be explained in the same way as that of the constituents of a cluster of monadic qualities. Considered as an object, each constituent would be logically inseparable from the other constituents. In fact such an explanation would seem to be needed only if the relation is a spatial or a temporal one or reducible to such relations. All other relations between quality-objects seem to be also necessary relations between the quality-entities, i.e., it is inconceivable that *any* object that is one of these entities should not be so related to an object that is the other entity. And, as I have remarked before, where the togetherness is necessary, it requires no explanation other than that of necessary truth in general. Spatial and temporal relations indeed do seem to hold contingently. The reason, of course, is that they are taken to hold between the individual things of commonsense and not between qualities. We have seen that to suppose that they hold between quality-entities as such, between universals, would be senseless. But the spatial and temporal relations between individual things understood as clusters of qualities would hold, respectively, between the shape-objects and between the duration-objects in the clusters. Precisely because ultimately they hold between objects, not entities, their holding, i.e., their togetherness with their relata, could be explained in the same way as the togetherness of the monadic quality-objects constituting a cluster.* Of course, the relations themselves would so hold qua objects, not qua entities, just as the constituents of a cluster are together qua objects, not qua entities. This is why their holding would not be described in necessarily true relational statements; the relations such statements assert hold between entities qua entities, even if also between objects (see above, pp. 221–22).

Such a generalized account of accidental predication would be accepted by almost anyone who would accept the specific account of monadic accidental predication offered in chapter eight. However, I find it grossly implausible. The reason has nothing to do with the views defended in this book. It has to do with the suspect character of the category of relation.

---

*This is why the purely dialectical Bradleyan arguments against relations are unsatisfactory. They are based on the assumption that the unity of a relational complex cannot be accounted for. But, as I have just argued, this is not so, given the distinction between objects and entities. For a recent dialectical argument against the category of relations, see Milton Fisk, "Relatedness Without Relations," *Nous* 6 (1972): 139–51; and *Nature and Necessity* (Bloomington and London: Indiana University Press, 1973), chapter VII.

Until about 1900, philosophers (with the notable exception of Aristotle) were reluctant to allow that relations constitute a distinct category of things, namely, a distinct category of qualities (of "accidents," in the Aristotelian terminology). *Pace* Russell, this was due neither to incredible metaphysical blindness nor to logical incompetence, but to certain important facts about relations that, under Russell's influence, twentieth-century philosophy has largely ignored. First, while one can single out and attend to a monadic quality without singling out or attending to anything else (an extreme but still important example would be the color of a uniformly colored visual field; one can single it out and attend to it without singling out and attending to anything else, not even the shape of the field, if it has one), it seems absolutely impossible to single out and attend to a relation and not also single out and attend to its relata. One can single out and attend to the shape of this page and not single out and attend to its color, or the page itself, even though one sees the latter, but one cannot single out and attend to the relation of being-longer-than that holds between the left edge and the top edge of this page without also singling out and attending to (both) the left edge and the top edge of the page. Second, even if monadic qualities as such, as universals, do not have spatial location, their instances, the respective quality-objects, do (see above, p. 193). But there seems to be no sense in which even the instances of a relation may be said to have spatial location, as Russell correctly observed.[1] If a is to the left of b, and a is here and b there, where is the relation between them? We may say that it is between them, but of course we would not mean by this that the relation is in the space between a and b, that it occupies the place or a part of it that is partially bounded by the shapes of a and b. Third, an immediate consequence is that we do not perceive relations. To perceive the relation to-the-left-of that holds between two visible things a and b could only be to see it, since a and b are visible things. But the idea of seeing something that is not (does not even appear to be) in space makes no sense. This is why the empiricist philosophers held that relations are "products of comparison," the result of thought.[2] Fourth, unlike monadic qualities, e.g., colors and shapes, relations, e.g., being-longer-than, seem to have no *specific* characteristics, although they can be named (e.g., "being-longer-than"). Their description seems limited to purely formal characteristics, namely, transitivity, symmetry, reflexivity, and n-adicity. Categorial characteristics, such as that of being a spatial relation, are more properly understood as characteristics of the relata, e.g., that of being a shape-object. A color, on the contrary, can be a specific shade of pink, or pink, or red; it can be darker or purer than another color; it has aesthetic characteristics and can evoke emotions. We expect a genuine entity to have such a wealth of characteristics, to have a *character*. Relations do not.*

Nevertheless, the reality of relations has seemed to twentieth-century philosophers undeniable. The reason, of course, is the indispensability of relational expressions for the description of the world.† But is it a conclusive reason? Let us make some distinctions.

First, even if the elimination of all relational expressions is impossible, only certain special such expressions may be indispensable, namely, those that should not, in any case, be thought of as standing for things in the world, but rather should be understood as transcendental in nature.† I have suggested, for example, that the expression "is identical with" is of this kind, and that togetherness and cluster-constituency can be understood in terms of identity.

Second, if spatial and temporal relations could be eliminated in favor of partial formal identities of shape-objects and duration-objects, as our discussion in chapter eight *suggests* that they can, then so also could all other relations that, for independent philosophical reasons, have been thought to be reducible to spatial and temporal relations. The relation of

---

*Even Russell, toward the end of his philosophical career, said: "For my part, I think it is as certain as anything that there are relational facts such as 'A is earlier than B.' But does it follow that there is an object of which the name is 'earlier'? It is very difficult to make out what can be meant by such a question, and still more difficult to see how an answer can be found. There certainly are complex wholes which have a structure, and we cannot describe the structure without relation-words. But if we try to descry some entity denoted by these relation-words and capable of some shadowy kind of subsistence outside the complex in which it is embodied, it is not at all clear that we can succeed." (*My Philosophical Development*, pp. 172–73.)

†Fisk (op. cit.) attempts to eliminate expressions for relations (e.g., "is larger than") in favor of expressions for monadic relational properties (e.g., "is larger than a") and what he calls foundations (e.g., the size of a). But I am not persuaded that the notion of a monadic relational property can be understood except in terms of the notion of a relation. The standard argument against the reducibility of relational statements to nonrelational statements, especially in the case of asymmetrical relations, was given by Russell in *The Principles of Mathematics*, sections 212–16, and repeated in several of his later works.

†Such a partial elimination of the category of relations would be, presumably, compatible with the fact that while the general functional calculus is undecidable, the monadic functional calculus (even with identity) is not. The indispensable relational expressions would occur in what formally would be relational statements, even though they would not stand for things in the world.

causality, if understood in Hume's way, would be an example of such a relation.

Third, the major remaining class of relations is that of relations among universals, e.g., those expressed in "Crimson is darker than pink" and "9 is greater than 2." It is these relations that would be ineliminable, if any relations are ineliminable. Such relations have been called internal, in the sense that if they hold, they hold necessarily, that they issue from the very nature of their relata, that the very conception of their relata requires that the latter be conceived as standing in the relation. This *suggests* that there is nothing to the relation except what is to be found in its relata, that it is not an additional third thing, somehow hovering between them. But, of course, it does not *suffice* for such a conclusion. We would need also to show how statements expressing internal relations may be reduced to nonrelational (or syntactically relational but metaphysically transcendental) statements, or to explain why such a reduction should be impossible even though there are no such relations.

Only the latter alternative seems to be not entirely hopeless. It would have the general form of an argument that the ineliminability of expressions for internal relations is due not to the nature of the world but to the nature of language, that it is, so to speak, a necessary feature of the *representation* of the subject matter, not of *what* is represented. Moreover, such an argument would apply also to expressions for spatial and temporal relations, as well as to the syntactically relational expressions for the transcendental concept of identity, e.g., "is identical with," and to the expressions for the concepts that can be understood in terms of that of identity, such as the concepts of togetherness (of qualities) and cluster-constituency. For, as we have seen, all of these apply to things only insofar as they are objects (even if they are also entities), and if the expressions stand for relations at all they only stand for internal relations in the sense explained above. For example, a certain shape-object that is to the left of a certain other shape-object cannot be conceived of as not being to the left of the latter. In both cases, the *formal* identity of the object, its being the object it is, requires that it be so related, just as the formal identity of the color crimson, its being the color it is, requires that it be darker than pink.

In the case of transcendental relational expressions, in particular those for identity, such an explanation of their ineliminability does not, of course, mean that the corresponding transcendental *concepts* are merely necessary features of language. (A concept is not an expression.) In fact it fits well with what we have meant by calling a concept transcendental: it applies to things in the world yet not in virtue of standing for some constituent of the world, be it a monadic property or a relation. On the other hand, to suppose that all relational expressions are such, that they all are transcendental, would be fantastic. The reason the concept of identity applies to the world even though there is no constituent of the world it represents, namely, a relation of identity, has to do with the special role of the concept of identity explored in chapter two. No similar explanation of the alleged ordinary relational concepts, e.g., being-to-the-left-of, can be given; therefore, the above explanation of the ineliminability of ordinary relational expressions would mean that such expressions are *merely* necessary features of language, not only that they do not stand for any constituents of the world but also that they do not even express genuine concepts that apply to the world. We need such relational expressions only because of the requirements of language, not because of the nature of the world. Relations belong not to the world but to the shadow that language casts upon the world.

When the suggested explanation of the ineliminability of relational expressions is so generalized as to apply to all syntactically relational expressions, it also amounts to an explanation of the ineliminability of the category of sentences.* From a formal standpoint, every atomic sentence, and thus ultimately all sentences, can be regarded as relational, since, again from a formal standpoint, even monadic predication, both essential and accidental, as well as identity, can be regarded as relational. A sentence expressing accidental monadic predication can be regarded as asserting the holding of a relation between an individual thing and a quality and a sentence expressing essential predication, if understood in the manner suggested in chapter five, can be regarded as asserting the holding of the *sui generis* relation between an object and the entity it is. Indeed, Russell explicitly (though not wholeheartedly) regarded predication as a relation between a subject and a predicate, a relation usually expressed by the verb "to be," which if so understood would be a relational expression.[3] Therefore, if relational expressions are merely necessary features of language, and stand for nothing in the world, then so are sentences. And if the notion of a state of affairs (or fact) is understood, as usual, in terms of the notion of an indicative sentence, then, if there are no entities such as relations, there are no entities such as states of affairs. Indeed, anyone who accepts the reasons we have given for doubting that there are relations would find doubt in the existence of states of affairs even more reasonable.

---

*I shall consider only indicative sentences and merely state my belief that other sentences can be understood on the basis of indicative sentences.

So far I have only described the extent and the implications of the above explanation of the ineliminability of relational expressions. The reasons for accepting it were the reasons given earlier for doubting that there is such a category of entities as relations. But the explanation must be filled out. How and why are relational expressions, and thus sentences, necessary for the linguistic representation of the world, even though they do not stand for constituents of the world?

I have already noted that it is impossible that there be genuine names of objects as such or of entities as such. Nor, it would seem, can we have genuine, reapplicable names of absolutely specific qualities (e.g., of the precise shade of white of this page); and most of our names of generic qualities (e.g., "white" and "round") have an indeterminate range of application (e.g., it may be neither correct nor incorrect to call a certain shade white). It follows that language is generally incapable of representing the world adequately in the most obvious and straightforward respect, namely, by containing genuine, precise, and unambiguous names of its constituents. To represent them at all, to be capable of connecting with them, to serve its function of drawing our attention to them, it must employ, so to speak, subterfuges. It can be argued that relational expressions, and thus sentences, are just such subterfuges, and not representations of things belonging, respectively, to the alleged categories of relations and states of affairs. If adequate names of the things we want to talk about were possible, then we would be able to represent whatever sentences, with their relational components, represent simply by listing the names of these things.* Such a list would not be a sentence, but what is in question is precisely the pervasive assumption of philosophers that the category of sentences is indispensable for representing the world in language. For example, I would not need to assert that this page is white, or, more fundamentally, that this white color-object, this rectangular shape-object, and whatever other objects constitute the page are together, if I possessed precise and unambiguous names of the objects in question as such. The mere listing of their names would show that the objects are together, not because it would show something additional to them, but ineffable, which relates them, but simply because each of the objects would be seen to be what it is in virtue of what the other objects are.

---

*According to Locke, the mind "gets all of its *ideas* of relations" by "bringing two *ideas*, whether simple or complex, together, and setting them by one another, so as to take a view of them at once, without uniting them into one." (*Essay Concerning Human Understanding*, Book II, Chapter XII, Section 1.)

Another example would be the sentence "Crimson is darker than pink," understood as being about the universals as such, and not about some instances of them (about entities as such and not about some objects that are those entities). "Crimson" and "pink" are not genuine, referentially used names, if so understood. What the sentence represents cannot be represented merely by the list "crimson, pink." But had these been genuine names, had they been capable of being used referringly, the list would have allowed us to *see* everything that the sentence *tells* us. Of course, it is not an accidental feature of language that we can have no such names; we cannot refer to entities as such because we cannot single out entities as such, because we can have only nonintentional consciousness of entities as such. Similarly, it is not an accidental feature of language that we can have no genuine names for objects as such, even though we can single them out and refer to them with demonstrative expressions and definite descriptions; we can have no genuine names for objects as such because objects by their very nature cannot be singled out twice. So the inability of language to represent the world adequately by containing genuine, precise, and unambiguous names for its constituents, its inability to express adequately the richness and detail of our experience and thought of the world, is itself due to the nature of the world and of our experience and thought of the world.

But even if we did have names for everything we want to name, would we not need relational expressions in order to distinguish what would ordinarily be described as different relational facts that are facts about the same things? Suppose that two objects enter into what would ordinarily be described as three different relations. Then, even if we did have genuine names of the objects, the mere pair of such names may succeed in drawing our attention to all three "relational" facts about the objects but would fail to distinguish these facts. And surely it is a feature of the world, deserving of representation in language, that there are these three distinguishable facts about the objects. I believe that this is the most serious objection to the thesis that there are no relations. It would seem that it can be met only if the following assumption is true. There are absolutely simple things, both as objects and as entities, of which all other things consist; and the simplicity of a thing consists not merely in its having no literal parts, or in its not being a cluster, but in its being, so to speak, perfectly one-sided, in the sense that if there were relations it could enter into only one relation with any other simple thing. If this assumption is granted, then, were names of two such simple things possible, the list of these names would express whatever any relational statement about them would express.

The assumption is not as fantastic as it may seem. There are, for example, independent reasons for regarding even absolutely specific shades of color as complex, in effect as subclusters consisting of a hue, a degree of saturation, and a degree of brightness. And, clearly, to assert that one shade is darker than another is to assert, more precisely, that the former's degree of brightness is lesser than the latter's degree of brightness. It is not at all clear that there can be another direct two-term relation between two degrees of brightness. And it is not implausible to suggest that to know that this relation holds between two actually singled out degrees of brightness is nothing but to have singled out both degrees at the same time and to attend to them concurrently.*

So, if there are simple things in the sense just explained, we may conclude that although relational expressions and sentences remain ineliminable, this is due not to the presence in the world of such entities as relations and states of affairs, but to the chasm that naturally and inevitably separates language from the world and from our experience and thought of the world.

See the quotation from Locke above, p. 245, n..

APPENDIX B

Idealism

The fundamental thesis of this book is that the notion of identity is a genuine concept, a principle of classification. That such is also the notion of existence, a much more controversial thesis, is a direct consequence of our account of existence in terms of identity. Much of the discussion in the first four chapters was concerned with arguments for these two theses and replies to the various objections they face.

But there is a deeper objection to both theses, which to my knowledge has not been explicitly made before, but which demands an answer. According to this objection, the classificatory nature of the notions of identity and existence is incompatible with unqualified realism and to accept it is to accept a variety of transcendental idealism.

That to understand the world we must apply to it concepts; that the application of concepts to things is essentially the classification of things, a concept being a principle of dividing all things into two mutually exclusive classes; that there is no unique classification of any subject matter (a classification can be arbitrary), even if only one classification adequately reflects the nature of that subject matter; and thus that there is a distinction of reason, though of course not a distinction of things, a real distinction, between things considered in abstraction from any classification of them and the things qua classified in a certain way—all this has been commonplace in philosophy at least since Kant and probably since Plato. It should be as evident as anything can be in philosophy. But it must not be confused with the view, which to my mind is incoherent, that the world has no objective, independent nature, objective similarities and differences, that determine the applicability of our concepts and the adequacy of our classifications.

The common solution of the problems of identity and existence that is provided by the distinction between objects and entities depends on taking seriously the fact that our notions of identity and existence are concepts, that they are principles of classification, and thus that we must

248

distinguish between things as they are independently of their classification in terms of these concepts, and things as so classified. But, it may now be objected, the measure of the adequacy of a classification to the nature of the world is the degree to which it reflects the similarities and differences, that is, as we saw in chapter seven, the identities and diversities, of things actually in the world, of existents. To suppose that these identities and diversities, and this being-actually-in-the-world, or being-an-existent, are themselves true of things only insofar as the latter are classified would be to make nonsense of the idea of the objective adequacy of a classification and thus of the idea of classification itself—for the objective world would itself be the result of a classification. Therefore, the notions of identity and existence cannot be classificatory, they cannot be concepts.

This important objection draws our attention to the fundamental difference between the concepts of identity and existence, on one hand, and all other concepts, on the other, which I have marked by calling the former transcendental. Paradoxically enough, this difference is the deeper motive both behind the realist's denial that the notions of existence and identity are concepts and behind transcendental idealism. Confronted with this difference, we feel compelled to deny that the notions of existence and identity are concepts. Yet we also feel compelled by our recognition of the special role of these concepts to embrace transcendental idealism. But there is a third alternative.

An application of the concept of identity or the concept of existence, like that of any other principle of classification, can be appraised as correct or incorrect by appeal to the independent characteristics of what the concept is applied to and to the objective similarities and differences between these characteristics and those of the paradigmatic cases of their application. That certain cases are paradigms of identity or of existence is the same as the fact that such is the content of the concept of identity or of existence. And while it depends on us with what word, if any, to express a certain concept, and on our intellectual development what concepts we in fact possess, the content of a concept and the paradigms of its application are an objective and quite impersonal, indeed *nonhuman* matter. Were we to change its content or its paradigms, we would have changed the concept only in the irrelevant sense that we would have acquired or shown preference for another, even if similar, concept.

To this extent our view is realist. But there is a sense in which it is idealist. Any judgment of the adequacy of a concept, or of a whole conceptual framework, is mainly a judgment of the degree to which it reflects, or helps to reflect, the similarities and differences, that is, according to the account of similarity in terms of universals, the identities and diversities, we find among the existents in the world. Therefore, the adequacy of the concepts of identity and existence themselves cannot be so judged.* We can have no notion of a world to which our concepts of identity and existence are inadequate.

The world thus does have a transcendental structure, if we mean by this the necessary applicability to it of concepts the adequacy of which cannot be judged by comparison with the world and with the objective similarities and differences one finds in it. But this transcendental structure is far removed from, far deeper than, such features of the world as space and time, or causality and substance, to say nothing of the existence of other minds or the world's having a history longer than five minutes. And the criterion for determining the transcendental features of the world is neither our ability to know them synthetically a priori nor their being necessary conditions of our understanding the language we speak. The criterion, I suggest, is that they be features the world must have if it is to be a world of entities.

If it seems, nevertheless, that our view is idealist in a much stronger sense than we have just admitted, that it considers the world to be our own mental creation effected by the application of the concepts of identity and existence, and ultimately just by that of identity, the reason would probably be the acceptance of a certain familiar conception of the self. For the supposition that the world, or at least a certain feature of it, is in some sense our own mental creation is intelligible only if by ourselves we understand something that can engage in such a creation. According to this conception, the self is a *sui generis* entity whose nature consists in the capacity for engaging in activities such as perceiving, or thinking, or experiencing, in the capacity for consciousness or awareness. Such activities may be regarded as monadic properties or states of the self that have their own intrinsic character, their "contents," which are what we express in language when we state what the perception or thought or experience is of or about; if so, then it becomes a significant question whether certain things, perhaps even Berkeley's "sensible things," might not be mere contents of such states. Or they may be regarded as asymmetrical relations in which the self alone can enter,

---

*"And that's what we *call* 'the same'. If there did not exist an agreement in what we call 'red', etc. etc., language would stop. But what about the agreement in what we call 'agreement'?" Wittgenstein, *Remarks on the Foundations of Mathematics* (Oxford: Basil Blackwell, 1956), p. 96.

and one may then speak, picturesquely, of the intentionality or object-directedness of the mind; if so, it can be a significant question whether the occurrence of such a relation produces a change in its referent, in the object.[1]

In 1739 Hume argued that there is neither evidence for, nor sense in, the supposition that there is such an entity as the self so conceived. I shall not repeat Hume's argument here;[2] suffice it to point out that he appeals not only to his inability to *find* such an entity, but far more fundamentally to his inability to form even an *idea*, a conception, of it. Superficially, the conclusion of the argument has generally been accepted, for example, by Kant, Mach, Husserl in the *Logical Investigations* (but not in the *Ideas*), Sartre, Wittgenstein, Strawson,* and the chief efforts of writers on the self have been directed, somewhat paradoxically, toward the elucidation of the nature of personal identity. But the implications of the Humean (though probably not Hume's) argument were seen, I believe, only by Wittgenstein in the *Tractatus*. It is these implications that constitute its chief philosophical importance. What Hume rejected was not merely the notion of a mental substance, whether introspectible or not, but the notion of the very sort of entity that can enter in activities such as perceiving, thinking, or experiencing, whether these be understood as monadic or relational. By implication, he therefore denied that there are any such activities. I believe that he would have agreed that when he looked within himself he not only did not find the sort of self he ironically allowed "some metaphysicians may have," but also did not find anything that could be described as a perceiving or a thinking or an experiencing. (What he says he found were perceptions, i.e., impressions and ideas, which for him are individual

---

*An exception in current American philosophy is R. M. Chisholm, who has argued (in "On the Observability of the Self," *Philosophy and Phenomenological Research* XXX [1969]: 7–21; and *Person and Object,* chapter 1) that the self is observable. His argument rests on the premise that in observing the properties or states of a thing one observes the thing itself. This premise cannot be evaluated unless it is buttressed with a particular account of predication, of the connection between a thing and its properties. (Chisholm provides no such account.) It would be useful to ask ourselves how convincing it would be as an answer to Locke's, Berkeley's, and Hume's thesis of the unobservability of *material* substance. According to Chisholm, at least some of the self's properties or states should be understood in accordance with the so-called adverbial theory, e.g., that we should speak of someone's sensing redly rather than of his sensing something that is red. I believe that Hume would have found the idea that such properties or states are observable even more fantastic than the idea that the self is observable.

things. Even if they were *objects* of perceivings, thinkings, or experiencings, they would not themselves be perceivings, thinkings, or experiencings.)* Indeed, if understood as a relation such a thing would lack the only relatum it could have (even if it did not lack a referent, i.e., the thing perceived, etc.).† And if understood as a monadic property or state it would lack the only sort of owner it can intelligibly be supposed to have. The fact is that the unintelligibility of the notion of the self goes hand in hand with the unintelligibility of the notion of such a relation and of the notion of such a property or state.

This view faces a difficult question. If we accept it, how should we understand terms such as "perceive," "imagine," "think," "experience," "consciousness"? Hume did suggest, though barely, what seems to me to be our only alternative. It is to regard them as ways of expressing what in fact are *monadic* characteristics of the *things* we ordinarily describe as perceived, or imagined, etc. What we call a perceived thing, for example, has the monadic characteristic of especial liveliness, according to Hume. A remembered thing has a lesser degree of liveliness. An imagined thing has the lowest degree of liveliness. And their being perceived, remembered, or imagined *consists* in their having a certain degree of liveliness. There can be no defense of Hume's terminology, nor need we accept his underlying theory of impressions and ideas, but

*It is significant that in his great defense of the distinction between consciousness and its objects, in "The Refutation of Idealism," G. E. Moore felt compelled to say the following: " . . . the moment we try to fix our attention upon consciousness and to see *what*, distinctly, it is, it seems to vanish: it seems as if we had before us a mere emptiness. When we try to introspect the sensation of blue, all we can see is the blue: the other element is as if it were diaphanous. Yet it *can* be distinguished if we look attentively enough, and if we know that there is something to look for." (*Philosophical Studies* [London: Routledge and Kegan Paul, 1922], p. 25.)

†Sartre's theory of consciousness seems to amount to accepting just this consequence. (Cf. *The Transcendence of the Ego* [New York: The Noonday Press, 1957], trans. Forrest Williams and Robert Kirkpatrick; and of course *Being and Nothingness*.) Yet it constitutes a great advance over Brentano and Husserl in its recognition of the fact that if the intentionality of consciousness is taken seriously then consciousness is seen to be nothing additional to its object, it exhausts itself in its object. "To say that consciousness is consciousness of something means that for consciousness there is no being outside that precise obligation to be a revealing intuition of something" (*Being and Nothingness*, trans. Hazel Barnes [New York: Philosophical Library, 1956], p. LXI). The view I shall sketch may be thought of as bringing Sartre's theory to its logical conclusion (which I have no doubt he would find distasteful).

the general point can be made clear and perhaps defensible in terms of our distinction between objects and entities. Let us call the monadic characteristics in question being-a-perceptual-thing, being-a-memorial-thing, and being-an-imaginal-thing. As long as we think of the things that may exemplify them as entities, the supposition that there are such monadic characteristics seems absurd. One and the same entity may be perceived, remembered, and imagined at different times by the same person or at the same time by different persons. It does not itself have any actual monadic, intrinsic characteristic such as being perceptual, memorial, or imaginal. But not so with objects. An object can be singled out only once, and its formal identity, the object it is, depends in part on how it can be singled out. And how it can be singled out is an actual monadic, intrinsic characteristic of the object itself. A visual object, for example, is not just an object that can be seen. It would not be the object it is unless it could *only* be seen. It may be *materially* identical with an object that can be imagined, or with an object that can be remembered, or with an object that can be felt, etc., but it cannot be *formally* identical with such an object, it cannot itself be such an object; its identity with such an object can only be material, the identicals necessarily appearing to be distinct, and the assertion of this identity can only be a material identity statement.

But even if it is acknowledged that objects do have such monadic characteristics, the difficult question the Humean view faces has not been answered. If there were no objects that are not singled out, then an object's being perceived would have been the same as its having the monadic characteristic of being a perceptual object, and analogously for an object's being remembered, imagined, etc. But if there are objects that are not singled out, then how are we to understand the difference, for example, between a perceptual object's being singled out, being perceived, and its not being singled out, not being perceived? And how are we to understand the difference between a perceptual object's being singled out, perceived by one person, say, me, and its being singled out, perceived, by another person? Hume could have answered both questions by adopting a solipsistic position and in effect denying that either difference exists. He did not do so in his writings, even if it was his conviction; Wittgenstein did seem to adopt such a position in the *Tractatus*. But we need not be forced into solipsism. I have pointed out (see above, pp. 62–63) that an object cannot be described either as causally or as logically mind-dependent. There can be no content, therefore, to the idea that there are no objects that are not singled out. But this is a general statement that cannot be instantiated in genuine singular statements. There is a clear sense in which we can neither think nor speak about objects that are not singled out, *as objects*. To think or speak about a certain object, we may therefore say, is to think or speak about an object that has been singled out. To speak about objects that are not singled out is to speak in general statements that, even though not about entities as such, are about objects only in the sense in which a general statement is about anything that is part of its truth-conditions. Therefore, we may say, while there can be no content to the idea that there are no objects that are not singled out, neither is there any content to the idea of *finding* a difference between an object that is singled out, and thus has a monadic characteristic such as that of being perceptual, and an object that is not singled out.

The second question could receive the following answer, which is closely related to the answer to the first question. One and the same *object* cannot be singled out, and thus perceived, or remembered, or thought, etc., by more than one person, since the judgment that what one has singled out is identical with what another person has singled out cannot be a formal identity judgment. But neither can it be a material identity judgment, since the description of what another person has singled out can never be used referringly by oneself. One may speak, therefore, of the objects someone else has singled out, and thus perceived, remembered, or imagined, only in general statements, and this already sharply distinguishes them from the objects one has singled out oneself.

But, of course, they share this characteristic also with objects that are not singled out at all. The explanation of the required *further* difference may be sought in the intimate connection between the objects that are singled out, whether by ourselves or someone else, and our bodies. The aches and pains you experience are in your body, the aches and pains I experience are in my body. The visual objects you see bear a certain necessary spatial relationship to your body, while the visual objects I see bear such a relationship to my body. The tactile objects you feel bear a necessary relationship to your skin, the tactile objects I feel bear such a relationship to my skin. And the objects of which you speak in singular statements, and of which I can speak only in general statements such as this one, bear a complex relationship to the activity of your body that we call your use of language; while the objects of which I speak in singular statements, and of which you can speak only in general statements, bear a complex relationship to the activity of my body that we call my use of language.

These answers to the questions a Humean theory of self faces are not solipsistic. For solipsism to be true, it is necessary that the general statements by means of which we speak of objects that are not singled out by oneself, and of objects that are not singled out by anyone, be all false or meaningless. Whether they are such is a philosophical question of great difficulty. But it is not the simplistic question of solipsism; it is the subtler question of the nature of generality.

If the so-called mental activities of the self can be understood in the manner suggested, then we can say that the mind is not an individual thing, whether one possessing monadic mental properties or essentially the origin of rays of consciousness; nor is it the Sartrean amorphous and contentless consciousness that attaches itself to and works upon the world in mysterious ways; nor is it the brain or any of its states. We can say, rather, that the mind is *in the things* we ordinarily describe as its objects, that it is nothing but the set of certain characteristics of objects in the world. These characteristics are very different from, say, colors and shapes, or zoological species. Yet they are quite familiar. They are such characteristics as being perceptual (including its species, being visual, being tactile, etc.), being imaginal, being memorial, perhaps being purely intellectual.

If the Humean theory I have sketched (I do not suggest that it is Hume's) can be developed and defended in detail, then philosophical idealism, if by this is meant the doctrine that the world, or its structure, or at least some features of it, are creatures of our own minds, must be rejected. There is nothing that can engage in such a sublime creation; there are only our bodies that occasionally, through their physical activities, make a modest difference to the world. And the presence of identity in the world would be analogous to the presence in the world of characteristics such as perceptuality and imaginality. But only analogous. Though in the world, it is not a constituent of the world. The reason is not that it is a mysterious self's conceptual secretion, but that, being the ground of the worldliness of the world, the measure of what it is to be a constituent of the world, it cannot itself rest on that ground, it cannot be the measure of itself. This is the only sense in which it should be described as a transcendental feature of the world. This is the only sense in which the central thesis of this book may be described as idealist.

NOTES

Introduction

1. A recent example of this unwillingness is provided by Nicholas Griffin's *Relative Identity* (Oxford: Clarendon Press, 1977); see especially pp. 161, 204–12. I consider the issue of relative identity in chapter three.

2. The recent (qualified) defense of Meinong by Leonard Linsky (*Referring* [London: Routledge and Kegan Paul, 1967], also *Names and Descriptions* [Chicago and London: The University of Chicago Press, 1977]), Roderick M. Chisholm ("Beyond Being and Non-Being," *Philosophical Studies* 24 (1973): 245–57, and "Homeless Objects," *Revue Internationale de Philosophie* 104/5 (1973): 207–23), and Charles Landesman ("Thought, Reference, and Existence," *The Southern Journal of Philosophy* XIII (1975): 449–58) has succeeded in meeting many of the usual specific objections but can hardly be supposed to have rendered the content of the key notion of the *Aussersein* of the pure object intellectually visible.

3. *Meaning and Necessity* (Chicago: University of Chicago Press, 1956).

4. "Some Problems About Belief" and "Reply to Quine," in *Essays in Philosophy and its History* (Dordrecht: Reidel, 1974).

Chapter One: The Apparent Distinctness of Identicals

1. *Tractatus Logico-Philosophicus*, trans. D. F. Pears and B. F. McGuinness (London: Routledge and Kegan Paul, 1961), p. 105.

2. *Philosophical Investigations*, trans. G. E. M. Anscombe (Oxford: Basil Blackwell, 1953), p. 84e.

3. *A Treatise of Human Nature*, ed. L. A. Selby-Bigge (Oxford: Clarendon Press, 1888), p. 200.

4. *Hegel Selections*, ed. J. Loewenberg (New York: Charles Scribner's Sons, 1929), pp. 135–37.

5. *Hegel's Science of Logic,* trans. A. V. Miller (London: George Allen and Unwin, 1969), p. 415.

6. Wittgenstein, *Philosophical Investigations,* p. 221.

7. *Translations,* pp. 57–61.

8. Cf. Michael Dummett, *Frege: Philosophy of Language* (New York: Harper and Row, 1973), pp. 154–59; and Reinhardt Grossmann, *Reflections on Frege's Philosophy* (Evanston: Northwestern University Press, 1969), pp. 156–57.

9. *Perceiving: A Philosophical Study* (Ithaca: Cornell University Press, 1957), pp. 44–52; *Theory of Knowledge* (Englewood Cliffs: Prentice-Hall, 1966), pp. 34–37.

10. Cf. "Naming and Necessity," in *Semantics of Natural Language,* ed. Donald Davidson and Gilbert Harman (Dordrecht: Reidel, 1972), p. 308.

11. Alfred Korzybski, *Science and Sanity* (Lakeville, Conn.: The International Non-Aristotelian Library Publishing Company, 1958), pp. 194–95.

12. "On Sense and Reference," *Translations.*

13. *Ibid.* pp. 57–61.

14. *Translations,* pp. 11–12. Cf. Dummett, *Frege: Philosophy of Language,* p. 102.

15. Cf. Carnap, *Meaning and Necessity;* also Alonzo Church, "A Formulation of the Logic of Sense and Denotation," in *Structure, Method, and Meaning,* ed. P. Henle, H. M. Kallen, S. K. Langer (New York: Liberal Arts Press, 1951).

16. Leonard Linsky, "Reference and Referents," in *Philosophy and Ordinary Language,* ed. C. E. Caton (Urbana: University of Illinois Press, 1963), and also *Referring;* Keith Donnellan, "Reference and Definite Descriptions," *The Philosophical Review* 75 (1966): 281–304.

17. Cf. Edgar Page, "Reference and Propositional Identity," *The Philosophical Review* 79 (1970): 43–62.

18. *Tractatus* 5.5321. Cf. Jaakko Hintikka, "Identity, Variables, and Impredicative Definitions," *The Journal of Symbolic Logic* 21 (1957): 225–45.

19. P. F. Strawson, "On Referring," *Mind* 59 (1950): 320–44; Donnellan, "Reference and Definite Descriptions." See also L. Jonathan Cohen, "Geach's Problem About Intentional Identity," *The Journal of Philosophy* 65 (1968): 329–35.

20. Cf. Strawson on identifying thought, in *Individuals* (London: Methuen, 1959), pp. 60–61.

21. *My Philosophical Development* (New York: Simon and Schuster, 1959), pp. 238–45.

22. Cf. W. V. Quine, "The Problem of Interpreting Modal Logic," *The Journal of Symbolic Logic* 12 (1947): 42–48. Quine does not argue for such a relation.

23. Cf. Ruth Barcan Marcus, "Modalities and Intensional Languages," in *Contemporary Readings in Logical Theory*, ed. I. M. Copi and J. A. Gould (New York: The Macmillan Company, 1967).

24. Cf. Hector-Neri Castañeda, "Thinking and the Structure of the World," *Philosophia* 4 (1974): 3–40; and "Identity and Modality," *Philosophia* 5 (1975): 141–50. I should observe, however, that there is much in these important papers with which I agree.

25. Cf. Leonard Linsky, *Referring*, p. 6.

Chapter Two: Objects and Entities

1. Cf. P. F. Strawson, *Individuals* (London: Methuen, 1959), p. 35.

2. *Being and Nothingness*, Introduction.

3. *From a Logical Point of View* (New York: Harper and Row, 1961), p. 4. Compare P. T. Geach, "Intentional Identity," *The Journal of Philosophy* 64 (1967): 627–32, but also L. Jonathan Cohen, "Geach's Problem About Intentional Identity." *The Journal of Philosophy* 65 (1968): 329–35.

4. *Theaetetus,*181b–183c.

5. *Philosophical Investigations*, ##243–412.

6. *Thinking and Experience* (London: Hutchinson's University Library, 1953). Indeed, Price defines concepts as recognitional capacities.

7. Cf. *The Problems of Philosophy* (New York: Oxford University Press, 1959), Chapter V.

8. *Sense and Sensibilia* (Oxford: Clarendon Press, 1962), chapters VII and VIII.

9. Cf. A. J. Ayer, *The Central Questions of Philosophy* (New York: William Morrow, 1975), pp. 75–76.

10. *From a Logical Point of View*, p. 153; "Reply to Mrs. Marcus," in *Contemporary Readings in Logical Theory*, p. 299.

11. Cf. Quine's account of this alternative in *Words and Objections: Essays on the Work of W. V. Quine*, ed. D. Davidson and J. Hintikka (Dordrecht: Reidel, 1969), p. 339; also *From a Logical Point of View*, p. 149.

12. "Perception, Belief, and the Structure of Physical Objects and Consciousness," *Synthese* 35 (1977): 285–351. See also his papers mentioned above, chapter one, n.24.

13. Cf. David Kaplan, "How to Russell a Frege-Church," *Journal of Philosophy* 72 (1975): 717.

14. Cf. Terrence Parsons, "A Prolegomenon to Meinong's Semantics," *Journal of Philosophy* 71 (1974): 561–81.

Chapter Three: Indiscernibility

1. Cf. David Wiggins, *Identity and Spatio-Temporal Continuity* (Oxford: Basil Blackwell, 1971), p. 3.

2. Max Black, "The Identity of Indiscernibles," *Mind* 61 (1952), reprinted in *Universals and Particulars*, ed. Michael J. Loux (Notre Dame and London: University of Notre Dame Press, 1976), pp. 250–62.

3. Cf. A. J. Ayer, "The Identity of Indiscernibles," in *Philosophical Essays* (London, 1954), also in Loux; Ian Hacking, "The Identity of Indiscernibles," *The Journal of Philosophy* 72 (1975): 249–56; for a rejoinder, see Gordon Nagel, *The Journal of Philosophy* 73 (1976): 45–50.

4. Cf. Linsky, *Referring*, pp. 79–80, and Cartwright, "Identity and Substitutivity."

5. "Naming and Necessity"; see also Marcus, "Modalities and Intensional Languages." For a valuable discussion of Kripke's general thesis that there are necessary a posteriori propositions as well as contingent a priori propositions, see Albert Casullo, "Kripke on the A Priori and the Necessary," *Analysis* 37 (1977): 152–59.

6. *Reference and Generality* (Ithaca: Cornell University Press, 1962), p. 39; "Identity," *The Review of Metaphysics* 21 (1967): 3–12; "Ontological Relativity and Relative Identity," in *Logic and Ontology*, ed. Milton K. Munitz (New York: New York University Press, 1973), pp. 287–302.

7. "The Same F," *The Philosophical Review* 79 (1970): 181–200.

8. *Identity and Spatio-Temporal Continuity*, pp. 3–4.

9. Cf. Stephan Körner, "Substance," *Aristotelian Society Supplementary Volume* 37 (1964): 79–90. Also Eli Hirsch, *The Persistence of Bodies*, pp. 29–30, and "Physical Identity," p. 361.

Chapter Four: Existence

1. Cf. Moore, "Is Existence a Predicate?" *Aristotelian Society Supp. Vol.* 15 (1936): 175–88. Richard Cartwright. "Negative Existentials," *Journal of Philosophy* 57 (1960): 629–39; P. F. Strawson, "Is Existence Never a Predicate?," *Critica* 1 (1967): 5–15.

2. See Czeslaw Lejewski, "Logic and Existence," *British Journal for the Philosophy of Science* 5 (1954): 104–19; H. S. Leonard, "The Logic of Existence," *Philosophical Studies* 7 (1956): 49–64, and "Essences, Attributes, and Predicates," *Proceedings and Addresses of the American Philosophical Association*, 1963–64, pp. 25–51; Nicholas Rescher, "Definitions of 'Existence,'" *Philosophical Studies* 8 (1957): 65–69, "On the Logic of Existence and Denotation," *The Philosophical Review* 68 (1959): 157–80, and *A Theory of Possibility;* George Nahknikian and Wesley C. Salmon, "'Exists' as a Predicate," *The Philosophical Review* 66 (1957): 535–42; Nino Cochiarella, "A Logic of Actual and Possible Objects," *Journal of Symbolic Logic* 31 (1966): 688–89. For the distinction between "exists" as a logical predicate and "exists" as a grammatical predicate, see William Kneale, "Is Existence a Predicate?" *Aristotelian Society Supp. Vol.* 15 (1936): 154–74.

3. John Woods, *The Logic of Fiction* (The Hague: Mouton, 1974). Cf. Richard Cartwright, "Negative Existentials," pp. 636–39.

4. For particularly useful recent discussions of fictional discourse, see John Woods, op. cit.; Alvin Plantinga, *The Nature of Necessity* (Oxford: Clarendon Press, 1974), pp. 153–63; J. O. Urmson, "Fiction," *American Philosophical Quarterly* 13 (1976): 153–57; and Peter Van Inwagen, "Creatures of Fiction," *American Philosophical Quarterly* 14 (1977): 299–308.

5. Bertrand Russell, "Some Explanations in Reply to Mr. Bradley." *Mind* 19 (1910): 373–78; F. H. Bradley, "Reply to Mr. Russell's Explanations," *Mind* 20 (1911): 74–76.

6. "A Defense of Common Sense," in *Contemporary British Philosophy*, Second Series, ed. J. H. Muirhead (London: The Macmillan Company, 1925), pp. 217–18.

7. *Perception* (London: Methuen, 1954).

8. I offer such a discussion in *The Concept of Knowledge*, Part Three.

9. Cf. Price's explanation of the notion of a sense-datum in *Perception*, p. 3, and my explanation of the notion of a pure perceptual object in *The Concept of Knowledge*, pp. 255–62.

10. "Form and Existence," in *God and the Soul* (New York: Schocken Books, 1969), pp. 55–56. See also *Reference and Generality*, pp. 163–64. A similar view was defended by Gilbert Ryle in "Systematically Misleading Expressions," *Proceedings of the Aristotelian Society* 32 (1931–32): 139–70, and in "Imaginary Objects," *Aristotelian Society Suppl. Vol.* 12 (1933): 18–43. But compare G. E. Moore's "Imaginary Objects," in the latter volume, pp. 55–70.

11. Cf. Russell, in *The Principles of Mathematics* (New York: Norton, 1903), p. 449.

12. "On Denoting," in *Logic and Knowledge;* also his review of *Unter-suchungen zur Gegenstandstheorie und Psychologie, Mind* 14 (1905): 530–38. Russell's argument that on Meinong's theory "the existent present King of France exists, and also does not exist" will be considered in my response to the ninth objection.

13. *Über die Stellung der Gegenstandstheorie im System der Wissenshaften* (Leipzig: Voigtlander, 1907), p. 14ff.

14. In his review of Meinong's *Über die Stellung der Gegenstandstheorie im System der Wissenshaften, Mind* 16 (1907): 436–39.

15. *Logic and Knowledge,* p. 45.

16. Cf. Plato, *Sophist,* 238ff. This objection is also L. Jonathan Cohen's chief reason for rejecting Lejewski's nonexistential interpretation of quantification. See above, p. 97, n.*.

17. See "In Behalf of the Fool," in *The Ontological Argument,* ed. Alvin Plantinga (Garden City: Anchor Books, 1965).

18. In "On Denoting" and the review of *Untersuchungen zur Gegenstandstheorie und Psychologie* in *Mind* 14 (1905). I agree with Russell (see his review of Meinong's *Über die Stellung der Gegenstandstheorie im System der Wissenshaften,* in *Mind* 16 [1907]) that Meinong's response that there is a difference between existing and being an existent, and thus that the existent round square need not exist, is inadequate.

19. Clyde L. Hardin, "An Empirical Refutation of the Ontological Argument," *Analysis* 22 (1961): 10–12.

20. I defend this view in detail in *Resemblance and Identity,* pp. 183–99.

21. Cf. P. F. Strawson, "A Reply to Mr. Sellars," *The Philosophical Review* 63 (1954): 221.

Chapter Five: Essence

1. Cf. Aquinas, *On Being and Essence,* 2d ed., trans. Armand Maurer (Toronto: The Pontifical Institute of Medieval Studies, 1968), pp. 32, 55, 57–58.

2. Aquinas, p. 66; also pp. 31–32.

3. Aristotle, *Categories,* 2b29–3a6. Cf. Baruch Brody, "Natural Kinds and Real Essences," *Journal of Philosophy* 64 (1967): 431–46, and Wiggins, *Identity and Spatio-Temporal Continuity,* pp. 27–28.

4. Cf. Alvin Plantinga, *The Nature of Necessity* (Oxford: Clarendon Press, 1974), pp. 70 ff.

5. A representative article is "Three Grades of Modal Involvement," in *The Ways of Paradox* (New York: Random House, 1966). See especially pp. 173–74.

6. Cf. Irving M. Copi, "Essence and Accident," *The Journal of Philosophy* 51 (1954): 717–19. Also Hilary Putnam, "Is Semantics Possible?" *Metaphilosophy* 1 (1970): 187–201. The view is discussed usefully by Paul Teller in "Essential Properties: Some Problems and Conjectures," *The Journal of Philosophy* 77 (1975): 233–48.

7. Cf. Plantinga, *The Nature of Necessity*, p. 79.

8. Cf. Kripke, "Identity and Necessity," in *Identity and Individuation*, ed. Milton K. Munitz (New York: New York University Press, 1971), p. 152; and "Naming and Necessity," in *Semantics of Natural Language*, p. 314.

9. *On Being and Essence*, p. 31.

10. Ibid., p. 37.

11. Ibid.

12. *Categories*, 1a 20 ff.

13. 1a 22–24, 3a 28–32. Compare 8a 13–8b 24.

14. *Metaphysics* 1007b 15–17, trans. Hippocrates G. Apostle (Bloomington and London: Indiana University Press, 1966). Compare *Posterior Analytics* I, 19–22.

15. Cf. Aristotle, *Metaphysics*, 1016a 25–1018a 10.

16. *Resemblance and Identity*, chapter 4.

17. *Categories*, 1a 19–34.

18. *Statement and Inference*, vol. 1, pp. 223, 375–76.

19. *Categories*, 1b 10–15, 2a 19–34, 3a 6–21.

20. Cf. *Selections from Medieval Philosophers*, vol. 1, ed. Richard McKeon (New York: Charles Scribner's Sons, 1929), especially pp. 224–25.

Chapter Six: Substances

1. Cf. Aquinas, *On Being and Essence*, p. 41.

2. Cf. Aristotle, *Metaphysics*, 1029a 20–26.

3. Cf. Aristotle, *On Generation and Corruption*, 317a 25–28.

4. G. E. M. Anscombe observes (in the context of a discussion of substantial change, i.e., of a parcel of matter that is a certain substance becoming a different substance) that we have no application for the notion of the annihilation of matter as such. ("The Principle of Individuation," *Aristotelian Society Suppl. Vol.* 27 [1953]: 83–96.) But this

suggests that neither do we have an application for the notion of its remaining the same.

5. Cf. Edwin Hartman, "Aristotle on the Identity of Substance and Essence," *Philosophical Review* 85 (1976): 545–61.

6. P. T. Geach and G. E. M. Anscombe, *Three Philosophers* (Ithaca and New York: Cornell University Press, 1961) p. 83.

7. See *The Concept of Knowledge*, pp. 82–83.

8. Book IV, 455–59, trans. Richmond Lattimore (New York: Harper and Row, 1965). For a detailed defense of the logical compatibility of such (and even more extreme!) changes with individual identity through time, see Marjorie S. Price, "Identity Through Time," *The Journal of Philosophy* 74 (1977): 201–17.

9. On this, Robert Coburn's "Identity and Spatiotemporal Continuity," in *Identity and Individuation*, ed. Milton K. Munitz, is a valuable guide.

10. David Sanford explores the connection and denies it, as well as the principle, in "Volume and Solidity," *Australasian Journal of Philosophy* 45 (1967): 329–40, and "Locke, Leibniz, and Wiggins on Being in the Same Place at the Same Time," *Philosophical Review* 79 (1970): 75 –82.

11. *Individuals*, p. 37; see also David Wiggins, "The Individuation of Things and Places," and Richard Swinburne, *Space and Time*, pp. 24–26.

12. Wiggins, *Identity and Spatio-Temporal Continuity*, p. 8.

13. Ibid., p. 10.

14. See Hugh S. Chandler, "Plantinga and the Contingently Possible," *Analysis* 36 (1976): 106–109; but also Richard A. Fumerton, "Chandler on the Contingently Possible," *Analysis* 7 (1976): 39–40.

15. *Individuals*, pp. 34–35. For a review of the extensive literature on the general nature of arguments such as Strawson's, see Moltke S. Gram, "Do Transcendental Arguments Have a Future?" in *Neue Hefte für Philosophie* 14 (1978): 23–56.

16. Cf. Price, *Thinking and Experience*, pp. 38–43.

17. *Perception*, pp. 218 ff.

18. See Karl Popper, "The Principle of Individuation," *Aristotelian Society Suppl. Vol.* 27 (1953): 97–120. Compare R. M. Chisholm. *Person and Object*, Appendix A.

19. *The Persistence of Objects*, p. 62.

20. W. V. Quine, *Word and Object* (Cambridge: The M. I. T. Press, 1960), p. 209.

21. Cf. N. L. Wilson, "Property Designation and Description, "*The Philosophical Review* 64 (1955): 389–404, and "Class Identity as

Presupposing Individual Identity," *Philosophical Studies* 11 (1960): 55–58.

Chapter Seven: Qualities

1. E.g., W. V. Quine, "On What There Is," in *From a Logical Point of View*, and Wilfrid Sellars, "Grammar and Existence: A Preface to Ontology," *Mind* 69 (1960): 499–533. Both are reprinted in Charles Landesman, ed., *The Problem of Universals* (New York and London: Basic Books, 1971).

2. In *Universals: An Essay in Ontology* (Chicago and London: The University of Chicago Press, 1970), p. 240.

3. Renford Bambrough, "Universals and Family Resemblances," *Proceedings of the Aristotelian Society* 60 (1960–61): 207–23; and D. F. Pears, "Universals," *Philosophical Quarterly* 1 (1951): 218–27.

4. Stephan Körner, *Experience and Theory* (New York: The Humanities Press, 1966).

5. G. F. Stout, *The Nature of Universals and Propositions* (London: Oxford University Press, 1921, British Academy Lecture), and "Are the Characteristics of Particular Things Universal or Particular?" *Aristotelian Society Suppl. Vol.* 3 (1923): 114–22; G. E. Moore, "Are the Characteristics of Particular Things Universal or Particular?" *Aristotelian Society Suppl. Vol.* 3 (1923): 95–113. All three are reprinted in Landesman, *The Problem of Universals*.

6. *The Problems of Philosophy*, pp. 96–97; also "On the Relations of Universals and Particulars," in *Logic and Knowledge*. Cf. John T. Kearns, "Sameness or Similarity," *Philosophy and Phenomenological Research* XXIX (1968): 105–15; Brand Blanshard, "Rejoiner to Mr. Kearns," *Philosophy and Phenomenological Research* XXIX (1968): 116–18; and especially H. H. Price, *Thinking and Experience*, chapter 1.

7. Cf. H. H. Price, *Thinking and Experience*, chapter 1.

8. An earlier, rather different version of this argument is offered in *Resemblance and Identity*, chapter 3 (partially reprinted in Landesman, *The Problem of Universals*).

9. Cf. D. J. O'Connor, "On Resemblance," *Proceedings of the Aristotelian Society* 46 (1945–46): 47–77.

10. For discussions of quality-orders, see W. E. Johnson, *Logic*, Part I, pp. 181–83, and Nelson Goodman, *The Structure of Appearance*, chapter IX.

11. "The Nature of Universals and Particulars," in Landesman, *The Problem of Universals*, pp. 155–56. Cf. Husserl's notion of a "moment"

in *Logical Investigations*, especially Investigation III; also Donald C. Williams, "The Elements of Being."

12. "Particulars and Their Qualities," *The Philosophical Quarterly* 18 (1968): 193–206. For criticism of Long's view, see Douglas Odegard, "Qualities and Owners," *The Philosophical Quarterly* 20 (1970): 248–52.

13. E.g., in "Russell on Particulars," *The Philosophical Review* 56 (1947): 59–72, and in *Realism: A Critique of Brentano and Meinong* (Madison: The University of Wisconsin Press, 1967), pp. 23–25. Cf. Russell's "On the Relations of Universals and Particulars," in *Logic and Knowledge*. The argument for bare particulars has been stated especially clearly by E. B. Allaire, in "Bare Particulars," *Philosophical Studies*, 14 (1963): 1–8. But see Herbert Hochberg, "Things and Descriptions," *American Philosophical Quarterly* 3 (1966): 39–47; Laird Addis, "Particulars and Acquaintance," *Philosophy of Science* 34 (1967): 251–59; Reinhardt Grossmann, *Ontological Reduction*, Part Three.

14. Cf. V. C. Chappell, "Particulars Re-Clothed," *Philosophical Studies* 15 (1964): 60–64.

15. Cf. "On the Relations of Universals and Particulars," in *Logic and Knowledge*, pp. 117–18.

16. Cf. *The Concept of Knowledge*, pp. 140–42.

17. Cf. Bergmann, *Realism*, Part I, Sections 2 and 3.

Chapter Eight: Accidental Connections

1. "Some Explanations in Reply to Mr. Bradley," *Mind* 19 (1910): 374.

2. "On the Relations of Universals and Particulars," in *Logic and Knowledge*, p. 108.

3. *The Principles of Mathematics* (New York: Norton, 1903), p. 50. In this work Russell regarded propositions as complex unities, not to be confused with anything mental or with cognitions (p. 49) and held that a proposition "does not itself contain words; it contains the entities indicated by words" (p. 47).

4. "Reply to Mr. Russell's Explanations," *Mind* 20 (1911): 74. See also *Appearance and Reality* (Oxford: Clarendon Press, 1897), chapter III.

5. *Logic and Knowledge*, pp. 108–109, 122–23.

6. *The Structure of Appearance*, pp. 200–204.

7. For the former, see "Ineffability, Ontology, and Method," *The Philosophical Review* 69 (1960): 18–40, reprinted in *Logic and Reality* (Madison: The University of Wisconsin Press, 1964). For the latter, see "Realistic Postscript," in *Logic and Reality;* "Diversity," *Proceedings*

and Addresses of the American Philosophical Association, Vol. XLI (1968): 21–34; and *Realism,* pp. 10n, 94–95. The two must not be confused. I discuss this aspect of Bergmann's philosophy in detail in "The Limits of Ontological Analysis."

8. *Appearance and Reality,* pp.27–28.

9. For a discussion of this point, see *The Concept of Knowledge,* pp. 54–61.

10. The pragmatic nature of most ordinary identity judgments was pointed out by Hume in his *Treatise of Human Nature,* Book I, Part IV, Section VI. See also Thomas Reid, *Essays on the Intellectual Powers of Man,* essay III, chapter IV. In the most recent literature see David Shwayder, "On the Identification of Bodies," *Nous* 10 (1976): 19–33; and E. J. Borowski, "Identity and Personal Identity," *Mind* 85 (1976): 481–502. Borowski, argues, in my opinion mistakenly, that all our applications of the concept of identity are based on pragmatic considerations. Compare R. M. Chisholm's notion of what he calls "the loose and popular sense of identity," in "The Loose and Popular and the Strict and Philosophical Senses of Identity," in *Perception and Personal Identity,* ed. Norman S. Care and Robert H. Grimm (Cleveland: The Press of Case Western Reserve University, 1969), pp. 82–106, and in *Person and Object,* chapter III.

Appendix A: Relations

1. Cf. *The Problems of Philosophy,* p. 98. Also *The Principles of Mathematics,* pp. 50–52.

2. Cf. Locke, *An Essay Concerning Human Understanding,* Vol. One, Book II, Chapter XXV, and Hume, *A Treatise of Human Nature,* Book I, Part I, Section V.

3. "On the Relations of Universals and Particulars," in *Logic and Knowledge.*

Appendix B: Idealism

1. For an account of these two alternatives, see Richard Aquila, *Intentionality: A Study of Mental Acts* (University Park and London: The Pennsylvania State University Press, 1977).

2. See my "The Self and Perceptions: A Study in Humean Philosophy," *The Philosophical Quarterly* 9 (1959): 97–115. (Reprinted in the Bobbs-Merrill Reprint Series in Philosophy.)

INDEX

Abelard, 152
"about," 48, 254
abstract singular terms, 184–85
accidental properties, 122–23
accusatives of consciousness, 59, 62, 145
acquaintance, 30; knowledge by, 50
actuality and potentiality: in Aristotle, 165
actuality, mode of, 90
Addis, Laird, 265
adverbial theory of sensing, 93, 251
Allaire, E. B., 265
angels, 192
Anscombe, G. E. M., 6, 94, 262–63
Anselm, 105
apparent distinctness of identicals, 12–28, 32–35, 39–40, 44–45, 54, 84, 88, 191–92, 194–95
apparent existence of nonexistent things, 13, 84, 88
Aquila, Richard, 266
Aquinas, St. Thomas, 135, 136, 162, 163, 165, 192, 261, 262
Aristotle, 2, 3, 4, 122, 137, 138, 139, 146, 152, 154, 158, 162, 163, 165, 169, 179, 241, 261, 262
Armstrong, D. M., 199
attributes, identity of, 183
Austin, J. L., 58
Ayer, A. J., 43, 181, 258, 259

Bambrough, Renford, 264
being, 2–3, 59, 90, 95, 98, 144
being qua being, 3, 4, 5, 235
Bergmann, Gustav, 90, 174, 208, 214, 265, 266
Berkeley, George, 172, 251
Black, Max, 56, 69, 259
Blanshard, Brand, 264

body, the human, 254
Borowski, E. J., 266
Bradford, Dennis, ix
Bradley, F. H., 90, 212, 214, 216, 217, 240, 260
Bradleyan regress, 216, 217
Brentano, 252
Brody, Baruch, 261
Butler, Joseph, 39

Carnap, R., 6, 60, 257
Cartwright, Richard, 65, 259, 260
Castañeda, Hector-Neri, 61, 258
Casullo, Albert, ix, 225, 259
category mistakes, 103–104
causality, 177–78
Chandler, Hugh S., 263
Chappell, V. C., 265
Chisholm, R. M., 14, 90, 93, 170, 251, 256, 263, 266
Church, Alonzo, 60, 257
class membership, 3
classes, identity of, 183
classification, 35, 52–54, 135, 139, 140, 141, 186–87, 248–49. See also concepts
Coburn, Robert, 94, 263
Cochiarella, Nino, 260
Cohen, L. J., 97, 257, 258, 261
complexes, unity of, 212–22
conceivability, 4, 20, 99, 130, 160, 189–90, 221–22. See also logical possibility, criterion of
concepts, 42, 43, 52–54, 79–80, 87, 98, 115–17, 130–33, 140–42, 147–48, 153, 159–61, 176–77, 186–87, 234–35, 248–50, 258; ostensible and genuine, 160; transcendental, 5, 110, 242–44, 249. See also classification

267